Journey of Faith

Maulana Abdul Majid Daryabadi

(1892-1977)

Editors

Akhtarul Wasey

Abdur Raheem Kidwai

SHIPRA

The volume is based on the journal *Islam and the Modern Age*, XLII No.1 (2011) and the book *From Darkness into Light* by A R Kidwai.

Rs. 800; US$ 40

ISBN: 978-81-7541-798-4

First Published in India in 2016

Journey of Faith: Maulana Abdul Majid Daryabadi

Published by:

SHIPRA PUBLICATIONS

LG 18-19, Pankaj Central Market, I.P. Ext.
Patparganj, Delhi-110092, India
Tel: 91-11-2223 5152, 2223 6152
E-mail: info@shiprapublication.com
www.shiprapublication.com

To

Maulwi Abdul Qadir

Maulana Abdul Majid Daryabadi's father, whose fervent prayers at Kabah during his Hajj contributed to Daryabadi's return to the fold of Islam

In the name of Allah, Most Compassionate, Most Merciful

Preface

We deem it as our great privilege to bring out this book highlighting the illustrious achievements of a leading Indian Islamic scholar of our time, Maulana Abdul Majid Daryabadi (1892-1977). A versatile and prolific writer as Daryabadi was, he enriched especially the field of Quranic and Islamic studies through his more than 70 valuable books and numerous articles in both English and Urdu. Among the Quran translators he holds the enviable distinction of having written two *tafasir,* one each in English and Urdu, and these are two entirely independent works, not the English/Urdu versions of the same work. Also, he was an eminent Urdu journalist, with his noble mission of vindicating the excellence of the Islamic worldview and of championing the cause of Muslim identity in the long, turbulent era through his popular Urdu periodical bearing the variant titles, *Sach, Sidq* and *Sidq-i Jadid* (1925-1977). While accomplishing this, he kept alive the glorious tradition of purposive journalism in Urdu, inaugurated by Sir Syed's *Tahzibul Akhlaq,* Maulana Muhammad Ali Jawhar's *Hamdard* and *Comrade*, and Maulana Abul Kalam Azad's *al-Hilal* and *al-Balagh*. Notwithstanding his substantial contribution to *tafsir* corpus, it is worth mentioning that Daryabadi was not a graduate of any Islamic seminary. Far from this, he earned his B.A. in Philosophy in 1912 from Canning College, Lucknow, then affiliated to the University of Allahabad. For his incomplete masters degree in Philosophy he studied at the M.A.O College, Aligarh and St. Stephen's College Delhi. In his early career, coinciding with his decade-long straying into the error of pseudo-rationalism and atheism (1908-1918) he wrote articles and books mostly in English on philosophy, logic, metaphysics and psychology. His first major work touching upon *al-Kalam* entitled *The Psychology of Leadership* was published from London in 1915. Under the influence of Hindu thought and Sufism initially and of Akbar Allahabadi, Maulana Muhammad Ali Jauhar and Maulana Ashraf Ali Thanvi at a later date, he returned to the fold of Islam and devoted himself heart and soul until his last breath to serving admirably the cause of Islam. His works bear out the unmistakable imprint of his mentors, Akbar Allahabadi, Maulana Jawahar and Maulana Thanvi, distinguished representatives of the twentieth century Indian Islam. For his life-long critique on Westernization and the resultant erosion of Islamic and moral values in the Muslim society of India, he drew upon Akbar Allahabadi's thought pattern. For his bold articulation of the plea for maintaining and strengthening Muslim identity he took inspiration from his ideal, Maulana Jawahar who had revitalized the Indian Muslims in the early 20th century India through his forceful speeches and writings and his steering the Khilafat movement. Daryabadi's long and close association with his spiritual and religious mentor, Maulana Thanvi equipped him with a fine understanding of the meaning and message of the Quran. From Allama Shibli, Daryabadi learnt the art and craft of composing effective, charming and idiomatic Urdu prose. Daryabadi thus represents the amalgam of the best intellectual traditions of Muslim scholarship in the 20th century India. Daryabadi's contribution to Urdu language and literature is equally impressive. Special mention must be made of his critical acumen, his stylistic charms and his broadening and deepening of the scholarly tradition in Urdu.

This book nonetheless focusses on Daryabadi's first-rate Islamic and Quranic scholarship. His English translation and *tafsir* of the Quran (1957) stands out as the first Quran commentary conforming to the stance of *Ahl al-Sunnah wa al-Jamah*. This distinction of his is aptly identified in Syed Abul Hasan Ali Nadvi's article on Daryabadi's *tafsir* in English, apart from underscoring its other laudable features. Daryabadi's through grounding in the domain of *tafsir* and his discerning sensitivity to the issues, challenges and problems in translating the Quran and more importantly, his realization of the role and responsibility of a Quran scholar are reflected sharply in the two articles of his included in this issue. As to the broad sweep of his enviable scholarship, especially of comparative religion, and his assiduity, these are evident from his heavily annotated *tafsir*-based piece, "Jesus and Mary in the Quran."

We believe this book spelling out the life and academic attainments of an outstanding scholar of Quranic and Islamic studies will inspire the budding scholars to emulate Daryabadi's glorious example and thus open new avenues of understanding better Islam and the Quran.

Let this be clarified that this book has grown out from the Special Issue of *Islam and the Modern Age* (42:1, February 2011) edited by Akhtarul Wasey, and Abdur Raheem Kidwai's earlier book *From Darkness Into Light.* (Springs, South Africa, Ahsan Publications, 2013).

Akhtarul Wasey
Abdur Raheem Kidwai

Contents

Preface *iv*

I
LIFE

1. Daryabadi's Family Background and Era 1
2. Daryabadi's Early Life 7
3. Daryabadi's College and University Education 12
4. Daryabadi's Quest for Truth: His Wandering into Error and his Return to Islam 17
5. Daryabadi's Mentors: Akbar Allahabadi, Allama Shibli, Maulana Muhammad Ali Jauhar and Maulana Ashraf Ali Thanwi. 28
6. Daryabadi's Family Life and Demise 47
7. Daryabadi's Mission and Message 52

II
WORKS

8. English Translation of the Quran: Issues and Problems 64
   Abdul Majid Daryabadi
9. *Tafsir* (The Quran Exegesis) in Modern Times: Pre-requisites and Challenges 69
   Abdul Majid Daryabadi
10. Jesus and Mary in the Quran 82
    Abdul Majid Daryabadi
11. MaulanaDaryabadi as a Quranic Scholar 103
    Syed Abul Hasan Ali Nadvi
12. Maulana Daryabadi's Contribution to Quranic and Islamic Studies 112
    Abdur Raheem Kidwai

Bibliography 152

Editors and Contributors 160

1

Daryabadi's Family Background and Era

Maulana Abdul Majid Daryabadi (15 March 1892 – 6 January 1977) hailed from a family of Muslim scholars and spiritual masters of north India. He was a descendant of Qazi Muiz al-Din, who had earned the appellation of "Qidwa al-Din wa al-Ilm" (the pillar of faith and knowledge) and was popularly known as "Qazi Qidwa". His descendants are accordingly known as Kidwais in our times. Many of them have held top public positions in the post-Independence India. According to popular reports, Qazi Muiz al-Din had arrived in India as part of Mahmud Ghaznavi's entourage and settled down in Ayodhaya, Faizabad, Uttar Pradesh. Annals of the day, however, provide more specific and authentic details about Daryabadi's forefather, Shaykh Muhammad Makhdum Chishti Nizami (d. 880H/1475CE). In recognition of his special concern for arranging for water for *wuzu* and for those in need of water, the title *Aab kash* (water carrier) was conferred upon him. His role as a spiritual master is acclaimed in the following chronicles of the day: *Mirat al-Asrar, Shaykh Nama* and *Khazinat al-Asfiya.*[1] At the behest of a noble man, Darya Khan, he moved to a new settlement in Barabanki district in 845H/1441 CE. The place later came to be known as Daryabad, presently a small town which made a mark in the academic world of the Indo-Pak subcontinent only because of Maulana Daryabadi's association with it. Makhdum Aabkash lies buried next to Daryabadi's ancestral house.

Makhdum Aabkash's grandson, Makhdum Bakhsh was Daryabadi's great grandfather. He had four sons: i) Hakim Nur Karim (d. 1871); ii) Mufti Mazhar Karim (d. 1873), iii) Haji Murtaza Karim (d. 1873) and iv) Maulwi Karam Karim (d. 1879). Of them, Hakim Nur Karim was Daryabadi's maternal grandfather whereas Mufti Mazhar Karim, his paternal grandfather.

Hakim Nur Karim had his early education at Firangi Mahal, Lucknow, and later studied *tibb* (indigenous medicine) as an apprentice of Hakim Nabba, a leading physician of Lucknow. Hakim Nur Karim, in turn, trained hundreds of *hakims,* including some from the central Asia, Iran and Afghanistan. He rendered into Urdu several works on *tibb*, originally in

Arabic and Persian. Some of these were prescribed as textbooks and hence frequently reprinted.[2] As a scholar of the classical Muslim era he led an exceptionally simple, pious and unblemished life.

Mufti Mazhar Karim, Daryabadi's paternal grandfather, studied at Firangi Mahal, Lucknow and specialized in *ifta* and *fiqh* (Islamic jurisprudence). He was in judicial service, posted at Shahjahanpur, when the first war of Independence was launched in 1857. The British charged him with treason, accusing him of having issued his *fatwa* (decree) for waging war against the British. In his account of the 1857 uprising, J. F. Fanthome identifies him as an influential Muslim cleric who had instigated the locals against the British.[3]He was sentenced to 14 years imprisonment and was exiled to the Andaman island. Several leading Ulema, as for example, Maulana Fazl Haq Khairabadi and Mufti Inayat Ahmad, had met the same fate. Mufti Mazhar Karim's sentence was slightly commuted in view of his constant scholarly pursuits even inside the prison. An instance in point is his Urdu translation of Safi al-Din Abd al-Mumin's work on Arab geography, *Marasid al-Itala' fi Asma al-Amkana.* His other writings embrace a wide range of topics on jurisprudence, devotional practices and Sufism.

Besides having such pious and highly educated ancestors, Daryabadi was fortunate enough also to be blessed with erudite, devout parents. His father, Maulwi Abdul Qadir (1848-1912) gained his early education at Firangi Mahal and later graduated in law. After his brief stint as the teacher of Persian in schools, he joined state judicial service. By dint of his hard work and integrity he rose to the coveted position of the day Deputy Collector in 1890s in many districts of UP. Notwithstanding his official engagements, he maintained close relations with Ulema and men of letters. He actively worked for community welfare projects. His daily routine, as recounted by Daryabadi, is very instructive, as it throws ample light on the way of life of an educated Muslim government official of 1890s:

> He used to get up at dawn and woke us (my elder brother and me) at Fajr time. Together we offered prayer in congregation. Then he turned to reciting the Quran and studying *tafasir* of Ibn Abbas and Jalalayn. After breakfast and browsing daily newspapers, he went to court. He used to say Zuhr prayer in his official chamber and returned home in the early evening. Asr and Maghrib prayers were offered by all of us in congregation. He usually went to the central mosque of the town for Isha prayer. Before going to bed he read literary magazines and books.[4]

As a civil servant he won a wide acclaim. He was held in esteem by the locals, most of whom were Hindus, for his integrity and piety. After his superannuation he proceeded to Makkah for performing Hajj in 1912. Soon after having performed the Hajj rituals he passed away at Mina and was buried in Makkah.

Daryabadi's mother, Nasirun Nisa (1853-1943) was a remarkably devout lady, fully devoted to Islamic faith and practices. She led a frugal life and gave in charity all that she had. Much of her time, as Daryabadi recounts, was spent on the Quran recitation and offering prayers. She treated well the large number of the members of Daryabadi's joint family. She inculcated the Islamic values among all her family members, especially her own children, including Daryabadi. Daryabadi appears to have imbibed in full the distinctive traits of his ancestors, grandparents and parents—their single-minded devotion to Islamic faith, scholarly pursuits, and working for the cause of Islam. These traits blossomed in his later career as he made a mark as a distinguished scholar devoted heart and soul to asserting and promoting the truth and eternal message of Islam through a plethora of his valuable writings in both English and Urdu.

Among Daryabadi's other family members who left some imprint on his supple mind in his childhood and adolescence, mention may be made of his two cousins: i) Abdul Haleem (d. 1903) who was an avid reader and had a refined literary taste. He introduced the very young Daryabadi to the fascinating, spell-binding Urdu classics and also to the Muslim intellectual history in which Sir Syed, Allama Shibli, Nazir Ahmad and Altaf Hussain Hali figured prominently. ii) Hakim Abdul Hasib (d. 1950), Daryabadi's material cousin, was senior to Daryabadi by 14 years. He generously helped the young Daryabadi buy books of his choice, which helped in cultivating in him a keen literary interest. Daryabadi has gratefully mentioned these benefactors who imbued him with literary interests at a very young age.[5]

Daryabadi had one brother and one sister, both elder to him by eight and six years respectively. His elder brother, Abdul Majeed (1884-1960) joined judicial service after doing his Intermediate and rose to the coveted position of the day, Deputy Collector in various districts of UP. He took a keen interest in the Muslim community educational and welfare projects and had close links with the leading Ulema of the day, including Maulana Ashraf Ali Thanwi.

Daryabadi's sister, Sakina (1886-1945) was an exceptionally pious lady who made it a point to offer regularly even supererogatory prayers. She was married to Muhammad Salim, a physician. Like Daryabadi she held Maulana Thanwi in great esteem.

Daryabadi was born on 16 Shaban 1310H/16 March 1892 at Daryabad. As was customary, at the age of four years he commenced his early education at home under the supervision of a *maulwi* (a teacher well versed in the Islamic faith and practices). His father was then posted in Lakhimpur as Deputy Collector. The commencement of education by a child in the Indo-Pak Muslim society was celebrated as a family ceremony, with strong Islamic overtones. Known as *bismillah* ceremony, a child recites first *basmala,* followed by reading out the Urdu/Arabic alphabets. His/Her initiation is celebrated by family members and friends as a feast. Needless to add, this custom aims at conveying to the child, rather imprinting this message on his/her mind that one's all activities, including studies, should be geared towards seeking Allah's pleasure. Allah should be invoked before one embarks on something. Moreover, in Islam there is no dichotomy between the "secular" and the "religious". All that one does, no matter how this-worldly it may appear, is an act of worship as long as he does not deny any Shariah norm. For example, one will be rewarded amply by Allah for all the time and energy spent by him on earning his bread lawfully for sustaining himself and his family. The same Islamic message accounted for the phenomenal contributions made by the Muslim scientists, physicians, lawyers and artists in the classical period, who broadened and deepened the body of knowledge as a religious duty.

It was in such Islamic setting that Daryabadi had his early education first at home. Apart from the Quran recitation, the young Daryabadi was taught by his personal tutors, Shaykh Sadi's *Gulistan*, *Bostan* and *Pand Nama*, and Maulwi Ismail Meeruti's series of Urdu readers, which abound in moral exhortations, guiding how to lead life, which may ensure the best for one in both the worlds. This instruction was reinforced by *tarbiyya* (upbringing in accordance with the best morals and manners), imparted constantly by his parents and the wider family. It is indeed a pity that such *tarbiyya* is now conspicuous by its absence in most of the Muslim homes. This has resulted in the mushrooming of the "lost" generations who have very hazy ideas about the purpose of their life and their ultimate goal. Their parents' ignorance of the Islamic way of life, their lack of attention to their own children on account of their extremely busy schedules and their apathy towards the meaning and purpose of life account, in the main, for the sorry state of affairs in most of the Muslim homes and societies today. A study of some valuable guides on parenting along the Islamic lines, which spell out lucidly the rights and duties of both the parents and children, may be of some help to the Muslim parents today.[6] Daryabadi's early childhood was spent in Gorakhpur where his father was posted then as Deputy Collector. He recalls his father's friends as regular visitors to his house. Most of them were religious figures and men of letters, as for example, Maulwi Subhan Allah Khan, a bibliophile who later donated his precious collection to the Aligarh Muslim University.[7] Maulvi Abul Fazl Ihsanullah Abbasi, the author of several works on Islamic history; and the celebrated poet, Riaz Khairabadi. These frequent religious and literary gatherings at home left an indelible impression on Daryabadi's young mind. It goes without saying that the ambience prevailing at home goes a long way in shaping the future personality of a child.

Consequent upon his father's transfer, Daryabadi, along with his family moved to Faizabad. The sensitivity of Daryabadi's father regarding *purda* (segregation of women) was so strong that while travelling by train, he used to get the whole second class compartment reserved so that the lady members of his family may not have to intermingle in any degree with men. Their covered carriages, known as *palki* (palanquin), carried on shoulders, were placed inside train compartment. In Faizabad too, Daryabadi benefitted from the religious and literary atmosphere at home. Hakim Shah Niyaz Ahmad, a Sufi master and Munshi Imtiaz Ali, the Urdu translator of Shakespeare's plays, often visited his father. Daryabadi's uncle, Abdur Raheem, took him to mosque at the appointed hours daily. This made Daryabadi regular in offering prayer from a very young age. Parents' attention to this important religious duty can make their children habitual of its regular performance.

In sum, Daryabadi had his early upbringing in a traditional Muslim family of scholars and literary figures.

Notes

1. For this and many other valuable pieces of information I am indebted to Tehsin Feraqi's *Abdul Majid Daryabadi: Ahwal wa Athar*, Lahore, Pakistan, Idara Thaqafat-i Islamia, 2006, p.13. In subsequent references this study is referred to as *Daryabadi*. Feraqi cites the following sources:
   i) Munshi Brij Bhokan Lal Muhib, *Tarikh-i Daryabad,* Lucknow, Nami Press, 1925, 101.
   ii) Ghulam Sarwar Lahori, *Khazinatul Asfiya,* Lahore, Pakistan, al-Marif, 1392H, 1, 396.
2. *Daryabadi,* p.15 cf. *Tarikh-i Daryabad,* p.88.
3. Ibid., p.16 cf. Abdul Majid Daryabadi, *Sidq-i Jadid,* Lucknow (9 December 1955), p.6
4. Abdul Majid Daryabadi, *Aap Biti*, Lucknow, Maktaba Firdaus, 1998, p. 35. This is Daryabadi's autobiography posthumously published first in 1978. Referred to as *Aap Biti* in all subsequent references.
5. *Aap Biti,* pp.55, 56 and 57.
6. Some of the titles on *tarbiyya* are
   - Ekram Beshir, *Parenting Skills: Based on the Qur'an and Sunnah: With Practical Examples for Various Ages.* Virginia, Amana Publications, 2009.

- Ekram Beshir, *Muslim Teens: Today's Worry, Tomorrow's Hope: A Practical Islamic Parenting Guide.* Virginia, Amana Publications, 2001.
- Umm Safiyyah Bint Najmaddin, *The Muslim Parent's Guide to the Early Years (0-5 years)*, London Ta-Ha, 2011.
- Norma Tarazi, *Child in Islam: A Muslim Parent's Handbook*, USA, American Trust Publications, 1995.
- Ruqaiyya Waris Maqsood, *Living with Teenagers: A Guide for Muslim Parents.* London, Ta-Ha Publishers, 1995.
- Iqbal Ahmad Azmi, *Muslim Manners: A Guide for*
- *Parents & Teachers of Muslim Children.* Leicester, UK Islamic Academy, 2003.
- Ekram Beshir, *Parenting in the West.* USA, Amana Books, 1999.
- Abdur Raheem Kidwai, *The Quran: Essential Teachings,* Leicester, The Islamic Foundation, UK, 2005. Chapters 15-19.

7. Subhan Allah collection is a valuable part of Maulana Azad Library, Aligarh Muslim University, Aligarh.

2

Daryabadi's Early Life

From Faizabad Daryabadi's father was transferred to Sitapur. It was there that Daryabadi received his school education. At the age of seven years he finished the recitation of the whole Quran. The Muslims of the subcontinent celebrate this event as well. Family members and friends gather on this day in order to felicitate both the child and his/her parents. Upto 1940s it was customary to admit a child to school only after he had finished the Quran recitation. Regrettably, in today's materialistic, competitive and career-oriented life, the Quran recitation by a child has been relegated to a secondary position. The focus now is on getting the child admitted at a very young of even 3 or 4 years to an English medium school. These schools under the management of Christian missionaries or other non-Muslims, of course, do not have any provision for the study of the Quran or Islam. As a result, these Muslim children are faced with a severe identity crisis. Their poor knowledge of their faith and religious practices renders them all the more vulnerable. Some parents, no doubt, take pains to arrange for the Quran recitation of their children in the after school hours. However, this arrangement often tends to be unsatisfactory. Of late, some English medium schools with some provision for the study of the Quran and Islam have been opened by some enterprising Muslim educationists in various parts of the country. The inadequacies in the above arrangement are too many and too serious.

Daryabadi received his early education from personal tutors who taught him at home. While the teachers of English, mathematics and other subjects engaged him for a couple of hours every day, his Maulwi stayed almost the whole day and served as his mentor as well. Urdu and Persian classics were taught to him, which included, apart from Shaykh Sadi's works,Mirza Qatil's *Ruqa'at*, Nizami's *Sikandar Nama* Jami's *Yusuf Zulekha* and Ghazali's *Kimya-i Sa'adat* in Persian. All these works helped the young Daryabadi imbibe morals and manners, and a literary taste. Ghazali's work stands out for its moralistic tenor ad for providing its overview of the

Islamic value system. While recalling to his study of these classics in his childhood, Daryabadi makes the following perceptive comments:

> *Kimya-i Sa'adat* is pregnant with meaning and message. However, it was taught to me in a rote manner, without making any allowance for my comprehension or mental level. At most, I gathered a faint idea of its text, without grasping its valuable contents. This work should be studied in one's mature years. If it is to be taught, a competent, discerning teacher should get the assignment of explaining it, not a conventional teacher who follows only the rote method and imparts only its literal meaning. As to Jami's *Yusuf Zuleikha* may Allah pardon Jami. It is hard to think how and why he has left behind such an obscene work. In view of his reputation, however, even this work of his is prescribed as a text book. There is some obscenity in Sadi's *Gulistan* too. However, its merits outweigh its defects.
>
> Another worth-noting point is that even the best writer or thinker is conditioned by his own ethos and era. It is impossible that a product of the human mind composed some hundreds of years ago be valid and relevant today. It does not and cannot fit in today's thought patterns. Even the best classic cannot be prescribed for study unless it is thoroughly edited. A new introduction and copious explanatory notes are essential. Moreover, its teacher should be intelligent, fully aware of the needs and mindset of his students. Without these precautionary steps even the elixir of yore may turn out to be worthless, even fatal.[1]

Apart from books, Daryabadi was surrounded in his childhood and later years by scores of domestic servants. One of the main factors responsible for this was the recurrent incidence of famines in north India. As a result of this, the poor used to abandon their children who were placed under state care home. Daryabadi's father, being a God-fearing senior civil servant officially brought some of them, especially girls to his home for their proper upbringing. In other houses and state care homes, however, they were treated like slaves. The Muslim nobility of the day was no exception in that they exploited these poor, hapless persons. Daryabadi's parents instructed him to be kind to them.

An instance of Daryabadi's keen interest in public affairs, especially those with a bearing on the Muslim issues, and his flair for writing is that at the age of only 8 years he wrote long letters in 1900, protesting against the anti-Urdu and pro-Hindi stance of then Lt. Governor of UP, Antony Mc Donnel. Even at such a young age he was a voracious reader. His interest was whetted by his cousin, Abdul Haleem, who provided him with a regular supply of moral, academic and literary works for study.

In 1901 when he was nine years old he was admitted to the IVth standard in school which was at some distance from his home. Even before entering school, he was grounded fairly well in such subjects as English, mathematics and science. Although Sitapur had a sizeable Muslim population, Daryabadi reports that there were only a couple of Muslim students in his class. Among his teachers there was not even a single Muslim. In education Muslims were non-existent in the early twentieth century. The situation improved somewhat by 1930s. The credit for this goes to the Aligarh movement set in motion by Sir Syed Ahmad Khan (1817-1898). The Muhammadan Anglo Oriental College was established by him in 1877 which rose to become the Aligarh Muslim University in 1920. The growing sense of identity among Muslims also turned their attention to education. It was at this school that the young Daryabadi came first into contact with Hindus. He relates his impressions about Hindus thus:

> There were only two or three Muslims in my class. Even in the British India Muslims did not figure in the Department of Education. My class teacher was a *Brahaman,* and the headmaster, a *kayasth* (names of two castes of Hindus). Both were thorough gentlemen and paid special attention to me as I was the son of a high official of the town. Most of my class fellows were Hindus. They, however, did not seem overawed by my social standing.
>
> It was for the first time that I came into direct contact with Hindus, who were my equal. Earlier I had been in touch with only some subordinate Hindus, as for example, the stable boy or office attendant or private tutor.
>
> The Hindu custom of greeting with the folded hands, their excessive respect for *Brahamans,* which bordered on veneration, their touching the feet of teachers and their practice of untouchability even among themselves struck me. They did not share food or drink among themselves, what to speak of eating or drinking with Muslims.
>
> Students had the option to learn either Persian or Sanskrit. Most of the students, who were of course Hindus, used to opt for Persian. Even the majority of the teachers of Persian were *kayasth* Hindus. At the insistence of the Arabic teacher, Hakim Mirza Muhammad Zaki Lakhnawi, however, I chose Arabic as the optional language.
>
> I was weak in mathematics. My Hindu head master was kind enough to ask a *kayasth* class fellow to help me overcome my weakness. He did this job almost as a religious duty and did not charge any fee. Although he was a needy student, he declined to accept the modest honorarium which I offered him after the examination. Later

on, he joined education department as a demonstrator. In 1960 when he learnt about the demise of my elder brother, he visited me after a gap of decades. While offering condolence to me, he said: "Today not only your brother, my brother too, has passed way. I stand by you in your grief."[2]

At school Daryabadi did fairly well; he had the distinction of winning the merit scholarship and was appointed class monitor in recognition of his good conduct. In 1908 he passed his high school examination. Reading voraciously was his only hobby in his school days. Under the patronage of his elder brother he participated in the local Friends' club which regularly organized group discussion and paper reading. Daryabadi recalls that he had presented on this platform papers on the topic of female education, which was a burning issue of the day. Such was his passion for reading that on return from school in the late afternoon, he read first the national English dailies and then took food. He ruefully reports that owing to his carelessness in reading even in dim light during his childhood, his eye sight was affected at a young age. Throughout his later life he suffered on this count and could hardly undertake any academic work at night. His school teachers, all of whom were Hindus, were highly impressed by the wide range of his knowledge. One of them exclaimed: "You are sure to make a mark in the world."[3] His Arabic teachers, Mirza Muhammad Zaki, Maulwi Hyder Hussain, and later, Maulwi Azmatullah of Firangi Mahal, Lucknow, showered affection upon him and had great expectations about his rising to fame.

The growing Westernization in the British India had its pernicious effects on schools. Students' participation in plays, cultural programmes and visits to theatre (cinema had not made its appearance till them) was fairly common. Worse, moral values had been eroding fast. Students had no scruples about using obscene, filthy language and indulging in immoral acts. Little wonder then that the phenomenal spread of Western education across the world in the last one hundred years has done precious little towards promoting or even maintaining morals and manners both inside and outside even the most prestigious and hallowed educational institutions. Modern education has, no doubt, helped man tap effectively vast natural resources and made life much more comfortable and enjoyable. Nonetheless, the loss of the value-based education, which once flourished in India, has wreaked havoc. Consequently we find ourselves today in a morass of social, psychological and spiritual crisis.

In sum, Daryabadi's school education prepared him better for embarking upon higher education and ambitious academic pursuits. It prepared him, to a degree, for the new emerging world of Western scholarship, of co-existence with non-Muslims, particularly the fellow Hindu countrymen, and of the formidable challenges of the new world order. Thus he moved away from the cocooned confines of his traditional family life which was steeped considerably in the Muslim faith and practices. His enrolment in a college in a big town as Lucknow signified his entry into a new world, dominated by the Western thought patterns and practices. It was a largely different world, of which Daryabadi's parents and even Indian Muslims of 1910s had almost no idea. Daryabadi was now on his own to charter the future course of his career and life.

Notes

1. *Aap Biti,* p.84
2. Ibid., pp.91, 92, 98, 101 and 102.
3. Ibid., p.107

3

Daryabadi's College and University Education

After having passed his high school examination in second division from a school in Sitapur in 1908, Daryabadi secured admission to Intermediate at Canning College, Lucknow, affiliated with the University of Allahabad, as the University of Lucknow had not come up by then. Most of its staff members were British academicians. It was customary in the day that the *taluqdars* (the landed gentry) having their houses in Lucknow and other major towns used to provide accommodation to the bright students free of charge or at nominal rent. Daryabadi managed to get a decent room in one of those houses in Qaiser Bagh, near his college. Since few students pursued education beyond high school in 1910s, getting admission to a college was not difficult. Entrance test or competition was something unheard of.

Amid Daryabadi's subjects at college, English was compulsory and his optional ones were Logic, History and Arabic. Of these, he was drawn most towards Logic. Apart from the college library, he drew heavily upon some rich libraries in Lucknow. In his testimonial, the Principal of the college stated that to the best of his knowledge no other student in the college had benefitted more from the college library than Daryabadi.[1] The department of Arabic at the College was very small, with only four students, including a Brahmo Samaj Hindu and it had only two teachers.

At the College he participated actively in elocutionary contests, especially paper reading sessions. His presentation on the thought of the British philosopher and statesman, John Stuart Mill fetched him the first prize. He excelled his class fellows in essay writing. Even at this young age some of his articles were published in the British journals. It was a rare distinction for a young Indian student. He had no interest in other college activities. Only once did he take part in the College Dramatic Society, as it staged Shakespeare's play, *The Mid-Summer Night Dream.* Western culture, especially its art forms, music, dancing and theatre had been then rapidly gaining ground in the Indian educational institutions. The educational system produced successfully the brown "Sahibs". Daryabadi passed his Intermediate examination in June 1910, with high second class marks.

Then he joined B.A. at the same Canning College. In 1910, particularly in north India, B.A. degree was a rarity. The then graduates commanded much respect, rather awe. For his graduation Daryabadi chose the following subjects – English, Philosophy and Arabic. Philosophy comprised these three branches – Metaphysics, Ethics and Psychology. Of these, he was attracted most towards Psychology. He read almost all the books on the subject available in the College library. Prestigious journals published from the West, as for example, *Nature* and *Mind,* were accessible to him, which both broadened and deepened his mental horizon. Some of his articles on psychology and philosophy were published in these journals. In these formative years of his he studied uncritically, rather with admiration the writings of Western scholars. Such was the sway and awe of the West in the day that these writings were taken by the Indians as the gospel truth. Among his favourite authors in his college days were Socrates (469-399BC), Plato (428-347BC), Aristotle (384-322BC), Bacon (1214-1299), Descartes (1596-1650), Locke (1632-1704), Hume (1711-1776), Hegel (1770-1831), Mill (1806-1873), Darwin (1809-1882) and Spencer (1820-1903). Of them, he was fascinated most by the thought of John Stuart Mill (1806-1873), the British philosopher. Mill opposed all forms of intuition, authority, custom or revelation. Some of his influential works are *System of Logic* (1843), *Utilitarianism* (1861), *On Liberty* (1859). Throughout he championed the cause of individuality and freedom. William James (1842-1910), the American psychologist and philosopher was Daryabadi's other favourite author. As the exponent of pragmatism, James defined truth thus: "Truth is what works for us, rather than a depiction of some structural relation between ideas and reality." His approach to religious and moral issues features in his *Varieties of Religious Experience* (1902) and *The Meaning of Truth* (1909). His writings were prescribed as Daryabadi's textbooks. M.P. Cameron and C.J. Brown were Daryabadi's teachers of philosophy, who were quite competent. The former rose to become the Vice Chancellor of the University of Lucknow.

Daryabadi's study of Arabic was, however, somewhat neglected owing to various factors. First, his fascination with the Western thought turned him indifferent to his legacy which seemed to him out of date and lacklustre. Moreover, his teachers of Arabic were regrettably not up to the mark. Selections from the works of Ibn Khaldun, Mutannabi and Abu Tumam and from *Maqamat-i Hariri* and *Maqamat-i Badi'* were included in the syllabus. Daryabadi's interest in Arabic was, however, revived by his friend, Abdul Bari, who was a graduate from Nadwatul Ulema, Lucknow. The friendship between the two lasted for more than sixty years. Both of them made a mark in later years as scholars devoted heart and soul to the cause of Islam. Abdul Bari was keen on learning English. So they decided to help each other in Arabic and English. At the age of only 14 Daryabadi was such an avid reader that when in 1906 the new eleventh edition of the *Encyclopedia Britannica* in 35 huge volumes, came out, this was his response:

> I learnt in the evening that the new edition of the *Encyclopedia* had arrived in the library. So intense was my interest in going through it that I could not sleep for most part of the night. It was a sheer pleasure to browse it the next morning. However, since the library opened for a few hours a day, my thirst was not quenched. Where there is will, there is a way. I came to know that a Hindu college fellow of mine, who was the son of an affluent aristocrat, had a personal copy of the *Encyclopedia.* Immediately did I approach him. He generously let me take home one volume at a time. Words fail me in conveying my delight when I took home its first volume. It was an elegantly produced work. I savoured it day and night. I felt on the top of the world as I read all its volumes. At that stage of my life I was nothing short of being a devotee of books.[2]

In his college days Daryabadi gained acquaintance with both his seniors and class fellows. Some of them turned out to be his life long mentors and friends. Allama Shibli had stayed in Lucknow up to 1913. Being an admirer of Shibli's works, particularly his prose style, Daryabadi regularly called on him. He gained much, especially the refined literary taste, from his close association with Shibli. Maulana Abul Kalam Azad was a frequent visitor to Shibli's place in Lucknow. Shibli introduced him to Daryabadi and this grew into a long relationship, notwithstanding some friction. Allama Syed Suleman Nadvi was another major literary, scholarly and religious figure with whom Daryabadi's rapport grew much with the passage of time. Others who deserve mention are: Abdul Halim Sharar, the Urdu novelist and historian; Mirza Muhammad Hadi Ruswa, the author of *Umrao Jan Ada*; Pandit Braj Narayn Chakbast, a leading Urdu poet; Akbar Allahabadi, another famous Urdu poet, who was instrumental also in bringing the young atheist and rationalist Daryabadi back to the fold of Islam quite tactfully; Maulwi Abdul Salam Nadvi and Maulwi Masud Ali Nadvi, who were to be Daryabadi's colleagues at Darul Musaniffin, the academy set up by Allama Shibli in Azamgarh, UP. Notwithstanding his growing interest in the Western thought, Daryabadi maintained close social relations with Ulema and Urdu men of letters. He attended the foundation stone laying ceremony, chaired by Allama Shibli and later in 1912 an important gathering chaired by Rashid Rida, the Egyptian writer on Islam.

Daryabadi graduated in 1912. As there was no provision for pursuing M.A. in Philosophy at Canning College, Lucknow, Daryabadi enrolled at the Muhammadan Anglo Oriental College, Aligarh, which was elevated as the Aligarh Muslim University in 1920. At Aligarh he developed close contacts with Dr Zafarul Hasan, Department of Philosophy, Joseph Horovitz, the German Orientalist working at the Department of Arabic, Maulwi Ahsanullah Khan, University Librarian, Shaykh Abdur Raheem who later made a mark as a lawyer in Pakistan and a great admirer of Daryabadi's writings, and Sahibzada Aftab Ahmad Khan. Daryabadi wrote his MA (Previous) examination in March 1913 in Allahabad, as the MAO College was then affiliated to the University of Allahabad. Even before appearing in the examination, he was doubtful about his passing it. For, the philosophy syllabus at the MAO College was not to his liking. He was grounded well in empiricist philosophy as expounded by the British philosophers, namely Hume, Mill and Spencer. However, at Aligarh he had to grapple with, for the first time, with the German idealist philosophers such as Kant and Hegel. Moreover, most of the text books were not available. He was not impressed by the competence level of his teachers as well. In short, he did not pass the examination. He, nonetheless, decided to do his MA (Philosophy) at St. Stephen College, Delhi. In August 1913 he joined the college. C.F. Andrews was associated with this College. Daryabadi embarked upon his studies earnestly and was happy with his teachers and the College.

After the sudden demise of Daryabadi's father in 1912, Raja Mahmudabad had generously deposited a lump sum for the education of Daryabadi in the People's Bank. In December 1913, a few months after his joining St. Stephen College, this private bank was abruptly declared insolvent, resulting in the loss of the money meant for his education. Daryabadi now faced acute financial crisis. His elder brother, then having a small, temporary job, could not support the substantial expenses incurred on Daryabadi's education in Delhi. With a heavy heart the helpless Daryabadi had to abandon his formal education. His lamentation, as recorded in his autobiography, is very moving:

> With this abrupt end to my studies I left Delhi for Lucknow. I tried to reassure, nay console myself that in a year or two I would publish such substantial articles on philosophy, which would bestow upon me the same stature which MA in Philosophy carries. Man's self is indeed both deceptive and deceiving. It conjures up something out of nothing and takes great delight in his world of fancy and fantasy.
>
> Man is created weak both in spirit and flesh. His plans and ambitions are hardly realized. Had I obtained my masters degree in philosophy, I might have ended up as a teacher of philosophy in some college. My life would then have been entirely different from what it is now. It is hard to say whether it would have been better or worse for me. It must have been nonetheless a totally different one.

Anyway, my formal education ended in 1913. Even now in the seventy-fifth year of my life, my level of knowledge is no better than that of a student, and that too of an immature one, with half-baked knowledge.

I embarked upon my studies at the age of four and finished my formal education at only twenty-one. Never did I realize in those long years that it was a very precious time. It never occurred to me then that I would not enjoy such care-free life later. I wish I had utilized even part of that time. To this day in my dream I often see myself as a student.[3]

Notes

1. *Aap Biti,* p.117
2. Ibid., p.134
3. Ibid., pp.152, 153 and 154.

4

Daryabadi's Quest for Truth: His Wandering into Error and His Return to Islam

Daryabadi's life is instructive in more than one way. At one level, it stands out as the account of a devout Muslim scholar who dedicated his whole life to presenting and promoting the Islamic way of life through his numerous writings in both English and Urdu which helped many grasp better the life-giving message of Islam. His elucidation of Islam stemmed, in the main, from the meaning and message of the Quran. He was versed so well in the Quran scholarship that he wrote two extensive *tafasir* (commentaries) of the Quran in English and Urdu. Let this be noted that both are independent works, aimed at different readerships and different mindsets. The distinctive features of his *tafasir* are discussed in Chapter 12.

What makes Daryabadi's life story all the more significant and full of lesson is his veering towards rationalism and atheism in his twenties under the influence of anti-Islam Western writings, and by Allah's grace, his return to the fold of Islam, facilitated by Akbar Allahabadi and Maulana Muhammad Ali Jauhar, and more significantly, his later spiritual development under the patronage of Maulana Ashraf Ali Thanwi. His life thus illustrates both the abiding appeal of the truth of Islam and also the pitfalls faced, especially by the young vulnerable Muslims who may wander into error, even disbelief under the pernicious influence of anti-Islam Western writings. His lapse into atheism underscores the strong and pressing need for the proper Islamic *tarbiyya* (upbringing) of the young Muslims to be ensured by their parents and the broader community. It calls for both introspection and vigilance.

As already stated, Daryabadi was born and brought up in a family of Muslim scholars. His parents and other family members and friends were practising Muslims who adhered fast to a traditional Islamic way of life. What was, however, regrettably missing was any mechanism to perceive the new, growing challenges and dangers inherent in the new, Western educational system, and in the ethos of the broader society. Complacency accounted, in the main, for the absence of any monitoring or mentoring of the young, especially those exposed to the currents and cross-currents of modernity and un-Islamic ways of life. The same threat stares the Muslim community in the face across the world today as well. Parents and community leaders should realize both the seriousness and enormity of the problem. They should be more vigilant, more sensitive and more responsive to the questions or issues agitating the mind of the young Muslims. Ulema, in particular, should be alive to the intellectual and civilizational threats confronting Muslims.

It would not be out of place to recount here the observations made by the American author, Francis Fukuyama in his best seller, *End of History (1992)* which critically analyses the rise and fall of various civilizations and, particularly the present inter-civilizational scenario across the world. While he acknowledges the resilience of the Muslim civilization down the ages which has not declined like others such as the Buddhist and Hindu ones, he triumphantly claims that the number of "cultural converts" and economic migrants to the West is very high among Muslims. Hence the Muslim civilization poses no threat to the dominant and deeply-entrenched Western civilization which wins over the mind and heart of Muslims.He thus takes great delight and pride in the steady march of Westernization all over the world:

> It is true that Islam constitutes a systematic and coherent ideology, just like liberalism and communism, with its own codes of morality and doctrine of political and social justice. The appeal of Islam is potentially universal, reaching out to all men as men, and not just to members of a particular ethnic or national group.
>
> Despite the power demonstrated by Islam in its current revival, however, it remains the case that this religion has virtually no appeal outside those areas that were culturally Islamic to begin with. The days of Islam's cultural conquests, it would seem, are over: it can win back lapsed adherents, but has no resonance for young people in Berlin, Tokyo or Moscow. And while nearly a billion people are culturally Islamic – one fifth of the world's population – they cannot challenge liberal democracy on its own territory on the level of ideas. Indeed, the Islamic world would seem more vulnerable to liberal ideas in the long run than the reverse, since such liberalism has attracted numerous and powerful Muslim adherents over the past century and a half (2006: 45-46).

Let us now return to Daryabadi's tragic yet instructive story: how a young Muslim born and brought up in a traditional Muslim family "lost" the way and groped into the darkness of skepticism, even atheism for a decade, harbouring a negative, hostile view of everything Islamic. The Orientalists' writings filled his mind and heart with revulsion towards Prophet Muhammad (peace and blessings be upon him) in particular.

As already stated, Daryabadi was born in 1892 in a traditional Muslim family acclaimed for its scholarship andpiety. His mother and sister never missed even *tahajjud* prayers. Notwithstanding being a senior and high ranking civil servant, his father was a practising Muslim who observed all religious duties. Daryabadi's grandfathers, both paternal and maternal, enjoyed fame as Muslim religious scholars and jurists. From the very young age Daryabadi had been performing prayers regularly. As he studied Arabic at home under the care of personal tutors who were Maulwi, it was assumed that his upbringing in the Islamic terms of reference was impeccable. Since he was a voracious reader, he took to writing at an exceptionally young age. While he was in school, he wrote rejoinders to the polemical assaults against Islam by the Christian missionaries, Arya Samajis and other Islam-bashers. He was fascinated, in particular, by the forceful writings of Maulana Muhammad Ali Monghyri and Maulana Thanaullah Amritsari in defence of Islam. Allama Shibli's scholastic works also impressed him much as these vindicated the truth of Islam.

It was in 1908 after having passed his secondary school and as a student of senior secondary at Canning College, Lucknow when Daryabadi's faith was dented first by a seemingly innocuous work, *Elements of Social Science* by Dr Dyresdale. Since Daryabadi loved reading everything, he studied this from cover to cover, unaware that its author was a die-hard atheist. This work was not directed, in particular, against Islam. Rather, it challenged all religious commands about morals and ethics. Under the pretext of rationalism and freedom, it made a strong case for a permissive, even promiscuous way of life, free from any moral or religious restriction. For example, it strongly argued that man's sexual urge being natural should be satisfied by all means: one need not wait for marriage. On the contrary, suppressing sexual desires results in psychological and physiological disorder. The moral code imposed by clergy is artificial and pernicious.It is pointless to observe such moral teachings which do not let man do what he wants. For a sixteen years old young boy of a traditional Muslim family this message was both radical and confounding. For it called into question all the assumptions and vague beliefs he had so far about morals, social order and religion. Since such a message appeals to man's base self, as it gives man unbridled freedom, it was of some appeal to the young Daryabadi. What was, however, crucial was that at this critical moment when the young Daryabadi faced this dilemma, he did not have any mentor to guide him. His parents and other family members had no inkling of this new challenge. Nor was there anyone among Daryabadi's family or Ulema who was mentally trained or prepared to tackle this problem. For the young Daryabadi the assertions in the Western writings were no less than gospel truths. For the Westerners then seemed to be superior, powerful and hence truthful. It did not occur then to the young Daryabadi that these writers were blatantly false, intent on discrediting Islam and the Prophet (peace and blessings be upon him) by all unfair means, which involved telling, rather inventing lies and calumny.

Such Western writings first shook Daryabadi's moral and ethical assumptions. Rationalism presented before him a new world, which challenged and rejected the old order. He realized, for the first time, that things could be viewed from a totally different angle. This newly found sense of power thrilled and eventually undid him.

Next, he came across such Western writings which directly attacked and belittled Islam, portraying the Prophet (peace and blessings be upon him) particularly in dark colours. For example, in a public library in Lucknow, the young Daryabadi laid his hands on the multi-volume *International Library of Famous Literature,* containing a selection of literary works from all parts of the world. The section on the Quran carried a full length photograph of the Prophet (peace and blessings be upon him), with the citation of its source. It gave a layman the impression that it was an authentic photograph which featured in a prestigious Western publication. That it was sheer forgery was something unimaginable for the young Daryabadi. The photograph depicted the Prophet (peace and blessings be upon him) in the traditional Arab attire. Worse, it showed him as a harsh bloodthirsty warrior carrying weapons, given to violence and bloodshed. It convinced Daryabadi that all the stories he had heard about the Prophet's mercy, love, affection and compassion were baseless. He felt his elders had cheated him, by imprinting on his mind a false image. For him, that Western publication was an authentic source. He had then little idea that the immensely rich Hadith corpus contains every minute detail about the Prophet's illustrious life and actions. Nor did it occur to him that this forged photograph bears no resemblance to the Prophet's character and conduct. Overawed by the Western supremacy in thought, technology and power, he rather felt that the Muslim version of the Prophet (peace and blessings be upon him) was only propaganda, and that the Prophet (peace and blessings be upon him), at best, was a tribal chief always engaged in warfare. This was a major blow to Daryabadi's faith. Without any active effort on any particular person's part, say a Christian missionary, his belief in Islam and the Prophet (peace and blessings be upon him) was almost razed to the ground.

Philosophy, psychology and logic were his subjects of study at College. Rational and atheistic philosophers were studied in detail by him, which weakened further his faith. He was influenced much by philosophical writings of Mill, Hume, Spencer and Bradley. Apart from their works,

Maudsley's text books, *The Physiology of Mind* (1876) and *The Pathology of Mind* (1879)[1] too, contributed to Daryabadi's loss of faith. While discussing the fit of epilepsy as a disorder, Maudsley referred to the experience of receiving divine revelation, as claimed by the Prophet (peace and blessings be upon him) as an illustration, though adding that an epileptic person may accomplish something outstanding. Such expert opinions by the specialists almost persuaded Daryabadi of the hollowness of religious assertions. Daryabadi's parents and well wishers had absolutely no idea that the textbooks at his college could be so lethal.

A little later, Daryabadi learnt about the inexpensive publications brought out by the Rationalist Press Association, London. These publications aggressively attacked faith, rituals and spirituality and strongly advocated rationalism and atheism. While these refuted in the main the Christian dogma, other religions were not spared either. Daryabadi enrolled himself as a member of this Association and regularly received a plethora of its publications. The constant supply of these publications hardened Daryabadi in his belief in pseudo-rationalism which bordered on atheism and revulsion towards every organized religion. Little wonder then that in his senior secondary examination form Daryabadi put "Rationalist", rather than Muslim in the column identifying his faith.

Notwithstanding the change in his outlook on matters of faith, Daryabadi did not sever his social and cultural ties with Muslims. He maintained close family relations, though it was an ordeal for his parents to put up with his non-observance of religious duties. Far from isolating himself completely with fellow Muslims, he reckoned himself as an enlightened member of the Muslim community. These social relations went a long way in facilitating his gradual return to the fold of Islam. For he had not moved away much further and farther. By Allah's grace, he did not take to drinking or any other vice forbidden by Islam. His early upbringing in consonance with the Islamic moral code may have deterred him from indulging in something which he had recognized since his childhood as a major sin. Moreover, he never imposed his atheistic views on anyone. A debate on his faith would have aroused hostility towards him and he too, would have turned more stubborn and defiant.

Owing to his thorough training in the Muslim religious ambience he faced some ironical, rather paradoxical situations during his atheistic phase. On listening to the anti-Islam outbursts of an Orientalist or a Christian missionary he instinctively and involuntarily defended Islam. For example, when in October 1911, the infamous Islam-basher, Orientalist and missionary S.M. Zwemer arrived in Lucknow for his presentation at a conference, Daryabadi called on him along with his friend, Maulwi Abdul

Bari Nadvi. In this informal meeting too, Zwemer criticized Islam on several counts. On each occasion both Daryabadi in English and Nadvi in Arabic refuted his objections.

Daryabadi's atheism nonetheless came to the fore in his critique in 1910 on Allama Shibli's *al-Kalam* in the Urdu periodical, *al-Nazir.*[2] Daryabadiused a pseudonym for the series of articles against Shibli's above work. Daryabadi contested the basic articles of Islamic faith, including God's existence, the institution of Messengership and the doctrine of the Hereafter. In doing so he appears as a brazen rationalist, not ready to grant any space to any religious truth. In the same phase he wrote his first full length book in English, *Psychology of Leadership,* brought out by a leading British publisher, T. Fischer Unwin, London in October 1915. It was favourably reviewed in the prestigious *Times Literary Supplement,* London. Maulana Ahmad Raza Khan Barelwi took a strong view of its derogatory stance on *wahy* (revelation) and *Sira* (Prophet Muhammad's illustrious life) etc and branded Daryabadi as a *kafir* (unbeliever). This decree was, however, challenged and refuted by such distinguished Ulema as Maulana Abdul Bari Firangi Mahali, Allama Syed Suleman Nadvi and Maulana Abdul Majid Firangi Mahali. They made some allowance for Daryabadi's offensive remarks. So doing they were presumably guided by this life-giving message of the Quran: "Call to the way of your Lord with wisdom and good advice. "(al-Nahl 15:125). Daryabadi's remarks betrayed the evil influence of the Orientalists upon his mind. Under their spell he hardly believed in the institutions of divine guidance and Messengers. Buoyed by the acclaim his *Psychology of Leadership* had won, Daryabadi published its enlarged version in Urdu under these two titles, *Falsafa-iIjtima* and *Falsafa-i Jazbat.* Since there was hardly any book available in Urdu on philosophy and psychology, these were received well, notwithstanding their objectionable and deplorable contents. These were prescribed as text books for setting in motion a new discourse, for introducing fresh, inventive terminology and for strengthening the genre of academic Urdu prose. After his return to the fold of Islam, however, Daryabadi ensured that these books of his were withdrawn from syllabus and were not re-issued. It is now hard to find even a single copy of these books.

The dark clouds of skepticism and atheism fogged Daryabadi's mind for almost a decade, from 1909 to 1918. His return to the fold of Islam is equally instructive. For it reflects the efficacy of certain strategies, of which the tactful use leads, by Allah's grace, to one's eventual realization of the truth of Islam. His account affirms also the importance of tact, perseverance and constancy on the part of those preaching truth. These qualities do impress and influence people and are essential to winning over the hearts and minds.

Daryabadi's unbridled study had resulted in his straying from the straight way. He did not have any mentor to allay his doubts and misperceptions. There was hardly any *'alim* around who could follow the language, and the range and tenor of the challenges posed by modern knowledge. The *Ulema* were not equipped at all to tackle this onslaught, as a result of which they could not provide any answer. This calls for sustained efforts to sensitize Ulema today to the new threats staring especially the young Muslims in the face. Today's Ulema should have a clear picture of the malaise afflicting the young Muslims and their vulnerability. Today young people, be they Muslims or adherents of any other faith, stand constantly exposed to the threats unleashed by both print and electronic media, internet, particularly the social networks and the ever-growing Westernization and globalization. Computer technology is actually an opportunity and a challenge for us, to be harnessed for preaching and promoting the life-ennobling message of Islam. Criticizing or boycotting the new technology will harm only us while the world would move one. What must be nonetheless ensured is that the young Muslims drawing upon these latest gadgets should be imbued with a strong moral sense, *taqwa* (awareness of accountability to God) and a definite direction and goal in life. Islam and monasticism are antithetical. We should tackle the challenges head on; we cannot merely wish them away. There was no one to answer the questions which troubled Daryabadi in his youth. For the Ulema had no inkling about the pitfalls. It is the crying need of the hour that Ulema and Muslim educationists and community leaders should have a nuanced understanding of the present way of life. Their rapport with the young should be robust and positive. They should be able to channelize the energy of the youth into positive, productive ways.

By Allah's grace, Daryabadi's own study of certain books made him rethink about his deification of rationalism. Up to that point he had studied the works of only Orientalists, rationalists and atheists. Under their spell he imagined that truth was represented only by them. His young mind was seemingly carried away by their powerful rhetoric, their quasi-logical arguments and pseudo-rational views. As already indicated, in his college or family no one offered him any guidance. His family members, who were pious and scholars in their own right, had no clue about the devastating contents of these new, modern Western writings. At college, most of the teachers were British, who had been fed on the secular liberal thought and hence were of no help.

As part of his keen and deep interest in philosophy, Daryabadi came across the writings of the German philosopher, Arthur Schopenhauer (1788-1860), whose ethical doctrines are influenced by Buddhism. His spiritual and ethical strain, rooted in Buddhism, struck Daryabadi and drew him to a detailed study of Buddhism. It convinced him that Buddhism is not some trash, consisting merely of superstitions. That much exists beyond the realm of matter came as a revelation to him. His interest in spirituality was developed and refined by his in-depth study of the Chinese sage, Confucius's moral and spiritual teachings, and more importantly, by his coming to grips with theosophy and Hindu thought and mysticism. The works of Mrs. Annie Besant and Dr. Bhagwan Das, who have elucidated Hindu mysticism, impressed him much. Besides, he read also the writings of Tilak and Sri Arabindo Ghosh. This led him to study the Hindu scripture, *Bhagwat Gita* in its English translation. This presented before him a new spectacle of spirituality and transcendence. Gandhi's writings, abounding in morals and spirituality, also struck him. Thanks to the study of this different set of books, within a year his mind was transformed. He now looked with disdain at materialism and rationalism. For he had come to realize that the Western rationalists and atheists cannot and do not decode or interpret the mysteries of nature. He found some better, convincing and cogent interpretations of life and the universe. By comparison and contrast he concluded that the views of Buddha and Krishna were not inferior in any degree to those of Mill and Spencer. To his good fortune he had now access to a new, different and comforting worldview. This eventually culminated into his total rejection of pseudo-rationalism and atheism. The intellectual edifice of the West, which once filled his mind and heart with awe, was no longer of any appeal to him. On his encounter with the Hindu mystic and scholar, Bhagwan Das, Daryabadi records these observations:

> On my way to Calcutta in June 1913 I stayed for a day or two in Benaras and met Dr Bhagwan Das there. I had been enthralled by his philosophical works. He appeared as a saint, with luster in his eyes and a halo around him. He was both a philosopher and practitioner of Hindu mystical and spiritual exercises. Throughout my discussion with him he talked about truth and its numerous manifestations and the higher reality. My atheism was considerably shaken by his spirituality. Had I not met him during that period, I would have been steeped in error for a longer time and might have been hardened in my atheism.
>
> Allah may direct anyone anywhere to guide others to truth, as it happened in my case.[3]

One big gain which Daryabadi had on account of his close study of mysticism and Buddhist and Hindu thought was his realization that certain things and experiences do exist beyond the realm of man's sense perception. In the Quranic parlance this is known as *al-ghayb*. Significantly enough, the Quran asks believers to have faith in *al-ghayb* which alone perfects their conviction. Daryabadi's spiritual experience helped him return sooner to Islam. It enabled him to free himself from the shackles of narrow materialism and pseudo-rationalism.

Soon Daryabadi's attention turned to the writings of Muslim authors, which gradually persuaded him fully of the abiding truth of Islam. Since his childhood he was a great admirer of Allama Shibli's stylistic charms and his chaste idiomatic Urdu prose. Around 1918 the first volume of Shibli's *magnum opus*, *Sirat al-Nabi* (The illustrious life of Prophet Muhammad (peace and blessings be upon him) came out. He was drawn, initially towards it for savouring Shibli's enviable command over Urdu. However, on studying it he eventually realized the greatness, nobility and perfection of Prophet Muhammad's character. Shibli's cogent account helped him dispel the misconceptions he had, based on the Orientalists' writings on Prophet Muhammad (peace and blessings be upon him). They had projected him only as a warrior, given to violence and bloodshed: Daryabadi's young, unsuspecting mind had bought this false story from them. However, on reading Shibli's work, he noted, for the first time, that the Prophet (peace and blessings be upon him) was essentially a guide *par excellence*, full of love, mercy and affection for everyone, including his enemies who were after his life. He was an exceptionally generous, noble person who resorted to war only in self defence. The false, negative image of the Prophet (peace and blessings be upon him) as conjured up by the Westerners, was exposed and Daryabadi's hostility was replaced by his tremendous respect for the Prophet (peace and blessings be upon him) whom he now regarded as the benefactor of mankind and as the role model for all time and place.

Daryabadi's study of Hindu mysticism and theosophy aroused his interest in Muslim mystical writings too. He no longer felt averse to the truth of religious and spiritual experiences which he earlier used to dismiss scornfully as something irrational and improbable. Apart from some titles on the subject available in English, he read many in Persian and Urdu. In 1919 he laid his hands on Rumi's *Mathnavi*. This work cast almost a spell upon him. Often was he so engrossed in its study that he forgot to take meals or even sleep. He cried profusely on reading some of its passages which are pregnant with truth, mysticism and spirituality. Its study helped him much in shedding his rationalism and atheism. Although he had by then not fully reverted to Islam, he recognized the truth innate in Islam. During the same period he studied a host of other Muslim mystical works such as Farid al-Din al-Attar's *Mantiq al-Tayr* and Jami's *Nafahat al-Uns*.

Another work which brought Daryabadi closer to grasping the true meaning and message of Islam was Shaykh Ahmad Sirhindi's, popularly known as Mujaddid Alf Thani's *Maktubat.* Like Rumi's *Mathnavi*, it had a spell binding effect on him. According to him, the following benefits accrued to him from the study of *Maktubat:*

> Rumi's *Mathnavi* had no doubt enthused me; awakening me to the truth of religious experience. *Maktubat*, nonetheless, guided me to the path of seeking and winning Allah's pleasure. It now dawned on me that I should not wander at shrines; the straight way is represented by Shariah alone. Obeying the Prophet's commands and teachings is the only way for attaining Allah's pleasure. Thus both these works, in their own ways, guided me to truth. I will never forget this debt of gratitude to them. Let me add that it was only a self-study, without any input from some teacher or guide.[4]

In October 1920 while Daryabadi was in Hyderabad, he came across Muhammad Ali's *English Translation of the Quran* (1917). Notwithstanding its Qadyani streaks, this translation being in English appealed much to him. Such was the servile mentality of Indians, including Muslims, in the British India that something written in English evoked far greater respect than a precious work in Arabic, Persian or Urdu. Anyway, when he finished reading this Quran translation, he had no mental reservation or doubt about Islam. By Allah's grace he returned to the fold of Islam, with the resolve to spread its message throughout his life.

Daryabadi then brushed up his Arabic and embarked upon his extensive study of *tafasir*, especially of Baidwai, Zamakhshari, Hadith collections, works on *fiqh* (jurisprudence) and Arabic language, especially lexicon. All this went a long way in equipping him well for his major undertakings at a later stage, especially in the field of *tafsir*. For, he holds the unique distinction of having authored two full length *tafasir* in English and Urdu. Since these are addressed to different readerships, the two works are almost independent of each other.

The valuable lesson to be learnt from the above account of Daryabadi's drifting into error and his highly welcome reverting to Islam is the importance and need of parental supervision or *tarbiyya* of the young ones. They should be alive to the intellectual needs of their children on the same scale on which they readily and willingly meet their children's material needs. It goes without saying that all parents may not have such competence or time and energy to cater to the intellectual challenges faced by their children. Yet the community as a whole should be alert to this danger. At least some Ulema and community leaders should shoulder this important responsibility of answering the questions agitating the mind of the young. This is needed all the more in today's globalized world. Consequent upon the explosion of knowledge in our time and thanks to internet, there are newer, more complex challenges. Parents and community leaders, especially Ulema should come to terms with the prevailing ethos and while making some allowance for the adolescent psyche, they should evolve a suitable strategy in order to minimize their drifting and delinquency.

A gruesome challenge today is radicalization which has placed the honour, life and even survival of the Muslim community across the world in jeopardy. We have to do soul searching as to why in the name of Islam some misguided youth go to the extent of killing wantonly, taking away the most precious gift of life, granted by Allah. The Quran unequivocally condemns mindless killing and places much importance on the sanctity and inviolability of life, as is evident from this Quranic assertion:

> If one kills a person, unless it be in punishment for murder or for spreading mischief on earth, it is as if he had killed all mankind. And if one saves the life of a person, it is as if he saves all mankind.
>
> (al-Maidah 5:32)

As we have noted, Daryabadi's unsupervised study proved to be his bane. Out of His mercy Allah directed him a little later to such a study which enabled him to appreciate and cherish the truth and supremacy of Islam throughout his later life. He was fortunate enough also to come into contact with some wise, tactful and noble personalities who served as Daryabadi's mentors. They influenced him in a variety of ways which helped him realize his error and embrace the truth of Islam. Let us now turn our attention to Daryabadi's mentors.

Notes

1. *Aap Biti,* p. 240.
2. Ibid., p. 243.
3. Ibid., p. 150 and Abdul Majid Daryabadi, *Muasirin,* Calcutta, Idara Insha-i Majidi, 1995, p. 54.
4. *Aap Biti,* p. 257.

5

Daryabadi's Mentors: Akbar Allahabadi, Allama Shibli, Maulana Muhammad Ali Jauhar and Maulana Ashraf Ali Thanwi

It has been part of divine dispensation that in every age and at every place there are pious, noble souls who guide and help the seekers of truth. Since the beginning of time this divine arrangement has been in place. The institution of Messengership is the culmination or perfection of the same. After the revelation of the Quran in full, Allah's declaration of Islam as the final religion for mankind until the Final Day and after Prophet Muhammad's demise, it has been the responsibility of the Muslim community as a whole to call people to the way of truth. Muslim history is characterized down the ages by the presence of numerous illustrious figures who have performed well the role of moral and spiritual guides for both fellow Muslims and non-Muslims alike. Their lifelong devotion has resulted in providing guidance to millions. Ulema and some Sufi masters have all along discharged this onerous duty. Little wonder then that such Ulema enjoy tremendous respect and admiration among Muslims.

As already noted, in Daryabadi's case his family members could not diagnose or remedy what ailed him. They had no idea of the crisis faced by the young Daryabadi as his study of Western writings had turned upside down his image of Islam, Prophet Muhammad (peace and blessings be upon him) and religion in general, which he had inherited from his devout parents and larger family. Being traditional Muslims of the late 19th century British India they had no idea of the poison spread against Islam and religion by the secular-liberal, Godless Western education.

Akbar Allahabadi (d. 1921), a highly popular and influential Urdu poet of the day acclaimed for his wit, pun and satire, was nonetheless an exception to the generality of Muslims with a conventional thinking mould. Being a judge associated with the British judicial system he had the first-hand knowledge of the Western way of life. More importantly, he was devoted heart and soul to preserving and promoting the Islamic way of life. He was acutely, rather painfully aware of the devastating effects of Westernization on the Indian Muslims. He foresaw the decline and loss of Muslim identity and way of life in the years to come. In the light of his study of the West he believed that the Westernization like a monster will soon trample upon and crush everything Islamic not only in the British India but also in the entire Muslim world. His forceful criticism against the threats posed by Westernization lies at the heart of his poetry, which is mostly satiric. As a satirist he knew well what things are and what they ought to be. The wide disparity between the ideal and real made him, at times, sarcastic. Notwithstanding the piety and sincerity of his intention, his was the lone voice amid the glitter and ascendancy of Westernization which made its way both rapidly and deeply into the Indian polity, including the Western- educated Muslims in particular. It is also a sad fact that his ire against the West signifies, at most, his fury over his fighting a losing battle. He did not and could not chart out the alternative Islamic way of life, a noble mission which was to be accomplished later by Dr Iqbal, Saiyyid Mawdudi and Daryabadi. They went a step farther than Akbar in spelling out extensively and convincingly the Islamic way of life, consisting of befitting responses to the challenges thrown by Westernization.

Akbar Allahabadi was essentially a friend of Daryabadi's father. The family terms deepened as in 1910 Akbar's son, Ishrat Hussain was posted as Deputy Collector in Sitapur, where Daryabadi's father was leading life as a retired Deputy Collector. The young Ishrat Hussain stayed at Daryabadi's house in Sitapur and became his good friend. Daryabadi's father took very good care of his friend's young son. So when Daryabadi visited Allahabad for writing his BA examination, as Daryabadi's Canning College was affiliated to the University of Allahabad, Akbar received him warmly and affectionately. Daryabadi's refined literary taste soon brought him closer to Akbar who was much senior to him in age. That was the same period in which Daryabadi had fallen a victim to pseudo-rationalism and atheism. Tactfully Akbar did not have any discussion with him on any religious issue. However, he got a fair idea of Daryabadi's mind and his disaffection with Islam and faith. Even after Daryabadi's return from Allahabad, Akbar remained constantly in touch with him through regular correspondence.

Notwithstanding the divergence of opinion between the two, Daryabadi was impressed by Akbar's conviction in monotheism and his friendly, non-confrontationist stance. Never did Akbar enter into polemics. Nor would he grow hysterical, using emotionally surcharged language, full of abuse against anyone who dared to question anything about Islam. Throughout the years when Daryabadi was averse to Islam, Akbar kept drawing his attention very wisely to truths inherent in Islam which made Daryabadi pause and think. His was an exceptionally soft yet eloquent and effective stance which often forced Daryabadi to think afresh about his own dogmatic and false position.

Daryabadi has cited several instances of Akbar's tactful handling of his audacious stance on Islam. For example, while commenting on Daryabadi's *Psychology of Leadership* he complimented Daryabadi for having highlighted man's mortality. A leader, no matter however successful and mesmerizing in his appeal, is after all a mortal human being, bound to die like any ordinary person. Akbar did not take issue with Daryabadi about some of the outrageous contents of his book which blatantly attacked religious sensitivities. For, he recognized that it would be counter-productive and might harden Daryabadi in his opposition. On the contrary, he praised the common ground between some of his views and the religious truth. This was his charming way to endear even his adversaries. Daryabadi too, felt drawn towards him in view of his affection and his tolerant attitude. He kept visiting and writing frequently to Akbar. However, both in his meetings and letters Akbar always made it a point to enlighten Daryabadi by way of mentioning some religious truth or posing a tricky question which rattled Daryabadi's rationalistic and atheistic assumptions. Once he enquired Daryabadi about the subjects, he had offered for his graduation. On learning that Arabic was one of his subjects, he expressed his great delight and a little later told Daryabadi: "For mastering Arabic, do read the Quran. It is a literary masterpiece and in the same capacity is accordingly prescribed in German universities. You need not perform *wuzu* (the ritual ablution) for its recitation. Read it as much as you like and when it suits you. Its study will help you master the Arabic language. Ignore those Quranic statements with which you cannot reconcile. However, do pay attention to those which strike a chord in your heart."[1] It illustrates how intelligently he urged the atheist Daryabadi to study the Quran attentively.

Akbar's letter of 19 February 1916 to Daryabadi reiterates the same: "Try to follow the Quran in original Arabic. This you can achieve by studying it regularly. As to *tafasir,* these are amazingly diverse in their approaches. Do not study the Quran for the sake of earning some divine reward. Read it for its literary hallmarks. I am sure some of its verses will leave their imprint on your mind."[2]

On another occasion, as Daryabadi recalls, he asked him:

> "You may have certain doubts about God, His existence and His attributes. Tell me, did you ever have any doubt about you as someone other than a human being? "His question took me by surprise. For I had never looked at the issue from this vantage point. Meekly I replied: "No, never did I have any doubt about my humanness. I think no one can at all contest this truth." Now it was his turn to shake me further: "This realization of humanness is enough. Keep affirming this. For, no one has ever fully grasped God's being and attributes. Even

outstanding scholars and gnostics differ widely on this issue. What really matters is man's consciousness that he is no more than a human being."

Akbar's above remarks kept haunting Daryabadi's mind for long time. Even after Daryabadi had returned to the fold of Islam which gratified Akbar much, he continued performing the role of his mentor, instructing him how to follow the best course in practising Islam. As already noted, in the transition phase between atheism and faith, Daryabadi had studied Rumi's *Mathnavi* and was deeply moved by its spiritual and moral tenor. Its study had facilitated his return to Islam. Out of gratitude for the same he recurrently mentioned Rumi's *Mathanvi* when he met Akbar. Akbar was first and foremost a monotheist, ever-conscious of Allah's greatness and glory. After listening repeatedly about Rumi from Daryabadi, he grew somewhat uncomfortable and asked him: "What do you think who is greater – Allah or Rumi?" This left Daryabadi speechless. Akbar then added: "In this session I have heard you speaking so highly of Rumi. This prompted me to seek your answer to the above question as to who is great – Allah or Rumi. You are under the false impression that Rumi has guided you to truth. Drop this idea altogether. It is Allah Who blessed you with guidance with Rumi's aid."[3] Daryabadi brings out this extra-ordinary trait of Akbar's personality thus:

> Hardly did I meet anyone other than Akbar who was so particular, so sensitive and so possessive about the basic Islamic doctrine of *tawhid* (Allah's Oneness and His matchless glory). Whatever be the topic of conversation, he would always link it with Allah's greatness and uniqueness. He could not put up with some extensive praise for any Sufi master or religious scholar, as he punctuated it with monotheism. To crown it all, on listening to even the Prophet's euology he would remark: "Look at Allah's creative wonder: how He created such a perfect man as Prophet Muhammad (peace and blessings be upon him)."[4]

On another occasion he made this valuable point which was immensely instructive for the young scholar, Daryabadi:

> Such men of letters who have displayed only their literary and stylistic accomplishments, they were never blessed by a wide acclaim. Their expertise has been appreciated only by the select few, as for example, the authors of *Shahnama* and *Sikandarnama*. In contrast, those who devoted themselves to proclaiming God's greatness and were self-effacing, Allah has made them highly popular. They are household names, as for example, Rumi, Sadi and Amir Khusrau.

Akbar believed even during the peak period of Daryabadi's atheism that he would one day realize the truth of Islam and turn into a devout Muslim. This is illustrated best by the following incident as reported by Daryabadi:

> In his letter to Akbar, Dr Iqbal remarked: "Daryabadi seems obsessed with Bergson, as he talks all the time about his philosophy." To this Akbar replied: "*Inshallah* (Allah willing) soon there will be a time when he would overwhelm Bergson."[5]

In his early, young days Daryabadi was impressed much by the spiritual strain in Gandhiji's political thought. He spoke highly of this many times in his meetings with Akbar. The latter, however, made him rethink over his excessive fondness, as he asked Daryabadi bluntly:

> "I believe the recitation of the credal statement of Islam (There is no god besides Allah) must be a prerequisite for joining Gandhi's non-cooperation campaign." When I replied in the negative, he quipped: "Your profuse and lyrical praise for Gandhiji's spirituality had made me believe that monotheism must be the cornerstone of his campaign."[6]

Akbar did not spare even Iqbal. While taking exception to Iqbal's occasional triumphalist assertions, he enlightened Daryabadi thus:

> One's victory or defeat in a war is something preordained. What Muslims are required to do is to adhere fast to Shariah. They should disregard the issue of any immediate gain or loss. What ails us is that we have neglected the Hereafter altogether. We are no more concerned about seeking Allah's pleasure.[7]

Daryabadi learnt much from Akbar's insightful view of life, especially with regard to the matters of faith, wholesale surrender to Allah's will and constant strife for winning His pleasure. Akbar enjoys reputation as an accomplished poet. Daryabadi drew upon his literary and artistic acumen. However, he benefitted much from Akbar's sound religious views. For Akbar dexterously inculcated these into Daryabadi's mind and heart. Consistently and strategically Akbar worked and achieved the hard task of bringing him back to the fold of Islam. Until his last breath Daryabadi recalled with utmost gratitude this big favour done to him by Akbar. His example illustrates the pivotal role of tact, wisdom and strategy in persuading someone of the truth of Islam. Polemics, heated debate or hostile confrontation do not help the cause of *da'wah* (call to Islam), though people are generally apt to taking instinctively a very hard and strong position on matters of faith. So doing, they make no allowance for the mindset and special circumstances of the addressee. In tackling Daryabadi,

Akbar, however, acted well on this Quranic directive: "Call to the way of your Lord with wisdom and good advice. Argue with them politely." (al-Nahl 16:125).

Muhammad Ali Jauhar (1878-1931) was like a hero for Daryabadi in view of his single-minded commitment to Islam, his enviable command over both the spoken and written varieties of English and Urdu, and his statesmanship. Daryabadi was introduced to Muhammad Ali in 1911 as a Muslim journalist *par excellence* in his capacity as the editor of the English weekly *Comrade*. At a later date he heard him as an orator and public speaker, particularly as a towering leader of India's freedom movement and the Khilafat movement. When Muhammad Ali brought out his Urdu weekly *Hamdard,* he came to know Daryabadi better as a competent contributor to his weekly. This was the beginning of Daryabadi's life-long association with and admiration for him. He acknowledges his indebtedness to Muhammad Ali in the following comparative note:

> In the religious and spiritual sphere I was attached most to Maulana Thanwi. No other religious scholar commanded from me such respect which I always had for Maulana Thanwi. However, as to my love and devotion, it was always reserved only for Maulana Muhammad Ali. Thanwi was my mentor, and Muhammad Ali my ideal.[8]

Daryabadi's tremendous admiration of and overflowing love for Muhammad Ali is reflected at its sharpest in Daryabadi's biography of Muhammad Ali in Urdu entitled *Muhammad Ali: Zati Diary ke Chand Waraq* (published between1954-1956). Far from being a conventional biography, Daryabadi records in this work his impressions about Muhammad Ali as his ideologue, in both political and Muslim community life. Muhammad Ali was one of the most distinguished public figures up to 1930s on the turbulent political centre stage of the British India. He made a mark as a first-rate journalist, a spell-binding orator, a freedom fighter, a pan-Islamist whose only loyalty was to the interests of Muslims. For almost two decades he was the unchallenged leader of not only Indians and Indian Muslims but also of the Muslims across the world, reeling then under British imperialistic tyranny. He obtained his education first at the MAO College which was elevated later as the Aligarh Muslim University, and later at the University of Oxford. Little wonder then that he had a remarkable flair for writing in English. His editorials in *Comrade* which usually consisted of scathing attacks on British imperialism, were acclaimed even by the British for their stylistic and presentation qualities, wit and mastery over English idiom and usage. As a student of history he was particularly alive to the nefarious designs of the British imperialism not only in India but also in

Palestine, Turkey and the Arab world. He eloquently warned Muslims against the impending threats, urging them to close ranks in their battle against the enemy. It is a pity that he faced bitter opposition from the sectarian groups within the Indian Muslim community. Most of his time and energy were wasted on tackling the opposition from within. He was often betrayed by even those close to him and he passed away in his middle age, without attaining any achievement to his credit. He nonetheless influenced Daryabadi in many ways.

In 1915 when Daryabadi sent him a copy of his book *Psychology of Leadership* published from London, Muhammad Ali sent him a long critique of 14 pages. While he complimented Daryabadi for his grasp over Western philosophy and modern thought, he minced no words in chiding, rather berating him for his fallacious, atheistic views:

> My criticism is directed in particular against your account of the Quran and Prophet Muhammad (peace and blessings be upon him). I thought you were a true, practising Muslim. Given this, I am utterly shocked over your belittlement of the divine scripture and of such an illustrious figure as of Prophet Muhammad (peace and blessings be upon him). Is it by way of infusing the so-called academic "objectivity"? Your tone and tenor smack of the same wickedness which vitiates the Christian missionaries' stance. You have crossed all limits in finding fault with the Quranic commands.[9]

His plea to Daryabadi to grasp and appreciate the truth of Islam is to the fore in his following letter:

> You are more familiar with Ghazali's philosophical corpus than I am. Had his *Ihya al-'Ulum* been translated into French at an earlier date, everyone would have taken Descartes as a plagiarist. Read again Ghazali's autobiographical notes. He arrived at the conclusion that the real observation transcends any logical argument and manifestation of this life. For God's sake, devote your knowledge, scholarship and talent to the cause of Islam alone. Do not be deluded by the deceptive modern thought.[10]

As a true mentor, Muhammad Ali advised Daryabadi on a number of issues. For example, he once told Daryabadi:

> I find you having gone too far in your veneration of Gandhiji. You take him even as a religious and spiritual master. Look at me, I do not have any such delusions. At most, I regard him as a political leader and would gladly follow him in that sphere. For he has surpassed all others in striving for the Independence of our country.[11]

Muhammad Ali's undivided loyalty to Islam is evident also from the following incident reported by Daryabadi:

> During his visit to Lucknow in 1923 a mischievous Araya Samaji newspaper flashed this provocative news item: "What kind of Indian is Muhammad Ali who publicly says that even an evil-doing Muslim is better than Gandhiji?" In the evening there was a crowded public meeting chaired by Chaudhri Khaliquzzaman. Someone sent him a slip, carrying the above question to be answered by Muhammad Ali. The Chaudhri disallowed the question so that a controversy be avoided. Muhammad Ali, however, insisted on responding to it. He proclaimed: "This question has two aspects. It first involves the issue of one's belief in God's oneness and the institution of Messengership. Whoever believes in these doctrines, I am bound to take him as a better, superior person. I am not concerned with his conduct, no matter what it might be. My only concern is with his faith. By contrast, one who does not subscribe to the above doctrines, is inferior in terms of his faith, though he may be a person of excellent character and conduct. I may regard Gandhiji as the best political leader and in that capacity he is superior to my respectable mother, and even my spiritual master. However, as far as faith is concerned, every Muslim is superior to him. Does Pandit Madan Mohan Malwiya not entertain the same view regarding Hinduism? If not, it would mean that Hinduism and Islam are alike for him. Given this, why does not he then accept Islam?"[12]

Daryabadi testifies that on numerous occasions he witnessed the same unadulterated devotion to Islam on Muhammad Ali's part. He made no compromise about on in what he regarded as matters of faith. As a result, he evoked the ire of many, including those who were at some stage very close to him. He personified boldness and nothing deterred him from saying what he reckoned as truth. Illustrative of the same is the following extract of his speech which he delivered before Sultan Abd al-Aziz, the ruler of Saudi Arabia in 1926 at Makkah al-Mukarammah:

> Some persons have warned me that opposing the Sultan amounts to violating and defying the norms of his court which may entail dire consequences for me. To them my reply would be: When I did not care for the displeasure of the much more powerful British Prime Minister, George Llyod, why should I be afraid of a fellow Muslim, and especially when I speak within the hallowed precincts of the Holy Mosque in which hunting even a bird is forbidden?"[13]

Likewise, Muhammad Ali parted company with his life-long spiritual master, Maulana Abdul Bari Firangi Mahali over a political issue. On being challenged, he bluntly told his detractors that his oath of allegiance to the

Maulana was only for the sake of winning Allah's pleasure. Since on that particular issue he clearly felt that the Maulana was in error and that his stance was discordant with truth, he was no longer obliged to follow him.

As already stated, Daryabadi was influenced by Muhammad Ali in more than one way. First, since Muhammad Ali was an Oxford graduate, with his first-hand knowledge of the Western way of life and a scholar in his own right, it was hard for Daryabadi to dismiss out of hand his censure of Daryabadi's fallacious ideas. The following incident is quite instructive. With great delight Daryabadi informed Muhammad Ali that the noted British journalist and chief editor of the overseas section of *The Times,* London, Valentine Chirol had commended much his book, *Psychology of Leadership.* For a young Indian of Daryabadi's background, his commendation was the highest honour imaginable. However, Muhammad Ali immediately informed him that Chirol was essentially an imperialist and hence his favourable review was not of any worth. Chirol's wicked mind comes out in the following secret memorandum he had submitted to the Political Department, India Office, London against the backdrop of the Khilafat movement spearheaded by Muhammad Ali:

> I doubt whether the menacing character of the Pan-Islamic propaganda has yet been sufficient appreciated. Had it had another ten or twenty years to extend and consolidate itself... it would have constituted an extremely serious danger to British power, and very scheme of dealing with the remnants of the Ottoman empire after the war should, in my opinion, be carefully studied from that particular point of view.[14]

In other words, Muhammad Ali's views carried weight for Daryabadi: For he was not a traditional Muslim religious scholar, insulated and isolated from the currents and cross-currents of Western intellectuality.

Muhammad Ali's genius reflected amply in his impeccable English, his rhetorical speeches across the country, his towering public figure and his journalistic accomplishments overwhelmed Daryabadi. What, nonetheless, struck him most about Muhammad Ali was his championing the cause of truth, at the expense of antagonizing even his near and dear ones. Daryabadi imbibed these two outstanding features of his character, and these characterize his later career and writings. Mention may be made here only of Daryabadi's journalistic ventures. His Urdu weekly bore the very title *Sach,* which was later changed for legal reasons to *Sidq* and *Sidq-i Jadid.* All these three Urdu expressions literally mean truth. Daryabadi indeed inherited from Muhammad Ali this devotion to truth which he kept championing throughout his later career.

Another sphere in which Muhammad Ali exercised deep influence over Daryabadi was politics. At one level, under his impact Daryabadi was drawn towards politics, as he actively participated in the Khilafat movement, of which Muhammad Ali was the moving spirit. Daryabadi attended its sessions held in various parts of the country and delivered Presidential address at the provincial conferences. However, as he watched the popularity and decline of both the Khilafat movement and Muhammad Ali's political career, it disillusioned him totally from active politics. After Muhammad Ali's demise he never attended any public meeting, what to say of undertaking any political activity. This also explains why he did not actively campaign for the Pakistan movement either at a later date, though his sympathy was for this cause. He believed that Muslims should have the right of self determination, including a state of theirs. Notwithstanding his aloofness from public life in his later life, like Muhammad Ali, Daryabadi closely monitored and followed all those political events which had bearings on Muslims in India in particular, and all over the world in general. His numerous comments in his Urdu weekly bear out his awareness of the issues that affected Muslims in any degree. Like Muhammad Ali, Daryabadi too, was a pan-Islamist who wished to see unity, prosperity and success for fellow Muslims the world over.

With his impressive academic credentials and his exalted status as an eminent public figure Muhammad Ali was effective in arresting Daryabadi's further drifting away and in facilitating both his return to Islam and his embarking upon a career which was inextricably linked to upholding and preaching the truth of Islam and to working for the cause of fellow Muslims on the academic and journalistic planes. Owing to his hectic public life and his demise at the age of only 53 years, Muhammad Ali could not write any sustained work highlighting the excellence of Islam. He, however, had plans to write such books, including the elucidation of the teachings of the Quran. He often shared these ideas both personally and in his letters with Daryabadi. This too, had its impact on the young Daryabadi who resolved to do all that he could which his ideal and mentor, Muhammad Ali was unable to take up. As to Muhammad Ali's devotion to Islam, it is reflected at its best in Daryabadi's following account. Let this be borne in mind that the following incident is of 1917 when Daryabadi was steeped in the morass of his error:

> In 1917 when Muhammad Ali was in Chindwara prison, he got parole to attend a family wedding in his home town, Rampur. He passed through Lucknow. I was among the big crowd that had gathered at the Lucknow railway station to have a glimpse of their dear leader. As the train stopped and the crowd started chanting: "Muhammad Ali *zindabad.*" (Long live Muhammad Ali), he asked them

to stop and requested one of his companions who was well versed in the art of reciting the Quran to read out this apt passage from Surah Yusuf:

"O my companions of the prison, who is better – several gods or the One True God Who cannot be defeated? Those whom you worship besides God are mere names. You and your fathers have named them. God has not sent down any authority for them. All authority is only for God. He commands you not to worship anyone besides Him. This is the right religion. However, most of the people do not understand."

(Yusuf 12: 39-40)

It was a spectacle to watch. The British passengers on board were awe-struck. I accompanied Muhammad Ali to the next railway station and presented him the latest issue of the *Times Literary Supplement* which I then rated very highly. Amused, Muhammad Ali told me: "Do you know what is my plan as soon as I am out of prison? I will visit Europe for preaching Islam there." He was very fond of Iqbal's Persian *mathnawis,* namely *Asrar-i Khudi* and *Rumuz-i Bekhudi.* He had almost memorized these. He often used to recite these, next only to the Quran.[15]

Such was Muhammad Ali's attachment to Islam and as his true disciple Daryabadi imbibed the same trait which is evident from his writings. To sum up, it may be said that while Akbar tactfully made dents in Daryabadi's atheism through his profound remarks, Muhammad Ali instilled religious fervor into Daryabadi, turning him into a deeply committed and unswerving champion of Islam. May Allah bless these noble souls for their valuable roles in having guided Daryabadi to the truth of Islam.

Apart from Akbar and Muhammad Ali, some others, in their own ways, contributed to Daryabadi's reverting to Islam. Mehdi Ifadi, an Urdu writer is known more for the aesthetic and liberal strain in his works than for his commitment to Islam. Yet, being close to Daryabadi, he, at times, censured Daryabadi for his anti-religion stance. He admired Daryabadi's thorough grounding in philosophy and his rationalism. He reacted strongly to Daryabadi's *Psychology ofLeadership*, especially its derisory treatment of the Messengers of Allah, as he ascribed selfishness and deception to them. Daryabadi recalls with gratitude how Mehdi took him to task, though as a sincere well-wisher of his:

In my book, *Psychology of Leadership* I had derided the Messengers, equating them with this-worldly, nationalistic political leaders. As an atheist I felt no qualms in heaping derision upon them. Had anyone

> criticized this stance of mine, I would have dismissed it as the emotional outburst of some religious bigot, unable to fathom my critique. Mehdi was a great admirer, rather a lover of my writings. When he visited Lucknow next, he called on me and told me: "Look, who can be a bigger fan of your book *Psychology of Leadership* than me? Since you are much junior to me, let me tell you sincerely that you have belittled the Messengers, especially Prophet Muhammad (peace and blessings be upon him). Leaving the issue of faith aside, such derogatory attitude does not befit a scholar. Civility and good manners demand that those personalities who are held in tremendous esteem by millions of people, be mentioned decently". He spoke these words with such sincerity and force that I was instantly convinced that notwithstanding my disbelief in them I must henceforth speak of them with some respect befitting their exalted stature.[16]

Likewise, in his letter of 20 June 1918 Mehdi advised Daryabadi:

> During my meeting with you in Lucknow I had drawn your attention to the streak of irreverence in your description of Prophet Muhammad (peace and blessings be upon him). You have not degraded him yet there is some belittlement of his on your part. This smacks of undergraduate attitude. It does not fit in with academic grace and seriousness. You can easily find a way out by changing a word or two, without compromising your stand. If you allow, I can revise it for you along the above lines.[17]

Mehdi continued performing this role of a sincere advisor and friend, as is clear from his following letter of 4 June 1919:

> While revising your writings you must ensure that in the heat of your philosophical thought, you should not betray even any indifference towards religion. I want to see the same generosity of attitude in your works which characterizes the works of the Orientalist, Le Bon. You should not refer to the Prophet (peace and blessings be upon him) only by his name. If you use some honorific title of him, all readers will be indebted to you.[18]

Syed Suleman Nadvi, Daryabadi's life-long friend, both advised and chastised him for his taking liberty in mattersof faith. Since he was Daryabadi's sincere friend and a widely read scholar, Daryabadi was not put off by his advice and exhortations. Moreover, like Mehdi Ifadi, he profusely complimented Daryabadi for his insightful scholarship. In his letter of 3 December 1915 Suleman Nadvi wrote to Daryabadi:

> Please do go ahead with your plan of writing on the Quranic psychology. However, it should be for bringing out the excellence of

> the Quran, not for finding fault with it. If you seek to strengthen the cause of Islam, do write this book at the earliest. If you have any other motive, please have mercy on us. The Muslim community already has too many woes to attend to.[19]

Even since his student days Daryabadi had a close relationship with Allama Shibli (1857-1914) who was his father's friend. The young Daryabadi regularly visited Shibli during his stay in Lucknow and imbibed his refined literary taste. Daryabadi was an avid reader of Shibli's writings. It was his dream to emulate Shibli's prose style. And he was highly successful in assimilating Shibli's stylistic charms into his own prose style. At a later date Daryabadi won a wide acclaim for his own inimitable prose writings.

Notwithstanding his great admiration for Shibli, in the peak days of his rationalism and atheism, Daryabadi harshly reviewed Shibli's *al-Kalam*, though under the pseudonym of "A student". His extensive criticism was published in seven instalments in a literary magazine, *al-Nazir,* Lucknow. Daryabadi questioned in the philosophical idiom and under the evil influence of the Western atheists, the very existence of God, the institutions of divine revelation, Messengership and the Hereafter. He tried to tear into pieces all the articles of Islamic faith. Even after learning that Daryabadi was the author of such a disparaging review on his book, Shibli graciously maintained his affection for and patronage of Daryabadi. He entrusted to Daryabadi several academic assignments during that period. Shibli's conduct impressed rather overwhelmed Daryabadi. Shibli's *Sirat al-Nabi* was read enthusiastically by Daryabadi, though he was then groping into the darkness of skepticism and unbelief. In his letter of a much later date to his spiritual master, Maulana Ashraf Ali Thanwi, Daryabadi recounts thus the impact which Shibli's book on Prophet Muhammad (peace and blessings be upon him) had on him:

> During my atheistic days I was hostile in particular to the Prophet (peace and blessings be upon him). For the study of the Western/Orientalist writings had persuaded me that he was, at best, a cruel, unjust warrior who managed to gain some victories. It was in the same period that Shibli's *Sirat al-Nabi*, volume one, came out. Its contents, style and presentation perfectly suited the taste of the Western educated persons like me. Its study served as an antidote to my misperceptions about the Prophet (peace and blessings be upon him). It rooted out my misconceptions. When I finished reading it, I had a refreshingly positive image of the Prophet (peace and blessings be upon him) — of being a great reformer, a generous, kind and

compassionate head of state who took recourse to war only as the last resort.[20]

In addition to Shibli's *Sirat al-Nabi,* Dr Iqbal's poetical works too, brought. Daryabadi closer to Islam. Iqbal's value-laden sublime poetry which is rooted deep into the universal message of Islam struck a chord in his heart, as he acknowledges the same:

> Maulana Muhammad Ali was a great admirer of Iqbal's poems. Under his influence I too, read Iqbal and was converted fully as his fan. With passion and veneration I read his collections which came out at regular intervals, *Payam-i Mashriq, Bal-i Jibrail, Zarb-i Kalim, Javed Nama* and *Armaghan-i Hijaz*. Reading these I profusely cried as these touched and moved my heart. Iqbal's *Mathnawis* were next only to Rumi's *Mathnawi* in being the source of guidance and enlightenment for me.[21]

All the above mentioned distinguished personalities, their books and their varied strategies were, no doubt, instrumental in the change of Daryabadi's heart. Let us, however, not disregard the role of the *du'a* (supplications from the depths of the heart) made by Daryabadi's devout parents. In a highly moving way Daryabadi has recounted it thus:

> My father passed away in November 1912 at Makkah Muazammah while performing Hajj rituals. He was tormented badly by my atheism. He contacted many Ulema with the request that they guide me back to truth. On their return my relatives who had accompanied him in the Hajj told me that while holding the curtain hanging on Kabah, he had fervently made supplications for my reform and guidance. A devout Muslim's prayer may be accepted by Allah sooner or later. It is on record that Prophet Jacob (peace and blessings be upon him) had to cry profusely and for years before his eventual reunion with his son, Prophet Joseph (peace and blessings be upon him). Allah could not deny the same joy to a member of Prophet Jacob's progeny and of Prophet Muhammad's *umma* (community). My father, Abdul Qadir could not be made to suffer forever, thanks to Allah's boundless mercy.[22]

Among Daryabadi's mentors and benefactors Maulana Ashraf Ali Thanwi (d. 1864-1943) figures most prominently. However, it should be noted that, Daryabadi came into contact with him in 1927, seven years after he had returned to the fold of Islam. It is therefore true that Maulana Thanwi did not contribute to Daryabadi's transformation from an atheist to a practising Muslim. Nonetheless, Daryabadi's post-1928 career is marked by a very strong and deep influence of Maulana Thanwi on his character and conduct, his spiritual development and his academic attainments. Daryabadi's numerous writings, especially his adulatory account of Maulana Thanwi running into hundreds of pages, entitled *Hakim al-Ummat: Nuqush wa Tathurat* (Sage of the community: some impressions and memoirs) published in 1952, stands out as a testament to Daryabadi's accolade showered on him. In unequivocal terms in his autobiography he has acknowledged Maulana Thanwi as his mentor *par excellence:*

> I stand indebted to many for their favours to me. However, two personalities in particular shaped me what I am. Both of them gave me a sense of direction and purpose in life. Had I not been fortunate enough to benefit from them I would have wandered into error hither and thither.
>
> Of the two, the first one is Maulana Muhammad Ali, the towering public figure of my days. I idealized him. Since my childhood I had been impressed much by his mastery over English and his enchanting flair for writing. I came into contact with him in 1912 and my love and esteem for him increased by the day in view of his intellectual prowess and his moral and spiritual greatness. From 1923 to his demise in 1931 I became very close to him. Never did I feel hurt by what he said and did. Rather, I grew fonder of him as my relations with him deepened and broadened. In terms of his total commitment to Islam and Prophet Muhammad (peace and blessings be upon him), his complete trust in Allah, his sincerity of purpose and God-consciousness, his aversion to hypocrisy and affectation, his standing by the truth at the expense of antagonizing even his near and dear ones, his wit and discernment and his wide and deep scholarship, he was my ideal. May Allah bless him abundantly with Paradise.
>
> However, the other personality who benefitted me much more was of Maulana Thanwi. In my young age I had some misperceptions about him, taking him as a fanatic, narrow-minded religious person who colluded with the British. When my friend, Wasl Bilgrami prevailed on me to, at least, read some of his sermons, my eyes became wide open. First I entered into correspondence with him and then visited him. My closer contact with him introduced me to several amazingly good aspects of his personality, his excellent conduct, his enviable erudition and his perfect blending of Shariah and Sufi practices in his life. Both in word and deed he was a perfect Muslim. He excelled all others in reforming and guiding the seekers of truth comprehensively. For me, before him other masters paled into insignificance.

> Whatever little I have contributed to the cause of Islam and whatever purgation my base self has been able to attain, I owe all this only to him. I had contacts with many saintly, devout persons. However, none matched him in being such a perfect mentor and guide. Muhammad Ali was, no doubt, my ideal but Maulana Thanwi was my spiritual leader and master. I love the former and extol the latter.[23]

Soon after his return to the fold of Islam, Daryabadi started looking for a *shaykh* (spiritual master) to help him attain self purification and mould his character and conduct in consonance with the teachings of Islam. Initially he was not inclined at all towards Maulana Thanwi in view of his unconventional political stance for, unlike others Maulana Thanwi was not actively associated with the national freedom movement. His passivity on this front sounded very strange, even unacceptable to Daryabadi. Furthermore, Maulana Thanwi's own disciples had spread exaggerated reports about his strict discipline and his harshness. In 1927, however, Daryabadi's friend, Syed Maqbul Hussain Wasl Bilgrami presented him a collection of Maulana Thanwi's sermons, requesting him to browse. Somewhat indifferently Daryabadi glanced through this work and was enthralled by Maulana Thanwi's penetrating, eloquent style. He appeared distinct from the traditional Sufi masters and gnostics. Daryabadi soon grew fond of his writings and sought appointment with Maulana Thanwi. In 1928 he visited him first at his monastery at Thana Bhawan, a small town in Muzaffar Nagar district in the western U.P. He was drawn more towards Maulana Thanwi after this meeting. From 1928 to 1943 i.e. until Maulana Thanwi's demise, Daryabadi kept visiting him regularly, and, at times, for longer periods of time. Moreover, he remained constantly in touch with him through his letters which cover a wide range of academic and religious topics.

Maulana Thanwi struck Daryabadi on many counts. During his stay at Thana Bhawan he observed with amazement Maulana Thanwi's balanced, well regulated way of life which represented a marvelous example of time management, moral training and religious and spiritual guidance. He followed strictly a set routine and prescribed the same for his disciples, which had absolutely no room for anything vain or discordant with Shariah. He was not very particular about observing or teaching spiritual exercises or incantations. He paid more attention to improving the morals and manners of his disciples, instructing them to be fair in their dealings with all fellow human beings. For him, one's obligations to Allah's creatures carried the same weight as the obligations due to Allah. So doing, Maulana Thanwi set in motion the much-needed social reform in the decadent, custom-ridden Muslim society. He denounced all innovations and accretions in Muslims' religious life and urged them to return to the pristine purity of Islamic faith and practices. Far from presenting religion as something complex and full of rituals, he elucidated faith and its dictates in a simple, easy to understand way. Little wonder then that both his *tafsir*, *Bayan al-Quran* and his compendium about leading everyday life in accordance with Islam, *Bihashti Zewar* were highly popular in early twentieth century after their first appearance. He authored a very large number of books and treatises which went a long way in enabling ordinary Muslims to grasp the essentials of Islamic faith and practices. For making his message accessible to all he allowed everyone to print his books, without any copyright or royalty for himself.

As to his erudition, Daryabadi's tribute is noteworthy:

> His scholarship, especially in the coveted field of *tafsir* is impressive, matched by only few. Both his *tafsir* and Urdu translation of the Quran [i.e. *Bayan al-Quran*] stand out for their very many qualities, especially eloquence.
>
> He excelled also as a spiritual master and guide, what to say of his substantial contribution to gnosis, spirituality and *tassawuf* (mysticism). For example, his *Tarbiyat al-Salik* is an outstanding work, superior to even Ghazali's work on this subject. How true he was who conferred upon Maulana Thanwi the appellation," the sage of the community." Indeed he was a sage *par excellence*.[24]

Maulana Thanwi's illustrious personality was multi-faceted. Combined in him were a first-rate Quran and Hadith scholar, jurisprudent, Sufi master, theologian and public speaker whose sermons transformed the mindset and lives of many. In his long, close association Daryabadi was captivated by both his sound erudition and his unblemished conduct. He was not interested much in the spiritual accomplishments ascribed to him which usually caught people's fancy. It is not therefore surprising that Daryabadi's biography unlike most of the works of this genre in Urdu, does not border on hagiography. On the contrary, it documents a free, frank scholarly exchange of views between the two on a range of issues, including some of Maulana Thanwi's opinions which Daryabadi did not endorse notwithstanding the high regard which he had for him. Daryabadi was gifted with a critical mind which had been honed further by his Western education. Accustomed to analysing things rationally Daryabadi found it hard, at times, to accept blindly Maulana Thanwi's all views or findings. So doing, Daryabadi, it appears, was inspired also by the example of his ideal, Maulana Muhammad Ali. The latter had parted ways with even his *shaykh* (the spiritual master), Maulana Abdul Bari Firangi Mahali on a political issue of the day – to support or oppose Saud or Sharif as the ruler of Hijaz. Little wonder then that Daryabadi's work documents also the divergence of opinion between Maulana Thanwi and him on several theological, juristic and literary issues. At another level, Daryabadi's biography of Maulana Thanwi represents some lively discussions, fresh perspectives and insightful comments on these topics such as the divine dispensation, the second coming of Prophet Jesus (peace and blessings be upon him), the identity of Yajuj and Majuj (Gog and Magog), divine recompense for man's deeds, man's free will and compulsions, authenticity of the Quran, and the story of the two angels, Harut and Marut. At places one notices the divide between the traditional and rational mindsets and the tension arising out of the unquestioning regard for the classical masters on Thanwi's part and the natural urge to explore new options, especially in the light of the latest archaeological historical and scientific studies on Daryabadi's part. Nonetheless, Daryabadi always held Maulana Thanwi in great esteem. His adulation for him permeates the whole work. Here are some illustrations of his fulsome tribute:

> Although technically I had *bay'a* (the oath of allegiance) at the hands of another luminary, for all practical purposes Maulana Thanwi was my guide and mentor. I turned to him for resolving all issues, be these domestic, academic, moral or spiritual. And on every occasion I derived invaluable help and guidance from him.[25]

It would not be out of place to mention here a contentious issue between Maulana Thanwi and Daryabadi. Partly owing to his exposure to rational and liberal thinking and partly owing to his naïve desire or dream of seeing all Muslims as members of a single, united community, Daryabadi did not initially share the popular view held by Muslims that Qadyanis are non-Muslims. He gave them, especially the group of Lahoris among Qadyanis, the benefit of doubt in branding them as believers as long as they did not openly deviate from the basic articles of faith, particularly the finality of Prophet Muhammad (peace and blessings be upon him) as the Last Messenger of Allah Maulana Thanwi, however, asked him to reconsider his stance in view of the false notions of Qadynanis which could misguide the unsuspecting people. At a later date, especially in response to Maulana Abul Hasan Ali Nadvi's request, Daryabadi avoided giving publicly any allowance to Qadyanis. For the Qadyanis were apt to misconstrue Daryabadi's stance as a serious division among Muslims themselves about their unbelief.

To recapitulate, Daryabadi returned to the fold of Islam after having wandered in error for almost a decade. It was mostly his self study, especially of Rumi's *Mathnawi,* Mujaddid Alf Thani's *Maktubat,* and above all, the English translation of the Quran which helped him perceive and appreciate the truth and light of Islam. The influence of Akbar Allahabadi,

Muhammad Ali Jauhar, Syed Suleman Nadvi and others too, contributed to the change of his heart. What is all the more important and instructive is that after having consciously embraced Islam in his late twenties, Daryabadi devoted the rest of his life, until his ripe age of eighty-five years, to serving admirably the cause of Islam in a variety of ways, which is discussed in the next chapters of this work.

Notes

1. *Muasirin,* p. 29.
2. Abdul Majid Daryabadi (Ed.), *Khutut-i Mashahir,* Lahore, Taj Company, 1944, p. 79.
3. *Muasirin,* p. 30.
4. Ibid., pp. 30 and 31.
5. Ibid., p. 31 and 64.
6. Ibid., p. 31.
7. Ibid., p. 32.
8. Abdul Majid Daryabadi, *Hakim al-Ummat: Nuqush wa Tathurat,* Allahabad, Sadi Book Depot, 1990, p. 144.
9. *Khutut-i Mashahir,* p. 197.
10. Ibid., pp. 226 and 231.
11. *Muasirin,* pp. 37-38.
12. Ibid., p. 38.
13. Ibid., p. 41.
14. *Secret Memorandum by Political Department, India Office:* No. B233 dated 25 May 1916, p. 4. Cited in Feraqi's *Daryabadi*, p. 299.
15. *Muasirin,* p. 36.
16. Abdul Majid Daryabadi, "Mehdi Ifadi" in *Nuqush*: *Shakhsiyat Number,* 1, 40.
17. *Makatib-i Mehdi Ifadi.* Edited by Mehdi Begum. Lucknow, UP Urdu Academy, 1982, pp. 57-58.
18. Ibid., pp. 80-81.
19. *Maktubat-i Sulemani:* Edited by Abdul Majid Daryabadi. Lucknow, Sidq Jadid Book Agency, 1967, 1, 47.
20. *Aap Biti,* p.248.
21. *Muasirin,* pp.63-64.
22. *Aap Biti,* p.244.
23. Ibid., pp.357-359.
24. *Muasirin,* pp.20-21.
25. *Hakim al-Ummat,* pp.188-189

6

Daryabadi's Family Life and Demise

After having discussed at some length Daryabadi's scholarly career, public life and writings, let us now recount in brief Daryabadi's family life, his children and his demise.

In line with the Islamic teachings extolling a cordial, happy family life and leading a value-based way of life, Daryabadi led an exemplary life as a member, and later on, as the head of an extended family life. His homage, soaked in love and affection, to his parents and his brother and sister and more importantly, his affectionate description of his other close relatives, as recorded in his autobiography,[1] speaks volumes about his adherence to family values. His obituaries of these family members too, reflect his deep attachment to his near and dear ones. Notwithstanding his keen interest in Sufism, there was no ioata of monasticism or dereliction of his family obligations in his life. Rather, under Maulana Thanwi's influence he grew more conscientious about fulfilling his obligations towards fellow human beings, including his domestic servants. The moral and spiritual training which he received from his mentor awoke him all the more to his role and responsibility as the head of family to cater for the *tarbiyya* (moral upbringing) of those under his care. Moreover, as a highly educated person himself, he realized the need for developing the potentials of the young ones which would impart them life skills, enabling them to lead life confidently, fruitfully and independently. As someone devoted heart and soul to Shariah, he was no doubt particular about the observance of Islamic norms and commands. He tried his best to sensitize people to Shariah norms yet he did not resort to coercion on such issues. As a trained psychologist, himself, he knew full the effectiveness of sincere advice and counselling, a role which he performed patiently notwithstanding his busy academic schedule in relation to his family members. Daryabadi was born and brought up in the Muslim society in which extended, joint family system was the way of life. The agrarian, land-based economy of the day accounted, in the main, for this practice, which otherwise did not have any Islamic sanction. Anyway, this entailed greater friction and tension in family life. Both as a member and head of an extended family Daryabadi acquitted himself well of this complex, delicate responsibility. Throughout his life he had such cordial, close relations with his elder brother and his wife and children that their mutual relationship was cited as a role model by others. Its more telling proof is that Daryabadi's four daughters were married to the four sons of his elder brother. Daryabadi's nephews, nieces, first and second cousins and his wife's close relatives too, received such patronage, love and affection that he was hailed by everyone for his warmth and concern for their welfare. Although Daryabadi's was a family of small scale land lords, he, unlike others, never entered into any litigation, leading a peaceful life. He was so particular about his role as the counsellor and moral trainer that despite his important scholarly engagements, he spared time for frank, friendly discussion with all of his family members, including his young grandsons and granddaughters. He would ask all of them to meet him individually, one by one, with a written report of what he/she read and did yesterday. It was an exercise in writing skills too. More importantly, it served as the perfect setting for discussion, especially his guidance about what and how to read. He personally taught English and Arabic to some of his family members, once again at the expense of deferring his own important and valuable assignments. He encouraged the young to ask questions on a range of issues which would clear their mental cobwebs. It was amazing on his part to descend to the level of immature, ill informed and semi-literate persons in order to answer their queries. Besides, he appreciated the young participating in games and sports as he believed in the development of both the healthy body and mind. As long as he could mange until his ripe old age, he himself carried out some physical exercises, including long walks particularly in early mornings.

His time management was exemplary. This enabled him to accomplish much more than others. His association with the disciplinarian Maulana Thanwi made him all the more conscious and careful about time management. Yet he managed to spare time for maintaining social relations, for attending to the emotional needs of those under his care and for interacting with his local acquaintances every evening between Asr and Maghrib prayers. He spent every day more than a couple of hours with his family members, though at the specified time. He was so particular about the making the optimum use of time that since his thirties he had given up taking lunch, and had high tea instead in the afternoon. Likewise, he would keep noting on paper all the points he had to discuss with his family members, which saved everyone's time. As he led a highly organized life, with its minute by minute engagements, he resented any guest barging in. On the other hand, he received warmly those guests who had informed him well in advance of their arrival, and he devoted much of his time to them. His time management and organized life style with its well defined priorities are quite instructive for everyone. For, in the peak of his career as a writer and when he was in his thirties, he moved away from Lucknow, the centre of academic, literary, political and cultural activities to his much smaller home town of Daryabad which lacked even such basic amenities as roads, electricity, means of transport and communication. He spent the rest of his life at Darayabad and set up his huge personal library there. A few years before his demise when he could no longer draw upon his library owing to his failing eyesight and other crippling ailments, with a heavy heart he gave out his precious collections of English and Urdu books to the libraries of Nadwatul Ulema and the Aligarh Muslim University respectively.

He was blessed with a happy, peaceful marital life. His wife, though belonging to a more prosperous family, adjusted herself remarkably to Daryabadi's standard of life which was not high, especially in early years of their marriage. She soon won over the hearts of Daryabadi's mother and widowed sister and other members of his extended family. Although she bore two sons to Daryabadi, both of them died in infancy, which hurt her much. The couple was nonetheless blessed with four daughters who outlived their parents. Moreover, as they were married to the sons of Daryabadi's elder brother, they had more opportunities to look after their parents in their old age. Daryabadi's sons-in-law, who were his nephews, were also a source of strength for him. For they held him in great esteem and served him well in their own ways until his last breath. After his demise all of them took good care of Daryabadi's publications. As a result, most of his works were re-issued and continue to appear to this day. His marital and family life did face a crisis for a short period when in 1930 he took a second wife, a widow, with a view to helping her. His detractors overblew it and his first wife too, was disturbed much. Since the second wife proved to be utterly incompatible for him, he divorced her only after one year. This again was taken as a scandal by those hostile to him in public life. His domestic, marital life, however, soon regained its bliss. Daryabadi's wife passed away in January 1969, after being his life partner for more than fifty-two years. He mourned her demise both publicly and privately and recalled her with much fondness and joy until his last days. He showered his love and affection even on his domestic servants. In his youth and under the evil influence of the then feudal mindset of landlords he may have been harsh towards his servants, as he himself has confessed in his autobiography. However, after his return to the fold of Islam when he realized the importance of one's obligations to fellow human beings in Islam, he grew repentant. For atonement he set a new record, by alloting a share to his servants in his bequest. This underscores his concern for accountability on the Day of Judgment and for earning Allah's pleasure.

His organized life is typified by his extensive correspondence with a host of persons, including the subscribers of his Urdu weekly. Notwithstanding his poor eyesight he made it a point to send replies on the same day. For ensuring that they may get a copy of his reply in case it was lost in post, he went to the extreme length of getting all of his replies copied by hand and preserved. Little wonder then that seven huge posthumous volumes of his letters entitled *Maktubat-i Majidi* have appeared so far.[2]

Although he did not take up any employment, he managed to earn his decent livelihood, of the standard of a middle class person. The literary stipend granted to him by the Nizam of Hyderabad, some income from ancestral land and farming and some proceeds from his Urdu weekly and books sufficed for him to support his family. As he was a pious, contented person, he did not aspire for much. Nor did he know the art and craft of self promotion, publicity and organizing and leading a coterie of his admirers and followers who would project and sell him. However, one serious disadvantage of his insulated, isolated life style, free from groupism, was that his writings, quite valuable in their own right, could not get any publisher. Since he did not belong to any well entrenched establishment of Ulema, or a politico- religious group, no one came forward to publish even his extensively revised *tafasir* in English and Urdu. For years he presented this problem in his Urdu weekly that as an author he would love to see his life long revised work, Urdu *tafsir* published yet it did not have the desired effect. With his own meagre resources he managed to bring out only one – third of his revised *tafsir*. This reflects poorly on the apathy of both the Urdu publishers and the reading public. Only after his demise, the Academy of Islamic Research and Publications, the publishing unit of Nadwatul Ulema decided to publish these. While the English *tafsir* in four volumes came out between 1981 and 1985, his Urdu *tafsir* is yet to be completed. Until 2013 its six volumes up to Surah al-Hujurat have been published. What a loss for the field of Quranic scholarship that a valuable *tafsir* initiated in 1930s and thoroughly revised in 1970s has not still seen the light of the day!

Daryabadi led a full, ripe life, thanks to Allah's mercy and blessings. More importantly, he led in a sense a missioned life, working willingly and tirelessly for the cause of Islam. Being an independent minded person he did not enter into any employment, which, in turn, made him fearless in taking to task all those individuals and institutions that deviated from the path of good, morals and Islamic faith and practice. Yet he managed to earn his livelihood.

Throughout his life he enjoyed good health. In his old age, generally during seasonal change, he used to suffer from high fever. As a devout person he branded it as expiation for his acts of omission and commission. In 1974, at the age of 83 years, however, he had a paralytic stroke which dealt a fatal blow to his academic career. Notwithstanding good medical care and best efforts he could not regain strength to resume his academic work. He kept contributing, though nominally, to his Urdu weekly, which was published owing to the sincere efforts of his eldest nephew and son-in-law, Hakim Abdul Qavi, who was a writer in his own right. With each passing day in 1976 his condition deteriorated. After the fracture in his hip he was bed ridden. At dawn on 6 January 1977 he breathed his last in Lucknow. Maulana Abul Hasan Ali Nadwi led his funeral prayer at Nadwatul Ulema. His body was then taken to his ancestral town, Darayabad where he had spent almost all his adult life. At evening he was buried in a small cemetry, next to his house, rather facing his study. He lies buried next to his ancestor, Shaykh Makhdum Aabkash Daryabadi. (880H/1475CE). It tellingly symbolises the very ideals which had been so dear to Daryabadi – indigenous culture and tradition.

Notes

1. *Aap Biti*, pp. 32-58.
2. *Maktubat-i Majidi*. Edited by Muhammad Hashim Kidwai. 7 volumes have been so far published by Idara Insha-i Majidi, Calcutta and Applied Books, Delhi.

7

Daryabadi's Mission and Message

Let us recapitulate in this final, concluding chapter of this book, the main contours of Daryabadi's mission and message.

His is an instructive story of the abiding, ultimate appeal and charm of Islam as the natural way in that after wandering into the error of psuedo-rationalism and atheism, Daryabadi eventually returned to the fold of Islam. His story serves also a wake up call to parents, Ulema and community leaders that they should readily perceive and address the challenges to faith in every age. Their call to Islam should take into account the current issues, mental reservations and anti-faith tendencies. As for example, the general worldview in our time is secular-liberal, Godless, with the consensus view that religion being a personal matter should be relegated to an individual's personal life only, and should not have any role or presence in public life. Today such misperceptions are to be removed, rather than getting engaged in petty, trivial juristic details or sectarian differences, and presenting scholastic/theological issues in today's idiom, measuring to the mental level of the audience or readers. There is a need for a revised, updated *Ilm al-Kalam* (scholastic theology defining and explaining the articles of faith and religious practices. *Mujaddidin* (Islamic revivalists) have admirably accomplished this task in every age. In the Indo-Pak subcontinent Shah Waliullah, Maulana Thanwi, Saiyyid Mawdudi and Abul Hasan Ali Nadwi have excelled on this count. When Daryabadi was passing through his spiritual and religious crisis in 1910s, regrettably there was no outstanding religious scholar or mentor or a discerning member of the family to realize and remedy his problems. At yet another level, his story alerts us to the threat of cultural invasion. This is exactly the thing about which Caliph Umar had drawn attention when vast non-Muslim territories had been falling under the banner of Islam. The Caliph expressed some apprehensions about their un-Islamic ethos and their bad influence upon the new Muslims. Same holds true about the influence of an alien tradition upon Muslims, especially the young in every age. Daryabadi's elders did not grasp and respond fully to looming threat posed by the then ascendant Western culture and learning. The naive, unsuspecting Daryabadi fell a prey to the shrewd, sophisticated tactics of the anti-Islam Western writers and in time, he almost abandoned his ancestral faith which he had imbibed well in his otherwise religious-minded family. This, once again, should serve as a note of warning to Ulema and Muslims community leaders. They should ensure some moral training (*tarbiyya*) system which must offset the un-Islamic influences. The need for this has grown all the more pressing in view of the economic migration of Muslims *en masse* to the West and in today's globalized world. Millions of young Muslims in the West, Australia, South Africa, and India stand in need of such balanced, up to date religious education both in and outside the formal *madrasa* (Muslim religious educational institution) system, and such all-embracing, vibrant *tarbiyya* (moral upbringing and training) which may help the young Muslims gain conviction about their faith and enable them to resolve the numerous challenges caused by the Godless society and modernity with which they are destined to co-exist. The need for the same is there in the same degree even in the Muslim world. For the religious discourse, generally speaking, is too dated and mostly blind to the new threats. Daryabadi's eventual return to Islam was facilitated considerably by the visible and palpable Islamic milieu of his immediate surroundings and the remnants of the Muslim culture around him. This helped him go not too far astray in error. More importantly, the force and appeal of the indigenous culture acted as a strong catalyst for his return to Islam. In other words, the importance of the overall, prevailing cultural ethos in a society should not be underestimated. Another significant point emerging from Daryabadi's story is the role played by the mystical writings and the mystical tradition, in general, including even its Hindu variety. This tradition, though not governed largely by Shariah, is helpful, to some extent, in drawing the genuine seekers to truth. In today's religion-bashing context this tradition has assumed greater value, and should not be dismissed outright. Daryabadi lost his faith in Islam owing entirely to his unguided study of books which were hostile to Islam. This underscores the need for supervised study and the benevolent role of guides and mentors. Again, Daryabadi mostly derived guidance from his own study of such spiritually revitalizing and profound writings as Rumi's *Mathnawi*, Shaykh Ahmad Sirhindi's *Maktubat,* Iqbal's poems and Maulana Thanwi's sermons. This points to both the adverse and benign facets of books, and in today's context, of the latest means of mass media communication, especially internet. Concerted efforts should be undertaken today in order to introduce and elucidate Islam with the quality presentation skills and in an acceptable style and idiom. Apart from Daryabadi's self study, his company with such illustrious representatives of Islam as Akbar Allahabadi, Maulana Muhammad Ali Jauhar and Syed Suleman Nadvi etc. contributed also to his return to Islam. Needless to say, it underscores the importance of good company, especially in the context of enhancing one's faith, piety and character. In the Islamic *tarbiyya* system, the pivotal role of a guide and constant association with the pious reinforces the above observation.

Nonetheless, the most important lesson to be drawn from Daryabadi's re-entry into the ambit of Islam is his zeal for and single-minded devotion to serving the cause of Islam as best as he could. He reserved his pen, his academic pursuits and his mental faculties only for vindicating the truth of Islam. In all that he wrote after 1918, i.e. after accepting Islam by choice his only vantage point was Islam. So doing, he recanted all of his earlier predilection for Western philosophy and psychology, play writing, and literary and political activities which did not have any nexus with Islam. Instances of such total and exclusive commitment are rare.

To begin with, his Urdu weekly *Sach,* which came out in 1925, illustrates best how he employed journalism as the effective medium of explicating the Islamic faith and practice, of social, moral and religious reform, and promoting value-based way of life as prescribed by Islam. As already detailed in chapter 7, his Urdu weekly *Sach*, which was later re-christened as *Sidq* and *Sidq-i Jadid,* was of the same mould as Maulana Muhammad Ali's *Hamdard* and Maulana Abul Kalam Azad's *al-Hilal* in that all of these were much more than conventional periodicals. All of these were wedded unflinchingly to the cause of Islam and Muslims, especially of India. At one level, these disseminated and vindicated effectively the message of Islam, and at the other, these infused into their Muslim readers a strong sense of Muslim identity, and guided them about socio-political matters of the day. *Hamdard* and *al-Hilal* were, no doubt, very influential weeklies, edited by two towering religio-political figures, and had almost mesmerizing effect on their readership. But these were short-lived ventures, and in time got increasingly tangled with the volatile politics of the day, and the concomitant controversies and factionalism. In comparison, Daryabadi's weekly was in circulation for more than fifty years (1925-1977), and, more importantly, it did not stoop to active politics, notwithstanding its own political stance. What is remarkable is that it steadily and ably convinced its readers about the relevance of the Islamic teachings in the day, projecting Islam as a vibrant, cogent, and natural way of life. This is illustrated best by the regular appearance of substantial articles and captivating notes by Daryabadi himself and a host of Ulema on topics such as governance, economy, polygamy, gender segregation, widow marriage, *riba* (usury), and articles of faith in Islam. Likewise, the range of articles on the Quran brought out the truth, stylistic features and various aspects of the Quran translations and *tafasir* in world languages. The focus on explicating the meaning and message of the Quran increased in depth and rootage in time on the pages of his weekly. For example, in his *Sidq* weekly (1935-1950), as many 650 pieces on the Quran appeared, including the serialization of his Urdu *tafsir*. So doing, his objective was to address and resolve the issues of the day in the perspective of the Quran. The following select list of the discourse on the Quran substantiates the above observation: Neglect of the Hereafter by us notwithstanding the recurrent Quranic references to our accountability in the Next life; our indifference to the Quranic command for giving women their due share in inheritance; exalted status of mother, in particular, and of women, in general, in the Quran; segregation of women as featuring in Surah al-Qasas 28:25; the Quranic advice on treating unbelievers with justice; patriotism in the light of the Quran; the veracity of the divine origin of the Quran; predestination and free will; Darwinism, Christology and a host of other issues examined with a special reference to Quran.

Comments on current socio-political issues and even everyday life happenings and situations figured regularly in a special column entitled *Sachchi Baten* (the truthful discourse) in his weekly. What lent this column its unique touch and force was its pointed reference to the Quran as the sole criterion for passing judgement. Apart from displaying Daryabadi's Quranic erudition, it urged readers to relate all the issues to the life-giving abiding message of the Quran.

Daryabadi's championing the cause of Islam is more pronounced and unequivocal in most of his books. Leaving aside some books and translations up to 1918 when he had not grasped in full the truth of Islam, all of his later writings are permeated with the overarching objective of elucidating the message of Islam in a variety of ways. As we noted earlier, even while engaged in penning down his travelogues, brief life sketches of his contemporaries, and his own autobiography, he always makes it a point to draw readers' attention to Allah's creative wonders, His boundless mercy, divine providence and dispensation, and Islam as the natural way. In all of his writings he is seen exhorting readers with all the force and persuasive charms to adhere to the way prescribed by Allah i.e. Shariah. More remarkably, his call is not in the form of some dry, prosaic sermon. Logic, argument, reasoning, wit, imagination, humour and irony, and stylistic charms are dexterously interwoven in most of his writings which strike a chord in every heart. Take his travelogue of Hajj as illustrative. Generally speaking, a Hajj travelogue relates one's experiences, including his account of the Hajj rituals. Daryabadi's version, however, goes far beyond the limits of this genre in situating and explaining the sacred geography and history, in delving deep into the essence and rationale of Hajj rituals, in detailing some of the benefits of this Islamic religious practice for humanity, in citing relevant juristic rulings on performing various rites, and in providing glimpses of the glorious Muslim history associated with Hajj and its sites. More strikingly, it records Daryabadi's emotional and spiritual journey, abounding in his rumination and repentance over his earlier lapses. It is a sort of confessional literature, representing a fervent plea for atonement and salvation. It then veers to the political domain, alerting Muslims the world over against the oppressive and manipulative, colonial West which had been wreaking havoc on the Muslim world in 1920s. His overflowing esteem and love for the Prophet (peace and blessings be upon him) characterizes his description of Madina, particularly the Prophet's grave. As a representative of the Muslim *ummah* (the worldwide Muslim community) he recounts impassionedly the plight plaguing the Muslims of his day. In his capacity as *shafi* (intercessor), as Shariah designates the Prophet (peace and blessings be upon him), Daryabadi invokes his recommendation both for his own forgiveness and for helping Muslims find a way out of morass in which they are trapped. It is a genuine seeker's heart-felt account, who is keen on his catharsis. At another, broader level, it raises questions about the decline of Muslims and reflects on the ways and means of Muslims regaining their lost power and glory. Written against the immediate backdrop of the abolition of the Ottoman Caliphate and owing to Daryabadi's active involvement in the Khilafat movement for the restoration of Caliphate, his tone against the imperialist West which had masterminded the fall of Caliphate, at times, turns acerbic. This travelogue is, nonetheless, markedly different, rather unique.

His other writings too, revolve around the axis of the Islam and the Quran. Many of his immediate predecessors and contemporaries too, have written both extensively and insightfully, in their own ways, on Islam and the Quran. What, however, sets him apart, rather above them, is his uncanny perception of the challenges thrown by modernity against faith, in general, and Islam, in particular. This valuable contribution by Daryabadi comes out most prominently in his English and Urdu *tafasir*, and his works on the Quran. There did exist some useful Urdu *tafasir* and a couple of good English translations of the Quran by Muslim scholars prior to his. However, none of these took a mental note of the intellectual needs and level of a new and very large constituency of Muslim readership that had come up by 1930s – of the Western-educated Muslims for whom the traditional interpretation of things Islamic had little appeal. In the wake of the aggressive missionary/Orientalist propaganda against the Quran, patronized by the Western establishment, unsuspecting Muslims were vulnerable to harbouring more mental reservations against the Quran, its Judaeo-Christian antecedents, its alleged incoherence, and its stance on war, violence gender bias, polygamy, miracles, and the Hereafter etc. The latest archaeological, historical and geographical studies were also utilized by them for calling into question the Quranic allusions to history and geography. Since Daryabadi had first hand access to the treasures of Western scholarship, and knew well the doubts agitating the minds of Western educated people, particularly about the institutions of divine revelation, Scriptures, Messengership and the whole edifice of man's resurrection and accountability on the Day of Judgment, he embarked upon this ambitious, noble project of interpreting the Quran with a view to guiding this particular category of readers. Ulema, with their enviable familiarity with the primary Islamic sources could not and did not respond to this big challenge. Instead psuedo-rationalist and apologist Muslim writers who projected a garbled version of things Islamic, had been regrettably gaining ground. Instances in point are of Sir Syed Ahmad Khan, Chiragh Ali, Muhammad Abduh, Rashid Riza, Ameer Ali and Abdullah Yusuf Ali. Had Daryabadi not risen to the occasion, most of the Western educated Muslims would have been carried away by the pseudo-rationalist and apologist interpretation of Islam. When Daryabadi embarked upon his English *tafsir*, the only available English translation with notes by a Muslim scholar was by Abdullah Yusuf Ali (published between 1934-1937). However, Ali's views on the Quranic eschatology, jinn, angels, joys of Paradise, punishment in Hell, houris, the divine throne and all that belongs to *al-ghayb* (what is beyond the ken of the human sense perception) smacks of blatant apologia. Overawed and unnerved by the Western pseudo-rationalism, he resorts to interpreting almost all the Quranic verses dealing with eschatology as "symbolic, allegorical or figurative." His appendix "The Muslim Heaven" seeks to refute

> some ignorant critics of Islam [who] imagine that Islam postulates a sensual heaven, and they press into service some garbled versions of what some of our material–minded brethren have said on the subject. Our doctrine of the Hereafter is not strictly a doctrine of Rewards and Punishments.[1]

The opening verses (8-11) of Surah al-Mursalat discuss in detail the great upheaval on the Last Day – the effacing of stars, cleaving of the sky and scattering of mountains. However, for Abdullah Yusuf Ali all this is merely allegorical.[2] In similar elusive, rather misleading terms of reference he explains the happenings of the Last Day (al-Infitar 82:1-4) thus:

> The metaphor behind the scattering of the constellation of stars is that in the present order of things we see many things associated together e.g. rank with honour, wealth with comfort etc. In the new Spiritual World this will be seen to have been merely fortuitous. The

oceans will overwhelm the whole globe. Figuratively, the different streams of knowledge, great and small, will be levelled down, for only One Knowledge, the Light Divine will hold the field.[3]

Far from so ruthlessly ruling out the palpable, physical forms of the Quranic eschatology, Daryabadi explains these in accordance with the authentic Islamic doctrines. Never does he shy away from presenting the message of the Quran as it is. Rather, on the basis of evidence and arguments culled from the Western sources he brings out the truth of the Quranic statements. He cites passage after passage from the Bible, illustrating how and why the Quran excels it, which, in turn, proves that the Quran is the final Word of Allah for all time and place and that the Bible has been altered and corrupted. He quotes also the latest Western scholarship in order to assert that all the Quranic commands, be these on *jihad*, women, or the Hereafter are perfectly compatible with the human nature. His *tafsir* helps Muslims realize that they should profess and practise Islam which alone would ensure the best for them in both the worlds. Moreover, throughout he presents the Quran as the book of guidance, which should govern both individual and collective life. His frequent references to Ahadith and classical *mufassirun* (*tafsir* writers) assure readers of the authenticity and reliability of his assertions. At the same time, he draws judiciously upon the latest, modern studies in order to vindicate the Quranic statements on almost every issue. As a result, his *tafasir* display a remarkable and highly welcome blending of tradition and modernity, and of classical *tafsir* corpus and modern learning. This constitutes a valuable addition to the tradition of *tafsir,* and a testament to Daryabadi's mission of serving the cause of the Islam/the Quran in today's context. The same prompted him to deliver a series of lectures and publish books such as *Qurani Mutala Biswin Sadi Mein* (Study of the Quran in the twentieth century) and *Qasas wa Masail* (the Quranic stories and other issues) which strongly urge Ulema and students of the Quran to take into account the advancements in modern knowledge and the challenges posed by modernity in order to explain the Quran more effectively. Ulema, in particular, tend to be indifferent to the new challenges, suffering from complacency. For them the classical tradition is sufficient and blessed for all time. Daryabadi, however, pleads, and rightly so, for forming first a clear picture about the mindset of readers and then explaining for them the meaning and message of the Quran in a way which may answer their queries, clear their mental cobwebs and help them resolve the challenges confronting them. Rather than rejecting and condemning modernity outright, the lesson imparted by Daryabadi as an Islamic/Quranic scholar is that we should study the issues and formulate a strategy for addressing these in the perspective of both Islam and modern scholarship. Since Islam is the natural way and the Quran is the final Word of Allah, we should not be apprehensive about the latest scientific developments or modernity. The truth of Islam is not, and cannot be eclipsed by these. What is, nonetheless, needed on the part of the Ulema is the critical study and understanding of the new challenges and offering their solution in accordance with the timeless Islamic Quranic directives. In doing so, there should not be any dilution of the Islamic stance.

Daryabadi's unflinching commitment to Islam and its value system is inscribed indelibly on his contribution to Urdu literature. Whatever poet, novelist or writer whom he discussed in his long literary career, his vantage point was always Islamic. Take his book reviews, published in his Urdu weekly, as an instance in point. The works he reviewed represent a broad range of genres and disciplines—Urdu short stories, poetry, Iqbal studies, literary history, chronicles, fables, sketches, collections of letters, drama, diaries, and journals, social studies, history, biography, humour and satire, and essays. More than 200 book reviews comprise only a selection of these.[4] What is more noteworthy than the number of hundreds of his book reviews is the running thread, or the unmissable imprint of his unswerving loyalty to Islam in his assessment of a book under review. Almost every work is evaluated against the touchstone of its Islamic content and context. Those advancing and reinforcing the Islamic worldview win his acclaim, and conversely, those found deficient on this count are branded by him as detestable. Daryabadi appears to have imbibed this outlook from his ideologue, Maulana Muhammad Ali Jauhar, who faced isolation in the political arena for his "crime" of being overtly religious. Daryabadi is seen commending those men of letters who abide by the Islamic moral code, and disparaging the recalcitrant and deviant ones. The former is exemplified by his adulation of Akbar Allahabadi, Iqbal, Hali and Rashidul Khairi etc. As to the latter, he did not spare anyone, no matter how influential. His moral courage, rather fervour seems to ooze in his, at times even vitriolic, attacks on such irreverent writers, though bearing Muslim names, as Niaz Fatehpuri, Azim Beg Chughtai, Sajjad Zahir, Rashid Jahan, Yagana Changezi, Nazir Niazi and Sajjad Ansari. He displayed amazing organizing ability too, in mobilizing Muslim community leaders and the reading public against blasphemous and sacrilegious writings. As a result of his concerted, and, at times, long, drawn out campaigns, most of these reckless authors recanted their outrageous ravings against Islam and tendered their unconditional apology. His boldness on this count is exemplified also by his occasional indictment of even those individuals and institutions who were otherwise very dear to him. Whenever he learnt about any deviation from the Islamic ideals and norms in the Pakistani public life, Maulana Mawdudi and Jamat-i Islami,

Pakistan, Aligarh Muslim University, Jamia Millia Islamia, New Delhi and Dr Zakir Hussain, he sincerely advised them to revert to the Islamic ideal. His public censure of some of the pseudo-secular actions of his erstwhile close acquaintance, Dr Zakir Hussain, the then President of India illustrates the above point all the more. It must be, nonetheless, immediately added, rather acknowledged that Daryabadi as a citizen of the democratic, republic of India, was placed in a much more enviable position than his counterparts in various parts of the Muslim world, in that he enjoyed, almost in full, freedom of expression. Accordingly, he wrote about what he felt strongly. Only in few instances he encountered some resistance from state, asking him to explain his stance which was objectionable in the eyes of state authorities. Nonetheless, as a whole he exercised in full his freedom of thought and expression. In comparison to the deplorable censorship and oppression inflicted upon journalists and religious scholars in the Muslim world, Daryabadi availed himself fully of a citizen's rights in the Indian democratic republic.

Another lesson to be learnt, especially by the young, from Daryabadi's illustrious career is his constant devotion to and his life long quest for knowledge. Even in the last days of his ripe age of more than eighty years he was as eager and curious as a budding scholar for the latest publications and new ideas. Throughout his life he was a voracious reader. More remarkably, he assimilated much of what he read and drew upon the same for serving the cause of Islam. For pressing home arguments, in his Urdu writings, he is often found citing an apt, effective part of an Urdu or Persian couplet which had its sway over readers. This rhetorical feature of his prose style added much appeal and charm to his writings. More significantly, it points to his retentive memory. Likewise, his writings of the last phase have plenty of internal evidence of his being abreast of the latest publications and new thought patterns. Some of his published letters to his acquaintances also point to this, at times, frenetic search for some important titles which he wanted to acquire at any price. Even while on a social or family visit to Calcutta or Lucknow, he used to spare time for visiting local libraries. All this made him alive to the current debates and developments around him, which is no doubt a prerequisite for a scholar.

Daryabadi led an exceptionally organized life, exercising excellent time management. He made the full use of his time, which enabled him to produce much and valuable work. His association with Maulana Thanwi and his assimilation of the Islamic stance on accountability in the Hereafter made him all the more particular and conscious about time management. His simple life style, away from much social interaction, public engagements also helped him utilize his time to the optimum. Furthermore, the domestic bliss, happy family life, free from litigation and other social evils, also enabled him to devote himself exclusively to his mission.

Daryabadi's life and career illustrate also the positive, benign influence of the pious, wise mentors and the long term benefits of good company. The credit goes also to Daryabadi for his receptivity and assimilation of all that was worthy of emulation. Daryabadi gained much, thanks to his contact at his early age with such literary stalwarts as Akbar Allahabadi, Shibli, Mirza Hadi Ruswa and Mirza Jalib, and such true embodiments of Islam as Maulana Muhammad Ali and Maulana Thanwi. This underscores the importance of the presence of some role models in society and their emulation.

Daryabadi's career epitomises a living example of the self sacrificing pursuit of a mission, without any lucrative interest. As a University graduate in 1910, when few Indian Muslims had this qualification, and with his remarkable, academic and literary credentials in that his book *The Psychology of Leadership* had been brought out by a leading British publisher in 1915 and was reviewed favourably there, a bright, rewarding career awaited him. He could easily earn a decent living and lead a comfortable life, with all material possessions. However, he opted for a self earning, free lance academic and journalistic career, which had a very low return value, and posed the threat of having even no income at all. However, this gave him independence of thought and expression, as he was not under obligation to any employer or patron. Nor was he bound to work for any organization or magazine, which would curtail or compromise with his freedom. As to the not so lavish literary fellowship (of Rs 125 per month in 1919) granted to him by the Nizam of Hyderabad, it did not put him either to any obligation to the Nizam. The fellowship entailed only the writing of a book every year, which was to be dedicated to the Nizam. He was perfectly free to choose the topic and contents of this work. Accordingly, he authored some distinctly religious and moral books as part of his fellowship. As a promising young man with immense potentials he got several offers. For less than a year each he worked as literary assistant at the Muslim Educational Conference, Aligarh, and at the Department of Translation, Osmania University, Hyderabad. However, he resigned of his own from these positions and led his life as a free lance writer devoted to the cause of preaching and promoting Islam. Such altruism is rare; if not altogether non-existent.

Another striking, rather laudable aspect of his life and career is his impartial, non-sectarian mindset, totally free from the shackles of groupism or factionalism. Muslim society of his day was divided and subdivided along the lines of numerous sects, political affiliations, religious establishments, juristic schools, and socio-cultural, linguistic and regional labels, and even personality cult and almost infallible hero worship. In his long public, journalistic career, Daryabadi's stance towards all was characterized by catholicity of mind. Throughout, he acted on the Quranic motto: "Cooperate with one another in good actions and piety. Do not help one another in any sin and wrong doing." (al-Maidah 5:2). Little wonder then that in his Urdu weekly he praised every Muslim organization, institution or movement which he deemed to be working for the interests of Islam and Muslims, be it Muslim League, Jamiatul Ulema, Jamat-i Islami, Tablighi Jamat, Ahl-i Hadith or Muslim Majlis: or Nadwatul Ulema, Darul Ulum; or Darul Musaniffin, Azamgarh or Nadwatul Musaniffin, Delhi: He spoke highly of those Shia scholars, publications and institutions that tended to support cordial Sunni-Shia relations. Likewise, though not formally or closely associated with Maulana Hamiduddin Farahi or Jamat-i Islami Hind leaders, he defended the former against the charge of blasphemy in 1930s, and the latter against the allegation of violence and sedition, as hurled by the Indian state during Emergency (1975-1977). His generosity, however, landed him into some trouble, as he complimented the Qadyanis too, for their missionary work in Europe and Africa. Furthermore, he did not endorse the consensus view that Qadyanis stand outside the fold of Islam, again out of his lenient view that some allowance should be given. He believed the tendency of declaring anyone a non-Muslim be discouraged. In this particular instance, it appears, his compassion was rather misplaced. Worse, it was misconstrued by some as his intransigence. Another price which he had to pay for his refusal to pledge his blind conformity to any one of the well-entrenched religious/sectarian establishments was that his contribution went largely unacknowledged. He was not owned by any, though he had kind words for everyone who served well the cause of Islam. As already noted, owing to this handicap, he could not get any publisher for his *tafsir* in his life time. Nor did anyone come forward to recognize and celebrate his sterling additions to Islamic scholarship.

To sum up, Daryabadi's mission and message consists in his scholarly refutation of the onslaughts on Islam by the Orientalists, in alerting Muslims of the subcontinent against the impending dangers of Westernization, in pressing home the excellence of Islam/the Quran in the context of comparative religion, and in a cogent, appealing manner, in boosting the morale of the decimated Muslim minority in the post-Independence India and in elucidating the Islamic faith and practices for a new constituency of readers — Western educated Muslims. He managed to accomplish all this with his gifted pen and his discerning, vast erudition.

His was the life and career of a genuine Islamic scholar, who was not carried away by any populist, political motive. Rather, he always derived inspiration and guidance from the Quran and Sunnah and articulated their life-giving message energetically and effectively through his periodicals, his books and above all, his *tafasir* in English and Urdu. His life and career encapsulate the meaning and message of the Quranic verse:

وَٱلَّذِى جَآءَ بِٱلصِّدْقِ وَصَدَّقَ بِهِۦٓ ۙ أُو۟لَـٰٓئِكَ هُمُ ٱلْمُتَّقُونَ

He who brings truth, and he who confirms and supports it, they are the pious.

(al-Zumar 39:33)

Notes

1. Abdur Raheem Kidwai, *Translating the Untranslatable, A Critical Guide to 60 English Translations of the Quran.* New Delhi, Sarup Book, 2011, p. 17.
2. Ibid., p. 17.
3. Ibid., pp. 17-18.
4. *Tabsarat-i Majidi.* Edited by Abdul Aleem Kidwai, New Delhi, National Council for the Promotion of Urdu Language, 2009

8

English Translation of the Quran: Issues and Problems

Abdul Majid Daryabadi

Of all great works the Holy Qur'ān is perhaps the least translatable. Arabic is not at all easy to translate into a language so widely and redically different from it in structure and genius as English, unless it be with the aid of loose periphrasis and lax paraphrase. Even so the fire of the original is quenched. Its vivacious perspicuity lost, and the so-called literal translation looks lifeless and dreary. That the language of the Arabs abounds in nuances and that both the noun and the verb are ultimately flexible, is a fact well known to every student of that tongue.

The difficulty is increased hundredfold when one has to render into English, with any degree of accuracy and precision, a work so rich in meaning, so pithy in expression, so vigorous in style and so subtle in its implications as the Holy Qur'ān. To reproduce even partially its exotic beauty, wonderful grandeur and magical vivacity without sacrificing the requirements of the English idiom and usage, is the despair of the translator and an ideal impossible to attain. The result is that every fresh attempt at translating the Holy Book brings home, in varying degrees, the truth of the old saying that nothing is so unlike an original as its copy.

The impediments confronting an honest translator may be summed up under six main headings and various sub-headings:

1. In the first place comes the comparative poverty of the English language. For instance:

   (i) There are a large number of Arabic verbs which cannot be translated into English as verbs, such as اسرف، ابطل، من، طغی، امات، استوی، صدق، بخل etc. and one has perforce to render each of these words not by a single word but by a combination of words. Thus یبخل has to be translated as niggardly, صدق as truthful, یستوي as equal, یسرف as extravagant, یبطل as to make vain or to render void, من as conferring a benefit, یطغی as exorbitant, and یمیت as causes death.

(ii) There is no equivalent for the Arabic مضارع (aorist) in English, or, for that matter, in any other language known to the translator. The Arabic مضارع combines both present and future tenses, whereas in other languages, including English, a tense is either present or future. Thus thousands of Arabic verbs can only be rendered incompletely into English.

(iii) In English grammar there are only two numbers, singular and plural, and there is no single word to convey the sense of the Arabic dual (تثنيه) in nouns as well as verbs, both in the second and third person.

(iv) There is comparative dearth of اسماء الفاعل (*nomina agentis*) in the English language, whereas they abound in Arabic. مستاخرون، مستقدمون، قانتون، معجزون، مفلحون آخرون، صادقون، شاكرون، متقون، مشركون، and many similar words have to be rendered as adjectives or participles, not as substantives.

2. Next, the repetition of synonyms, chiefly for the sake of emphasis, is a frequent occurrence in Arabic; in fact, at times it is of considerable literary merit and beauty. In the English language there is no sanction for it. Thus many such expressions as (literally, Verily, We! We! We! quicken the dead) or انا نحن نحي ونميت (literally, Verily, We! surely We! We! quicken and cause death) or انا نحن نزلنا الزكر (literally, Verily, We! We! We have revealed the Admonition) remain only partly translated.

3. Another serious difficulty is caused by the case with which ellipses occur in the best and finest Arabic style and where both words and phrases have to be supplied by the reader to make the sense complete. Sometimes, only the subject is mentioned and the predicate entirely suppressed, whilst on other occasions, the reverse is the case. The obvious duty of the translator in all such instances is to supply the omission, although his attempts in many cases must be hazardous.

4. Yet another perplexity faced by the translator is the abrupt grammatical transition, in one and the same sentence, frequently found in Arabic:

   (i) of person, as from the first and second person to the third, or *vice versa*;

   (ii) of number, from plural to singular, or *vice versa*.

5. A further complication is caused by what is known as (انتشار ضمائر) i.e., a personal or relative pronoun having a different antecedent in one and

the same sentence. The translator cannot afford to allow such ambiguities; he has to make a choice.

6. Finally, there is no real equivalence in the import of many Arabic and English words generally held to be synonyms. The Arabic word زنى for instance, has no equivalent in English, both adultery and fornication being of much narrower import. Similarly, English has few words to express such closely related Arabic terms as, ترهيب، خشيت، خوف and, as in the phrase تقوى (as in the phrase تقوى الله). Nor is English perhaps rich enough to clearly indicate the shades of meaning of such sets of words as قادرقدير، and مقتدر or رحمن and رحيم or حية، ثعبان and جان .

As to the genius of the Arabic language, it may not be amiss to recall a few observations made by the distinguished Arabists, Arnold and Guillaume: 'Arabic is fitted to express relations with more conciseness than the Aryan languages because of the extraordinary flexibility of the verb and noun. Thus the ideas in break, shatter, try to break, cause to break, allow to be broken, break one another, ask someone to break, are among many variations of the fundamental verbal theme which can, or could, be expressed by vowel changes and consonantal augments without the aid of the supplementary verbs and pronouns which we have to employ in English. The noun, too, has an appropriate form for many diverse things, such as the time and place of an action, bodily defects, diseases, instruments, colours, trades, and so on. One example must suffice. Let us take the root *d-w-r*, which, in its simplest form, means to turn or revolve (intransitive).

dawwara, to turn a thing round. *dāwara*, to walk about with someone.
adāra, to make go round, and so to control. *istadāra* to be round in shape.
dawr, turning (noun). *dawrah*, one turning.
dawarān, circulation. *duwār*, vertigo.
dawwār, pedlar or vagrant. *dawwārah*, mariner's compass.
madār, axis. *mudārah*, round water-skin
mudīr, controller.

None of these forms is fortuitous, but is predetermined by the structural genius of the Arabic language.' Arnold and Guillaume, *The Legacy of Islam*, pp.vi-vii.

To take another instance:

'From the root *KTB* "write", we have *KaTaBnā*, "we wrote", *naKTuBu*, "we will write", *KāTiBun*, "written, a writer", *KiTāBun*,"a book", *maKTaBun*,"a place of writing, a school," *muKTiBun*"a teacher of writing."

taKāTaBā "they two corresponded with one another", *astaKTiBu*, "I will ask (him) to write", *waKtaTaBa*, "and he got his name written down (in the register)," *KuTTāBun*, "scribes", *muKāTaBatun*, "correspondence", etc. (*Encyclopaedia Britannica.* 2, p. 192).

Add to these inherent handicaps my own incompetence, my meagre knowledge of English and only a passing acquaintance with Arabic and the audacity of the enterprise becomes apparent. Further, it has been my lot to work almost unaided and single-handed. The outcome of this seven year labour of love is before God and man, and certainly it is not for me to pass any judgement on my own work. Had I been able to foresee at the commencement of the task the amount of labour it would involve and the length of time it would necessitate, my courage would surely have failed me and I would not have undertaken the work at all. If there is any merit discernible in the work, it is absolutely owing to the grace and mercy of the Almighty and if there are faults (and undoubtedly they are many and serious ones), they must be credited to my own incapacity. My constant endeavour has been to give as literal and as faithful a rendering of the Holy Qur'ān as is consistent with tolerable English. Accuracy, rather than literary embellishment, is what I have aimed for throughout. I have also attempted, in my own humble way, to follow closely the style and phraseology of the Authorized Version of the English Bible, though it would be nothing short of temerity to expect that that standard has been even appreciably achieved.

In regard to the arrangement of the commentary, a word or two will suffice:

(i) Comments on lexical, grammatical, historic, geographical, and general exegetic interest are given in the footnotes.
(ii) Where an elucidation seemed necessary in order to complete the sense, it has been placed in parentheses, again in the footnotes. The reader is requested to treat such matter as if it formed an integral part of the text and to read the two side by side.
(iii) Ellipses have been supplied in the text itself.

A few characteristics of my translation and transliteration may be briefly noted. The word 'Allah' in the monotheistic context has always been retained in translation as Allah, and only rendered as 'God' when the content is distinctly pagan or polytheistic. The words نصراني and نصارى I have invariably translated as Nazarene and Nazarenes, not as Christian. The Holy Qur'ān allows no status to Christianity as such. The religion of the Qur'ān and the Prophet is always referred to as Islam, not as Muhammadanism.

Now remains the pleasant duty of acknowledging obligations and recording thanks. To several of my precursors I am more or less indebted, but in particular to Sale, Lane, Pickthall and Nawab 'Imad-ul-Mulk Bilgrami (whose unfinished and unpublished translation, up to Sūrah Tā Hā, I have the good fortune to possess). To Dr. Bell, the latest of the English translators, my debt is especially great. In exegetical and explanatory notes I have found Ashraf Ali Thānwi's Urdu *Bayān al- Qur'ān* (12 Vols.) of invaluable help, and I have also drawn largely upon Wherry's Commentary and, in a lesser degree, upon Abdullah Yusuf Ali's. Many other authors, both classical and modern, besides those explicitly quoted in the following pages, must, I fear, remain unacknowledged by name. In many cases, they impressed themselves so indelibly on my memory that their very words became part and parcel of my phraseology, but I could not in every instance remember whence they came. This is a general acknowledgement of any unconscious plagiarism that I may have committed. A list of the principal books cited and referred to by me, given at the end of this work, may, however, to some extent, extenuate my crime.

I have been considerably benefitted by the suggestions of several of my esteemed friends and scholars to whom part of this work was submitted for detailed criticism. To Dr. Muhammad Hafeez Syed and Dr. Abdul Sattar Siddiqi, both of Allahabad University, I owe not a few improvements in language and transliteration respectively.

Originally this is Daryabadi's Preface to the first edition of his English translation of the Quran (1957)

9

Tafsir (the Quran exegesis) in Modern Times: Pre-requisites and Challenges

> *"It is He (God) Who sent among the unlettered a Messenger from among themselves, to rehearse to them His signs, to sanctify them, and to instruct them in the Book and wisdom."*
>
> (*al-Jumuah* 62:2)

Apart from conveying the verses of the Qur'an and purifying his Companions, it was also the job of the Prophet Muhammad (peace be on him) to instruct his Companions in the Qur'an. Since such an instruction was needed for the immediate addressees of the Qur'an, its need for the non-Arabic speaking people of far-off places and of a much later date becomes all the more pressing. 'Instructing in the Book' embraces the whole gamut of *tafsir* literature, Apart from a faithful representation of the text, tafsir should elucidate as clearly as possible all the Qur'anic doctrines, commands and concepts.

With the gradual revelation of the Qur'an the Companions put many queries to the Prophet Muhammad (peace be upon him) about the intended meaning and message of the Qur'an and this laid the foundation of the discipline of tafsir. Tafasir literature produced by the Companions made its appearance in the first century of the Hijra calendar. By the third century Hijra several *tafasir* had been written, including some voluminous ones. The history of tafsir literature is a fascinating study in itself. Leaving aside its historical evolution, what needs to be emphasised at the very outset is that each *mufassir* has sought to interpret the Qur'an according to the milieu of the day while making full allowance for the mental level of his readership. Razi's *tafsir* is an outstanding example of *tafsir* literature. Written between the last decade of the sixth century Hijra and the beginning of the seventh century Hijra, it reflects the ascendancy of the Greek philosophy in the day, somewhat similar to the preponderant position of science and technology in our times. Little wonder then that Razi is found, at times, seeking to make his arguments compatible with the Greek thought.

There has been information explosion in the twentieth century. The challenges posed by modern scholarship were, therefore not faced by them. Nor were they troubled with the questions that stare in the face of the students of the Qur'an today. Many historical, geographical and archeological issues need to be investigated which were non-existent a century earlier. Of all the earlier *musfassirun* Mahmood Alusi, writing in the middle of the nineteenth century, has tackled some of the modern astronomical issues in his exhaustive *Tafsir Ruh al-Maani.* He seeks to discuss the revolving of the earth and other scientific issues and problems in the Islamic terms of reference. His work won a wide acclaim in the Muslim world. However, much time has elapsed since his death in 1853. His tafsir was completed in 1846, whereas modern knowledge has advanced by leaps and bounds in the last one and a half century. His tafsir now inevitably stands dated. With reference to the precedents set by such illustrious figure as Razi and Alusi, it may be argued that tafsir in our times should address the pressing issues and challenges of our times, especially in the following domains.

History holds the pride of place as a discipline in that the Qur'an cites several historical communities and personalities as representatives of both good and evil. The historical antecedents of these Qur'anic figures are worth exploring. Pharaoh is mentioned many times in the Qur'an. He cannot be simply explained away as an Egyptian king. With the help of the latest studies in history and archaeology, it is to be found out that Pharaoh was not the personal name of an individual; rather it was the official title of the royal Coptic family, exactly in the same way as the appellation Ceaser and Khedive were employed by the Roman and Egyptian rulers respectively. Many rulers in the ancient Egypt bore the title of Pharaoh, though they had their own personal names. This title was derived from the Egyptian belief that the ruler was an incarnation, rather the incarnation of the most overwhelming god, i.e. sun god.

According to the Bible, there were two Pharaohs contemporaneous with the Prophet Moses (peace be upon him). And it was during the reign of the former Pharaoh that the persecution against the Egyptians was unleashed, which assumed such an unendurable pitch that the Israelites had to migrate from Egypt, whereas the latter Pharaoh was drowned while pursuing them.

As to the figures of the Prophets John and Zakariah (peace be upon them) the latest historical studies have unearthed a mine of information. With the appearance of scrolls and other archives material, more and more is known about them. What is needed is that the new sources should be tapped irrespective of their divergence from the account of the classical *mufassirun* about these matters.

Likewise, a great deal of new information is now available about the life and times of earlier Messengers such as Jonah, Jacob, Abraham and

Noah (peace be upon them). A few centuries earlier, these figures were very much clouded in oblivion. The statements of classical *mufassirun* regarding these figures are not sacrosanct; only the Word of God is unaltered and unalterable. Many events related to the life and times of the Messenger Solomon (peace be upon him) are known now while many are yet to be ascertained. That Solomon (peace be upon him) possessed ships and boats is a historically established fact. However, it is not confirmed whether he flew also. Presently his sea voyages are sufficient enough to bring into sharper relief the veracity of the Quranic statement. The Quran does not specifically mention his ability to fly. What the Qur'an says is that Solomon (peace be upon him) exercised control on the wind hence his sea voyages are to be cited as historical proof.

Crucifixion is central to the discussion on the Prophet Jesus (peace be upon him). Unequivocally does the Qur'an deny that he was killed or crucified. Rather his enemies were deceived. This Qur'anic statement is to be elucidated with reference to historical material. In such matters one should not rely on the opinion of an individual, however, respected he may be. Jesus had lived only two thousand years ago in the full glare of history. The Roman and Judaic historical works of the period are easily available, Jesus (peace be upon him) hailed from Palestine, which was then ruled by the Romans, who were pagans.

Palestine was a semi - autonomous state under the control of the Roman empire, with an overwhelming majority of Israelites. Israelite rabbis were, in particular, deadly opposed to Jesus (peace be upon him). After arresting Jesus (peace be upon him), they first persecuted him in their supreme religious court and sentenced him. However, they were not authorized to enforce sentence in civil matters. It was the prerogative of the state court. So a fabricated case of treason and sedition against him was presented before the state court. The judgment was to be delivered incidentally on a Friday evening with the Jewish Sabbath approaching after a few hours. The court was about to set Jesus (peace be upon him) free on finding him innocent, but the court was besieged by the Jews, who insisted on the award of the capital punishment to Jesus (peace be upon him), otherwise they would appeal to the Roman empire. Eventually the judge gave in and sentenced Jesus (peace be upon him) with crucifixion in that it was the prescribed punishment for his alleged crime.

The place of crucifixion was a few miles away from the court and the convict had to carry the cross from the court to the place of crucifixion. Being physically weak, Jesus (peace be upon him) found it difficult to carry the cross all the way. Moreover, he was constantly harassed by the unruly Jewish mob. As the Sabbath was approaching fast, which would suspend all activity for the next twenty-four hours, the Roman soldiers escorting Jesus (peace be upon him) got hold of a Jew and forced him into carrying the cross. For the Roman soldiers all the Jews looked alike. When they reached the gate, the soldiers on duty mistook the person carrying the cross as Jesus (peace be upon him) himself. Notwithstanding his loud protest in a foreign tongue, the soldiers crucified him whereas Jesus was saved.

Next to history, a *mufassir* in our time should make much use of the latest studies in geography, The Qur'anic events are rooted in history with place fixities. In the account of Pharaoh and the Israelites, the Qur'an uses the expressions both for the ocean and the river which the Israelites had to cross. Classical *mufassirun* have explained this allusion with reference to the river Nile. However, Israelites then lived in Goshen which was far away from the river Nile and lay in the opposite direction. Palestine and Syria lay to the east of Egypt, the destination of the Israelites. The river Nile was situated to the west and it could not be on the way of the Israelites. As Israelites moved away from Goshen, they lost their way in the darkness of the night. Instead of going eastward they reached a place on which was situated the triangular part of the Red or the Caspian sea as a gulf. As it dawned, they stood facing the sea. Inspired by the divine revelation Moses (peace be upon him) asked the Israelites to march straight into the sea and the waves formed walls on both the sides while the Israelites crossed it safely and comfortably. On looking at the map, this fact emerges unmistakably and clearly.

Similarly, much is to be gained from geographical information regarding Prophet Jonah (peace be upon him). He lived in the middle of the eighth century BC during the reign of the Israelite ruler Jermina, who ruled from 791 BC. Jonah (peace be upon him) was based in Nineveh, an Iraqi town which was the capital of the Assyrians. Baghdad now stands close to the place where once Nineveh was situated. The river Tigris passed through the town. Exasperated with his people, Jonah (peace be upon him) left the town without waiting for the divine leave and went for a sea-voyage. While he was aboard, the ship was wrecked. In accordance with their belief, those on the ship cast lots and Jonah (peace be upon him) was held the culprit. Consequently, he was thrown into the sea and a huge fish swallowed him. Since he was a Messenger of God, he prayed in the darkness of the fish belly and was eventually salvaged.

Regarding the Qur'an, one learns that the Prophet Moses (peace be upon him) was directed to reach a place where the two rivers converged and there he was to meet a specially appointed person. It is yet to be established as to what was this exact place where the two rivers met. If this event happened during his stay in Egypt, it is likely that it was the place where the two branches of the river Nile meet each other and on the bank of which the town of Khartoum is situated, if this event happened after his Egyptian phase and in the Sinai Peninsula, the above mentioned place might refer to the meeting point between the Aqabah Gulf and the Suez Canal. There is also a remote possibility that if this event happened before his Egyptian days, this place might be in Abyssinia.

Apart from numerous historical allusions in the Qur'an, there are many geographical allusions to towns, places, rivers, mountain and buildings, for example, Makkah. Madina, Yathrib, Midian, Egypt, Babylon, the Mount Judi etc. In sum, there are many geographical allusions, which are yet to be elaborated. Recent archaeological excavations have solved many puzzling questions. But these Quranic allusions be explained better in the light of this new knowledge. It might take some time but a *mufassir* should draw on all sources of knowledge in the pursuit of elaborating Qur'anic allusions.

Comparative religion, especially Christianity and Judaism, is also pivotal to understanding the Qur'an better. Being Abrahamic faiths, Christianity and Judaism have much in common with Islam in the domain of belief and articles of faith. Particular reference may be made to the oneness of God, Prophethood, Messengership, revelation, angels and reward and punishment in the Hereafter. Although both the Christians and Jews have distorted these fundamental beliefs in that they have reduced Messengership to soothsaying, denied the sinlessness of angels and tampered with the doctrine about the Hereafter, the Qur'an has recounted their beliefs at length and described their history. At places, the Qur'an recounts their faith and beliefs and reproaches them for their misdeeds. Classical *mufassirun* have painstakingly discussed threadbare numerous juristic rulings derived from the Qur'an. However, since they had almost no interaction with other faiths, they have often failed to grasp the Qur'anic allusions to comparative religion.

The Qur'an specially deals with two polytheistic beliefs: sonship of Jesus and Jesus as the child of God. Whereas the former notion is obviously the most serious and worst form of polytheism in that the Qur'an denounces in it in the strongest possible terms. For example, reference may be made to this Qur'anic passage:

> They say: "Allah Most Gracious has begotten a son!" Indeed you have put forth a thing most monstrous. As if the skies are ready to burst, the earth to split asunder, and the mountains to fall down in utter ruin that they should invoke a son for Allah Most Gracious.
>
> (Maryam 19:88-91)

The Bible speaks of Jesus (peace be upon him) as the son of God and this is believed by the majority of Christians. Another belief, which is also polytheistic, relates to taking Jesus (peace be upon him) as the child of God. As compared to Sonship, this belief is not so loathsome as the former, Accordingly, the Qur'an condemns it in somewhat milder terms. The expression 'child' is much more general than the son. In the Bible it is used in both singular and plural forms and in a metaphorical sense. It connotes someone as God's a favorite and the chosen one. Christians alone are not guilty of it in that Jews laid a similar claim. Jews believe that the children of Abraham and Jacob (peace be upon him) have been specially favoured by God and they believe that they will not be punished. The Qur'an recounts their claims:

> Both the Jews and the Christians say: "We are children of Allah and His beloved.
>
> (al-Maida, 5:18)

The Bible mentions Ezra and in the Judaic tradition he figures as a Messenger and scribe of the Torah. He lived in the middle of the fifth century BC and most probably died in 455 BC. After the reign of the Babylonian king, Nebuchadnezzar (605 BC-562 BC) and his invasion and destruction of Jerusalem (586 BC) and of the Torah, he compiled afresh the Torah with his memory. In recognition of this great service rendered by Ezra, Jews took him as another Moses. Some went a step further and looked upon him as all-in-all and the Lord.

The Jews deny that they ascribe Sonship to Ezra and accuse the Qur'an of charging them with something of which they are not guilty. Their misunderstanding stems from their misconstruing the relevant verse. The Qur'an does state a fact and a *mufassir* while taking into account the distinction between the son and the child, may silence these Jewish detractors of the Qur'an. This view is supported further by the following Qur'anic verse:

> The Jews call Ezra (Uzayr) a son of God, and the Christians call Christ the Son of God. That is a saying from their mouth; in this they but imitate what the unbelievers of the old used to say. Allah's curse be upon them: how they are deluded away from the truth.
>
> (al-Tawbah 9:30)

The Qur'an criticizes the people of the Book for behaving like other polytheists guilty of believing in the divine incarnation and transmigration of the souls, for example, the Greeks, the Romans and the Egyptians. Earlier pagan communities took pride in their divine descent, for example, the Brahm and Suryavanshi and Chandravanshi Rajputs of India.

Although the twentieth century scholars of comparative religions are credited with making a critical study of earlier Scriptures and for pointing out the common points among adherents of earlier faiths, the Qur'an pointed to the same fact more than a thousand year ago. This alone is sufficient enough to corroborate the miraculous nature of the Qur'an. Often does the Qur'an record the statements of the Jews. For example, it recounts the Jewish notion that the Jews will have to live in hellfire only for a few days: "They say: "The Fire shall not touch us but for a few numbered days." (Ali Imran). A *mufassir* should in our times identify such passages in the Torah and other Jewish religious traditions. Apart from several references to the people of the Book, the Qur'an occasionally mentions other faiths. In addition to Judaism and Christianity the Qur'an makes specific mention of two other religious communities, Magians and Sabians. Both these religious communities inhabited places around the Arabian peninsula at the time of revelation of the Qur'an. The Arabs had cultural and business contact with them. A thorough familiarly with these faiths is essential for a *mufassir* in our times. In Surah al-Maidah the Qur'an alludes to some earlier religious communities:

> O people of the Book! Exceed not in your religion the bounds of what is proper, trespassing beyond the truth. Nor follow the vain desires of the people, who went and strayed wrong in times gone by, who misled many, and strayed themselves from the even way.
>
> (al-Maidah 5:77)

The above Qur'anic passage is directed specially at the Christians as pointed out by al-Tabari. Western scholars concede the point that early Christianity was influenced greatly by the Egyptian, Greek and Roman varieties of polytheism, Moreover, the Pauline doctrines betray an unmistakable mark of Hellenism. We should draw on Biblical Criticism in dealing with such issues.

At places, the Qur'an makes generalized comments which need to be ascertained precisely. For example, in Surah al-Maidah 5:78, the Qur'an says that both the Messengers David and Jesus (peace be upon them) condemned Israelites for their misdeeds. This condemnation is to be established with reference to both the Old and New Testament. The Israelites defied the Messengers; they broke the Sabbath in the days of the Prophet David (peace be upon him) and cried lies to the Messengership of Jesus Christ (peace be upon him). With a particular reference to the Torah and the Gospel, the Qur'an spells out the outstanding features of the believing Companions of the Prophets.

> Muhammad is the Messenger of Allah, and those who are with him are strong against unbelievers, but compassionate amongst each other. You will see them bow and prostrate themselves in prayer seeking grace from Allah and His good pleasure. On their faces are their marks being the traces of their prostration. This is their similitude in the Torah and the Gospel is like the seed which sends forth its blade, then makes it strong, it then becomes thick, and it stands on its own stem, filling the sower with wonder and delight. As a result, it fills the unbelievers with rage at them.
>
> (al-Fath 48:29)

For appreciating better the import of the first part of the above passage, one should turn to the Torah. As regards the concluding part of the Qur'anic verse, it can be elaborated with reference to the relevant Biblical passage. In addition to the beliefs of other faiths, their history is equally important in that the Qur'an pays special attention to the moral, social and religious life of the Israelites. A *mufassir* should be well-conversant with the Israelite history. As compared to other communities, the Qur'an deals at length with their beliefs and life. The vicissitudes in the history of the Israelites are recorded in the Qur'an, which should be studied along with the latest historical writings and this comparative study would bring about the miraculous nature and divine origin of the Qur'an. A point worth quoting in this context is related to the Prophet Solomon (peace be upon him). Notwithstanding the damaging passages in the Bible, the *Encyclopedia Britannica concedes*: "Solomon was a sincere worshipper of Jehovah." The same point is endorsed by the *Encyclopedia Biblica.*

While the Qur'an is the Word of God, hence miraculous and all embracing, some *mufassirun* have accomplished partly the task of unravelling some of its numerous marvels. Notwithstanding their limited knowledge, Al-Tabari, who lived in the third century Hijra and did not have specialized knowledge of Judaism and Christianity, records this report on the authority, of Muhammad bin Ishaq that the verse about the Prophet David (peace be upon him) is in fact the refutation of the Jews' charge that Prophet Muhammad (peace be upon him) was totally mistaken in presenting Prophet David as the Messenger of God, while he was a mere sorcerer. The relevant Qur'anic verse takes the Jews to task for this baseless charge.

Another instance in point is found in Surah Yusuf. According to the Qur'an when the Egyptian official provided the sons of Jacob with food grain, he returned their *bidah* (stock in trade/merchandise). The above Qur'anic expression (*bidah*) used in this context is specially related to some material used in exchange. In an earlier verse (20) of the same Surah Yusuf the Qur'an, however, uses the expression *thaman* which is specific to money. Those *mufassirun*, who mistake the two expressions as synonyms, betray their ignorance about the ancient commercial practice of bartering. In the day of the Prophet Yusuf (peace be upon him), cash dealing had not gained universal currency. While money was in circulation in Palestine, the older practice of bartering prevailed in Egypt, hence the Qur'an uses apt expressions for two different situations. Human knowledge and wisdom cannot simply fathom the marvels of the Qur'an.

At one time the articles of faith held the central position in that the detractors of Islam evaluated the Qur'an with reference to the beliefs it prescribed, such as monotheism, the Hereafter and the divine attributes. The classical religious discourse is, therefore, devoted mainly to these issues. However, with the passage of time, there is now a greater need for a discussion on matters related to social life and individual conduct. Public affairs have now assumed greater importance and urgency. These issues need to be addressed, as for example, the form of government, slavery, jihad, interest and economy, gender equality, war on religious grounds and the policy of total prohibition of wine. In sum, numerous ramifications of ethics, politics and economics have to be discussed and resolved in the terms of reference set by the Qur'an. Obviously, the Qur'an has as its own specific viewpoint on these issues. Some of them are crystal clear in that the Qur'an explicitly brands some of them as lawful and others as unlawful and some are recommended as desirable deeds. A *mufassir* is bound to abide by the norms set forth by the Qur'an on these issues. However, such matters, which are no longer extant need not be emphasized, for example, a discussion on slavery is now obsolete in that this institution does not exist any longer. Only a passing reference to it is sufficient, for slavery may reappear at some stage with the change in conditions. However, the categorical Qur'anic comments related to law of inheritance, polygamy and divorce should be elucidated with full conviction without being overawed by the prevailing Western model. Rather new arguments in line with our own times, should be advanced in support of the Qur'anic commands. A *mufassir* has to be on his guard against the manifestation of sexual promiscuity, obscenity and nudity, for, being the custodian of the Word of God; it is his utmost responsibility to state the Qur'anic position firmly without making any allowance for the rampant immorality. The sheer incidence of evil cannot obviously justify or legitimize evil.

Leaving aside the categorical Qur'anic commands, flexibility or elasticity is an outstanding rather miraculous feature of the Qur'an. It is no exaggeration to say that each and every word of the Qur'an is pregnant with several meanings. This feature is all the more marked in the Qur'anic verses dealing with matters related to science. As long as the Ptolemaic worldview obtained, *mufassirun* drew attention to several Qur'anic verses, which were in accordance with it. With the dawn of modern science, several Quranic verses were identified which support modern science, as for example, regarding such Qur'anic passages:

> Allah has made subject to you the sun and the moon, both diligently pursuing their courses.
>
> (Ibrahim 14:33)

> The sun and the moon follow courses exactly computed.
>
> (Al-Rahman 55:5)

> And the sun runs its course for a period determined for it. That is the decree of Him, the exalted in might, the All-Knowing.
>
> (Yasin 36:38)

> It is not permitted to the sun to catch up the moon, nor can the night outstrip the day, each just swims along its own orbit.
>
> (Yasin 36:40)

In the case of the above mentioned verses, a *mufassir* must exercise utmost caution and moderation. As it is, the Qur'an is not some text book of science. Nor does it seek to impart knowledge about the laws of nature. Essentially, it deals with faith and moral teachings with the objective of providing guidance to everyone. Matters related to science are incidental to the Qur'an. A *mufassir* should adopt a balanced approach in that the Qur'an should not be presented as opposed to science. Nor should the current scientific theories be emphasized so forcefully that the Qur'anic message tends to appear supporting it fully. In the early history of Islam, some classical writers betrayed an excessive regard for the Greek thought while it dominated the intellectual scene. A *mufassir* in our time should not betray an obsession with modern science. For, this basic reality should not escape our attention that any human discovery, however great, is after all the product of the human mind and subject to change, alteration and even total refutation. And this is a fairly common phenomenon. Yet is should also be realized that the Qur'an is not *per se* opposed to any sound philosophy or theory or formula. It should not be, however confused with laying the claim that the Qur'an endorses the Greek or the Egyptian or the Indian or the Roman or European version of science. There is a tremendous difference between the two positions. This distinction should be realized and should not be blurred in the elucidation of the Qur'an.

Notwithstanding the exact meaning, even the Qur'anic words have to be explained carefully and cautiously. For example, the Qur'an says that Allah taught Prophet David (peace be upon him) to manufacture coats of mail. He, of course, excelled in this art. Yet it does not prove in any way that he was the first to do so or that it was something unknown in the days before him. For an insistence on suggesting Prophet David (peace be upon him) to be the pioneer in this art might run counter to some historical research pointing out that the coats of mail existed a date earlier than that of Prophet David (peace be upon him). The Qur'anic statement need not be extended illogically.

Similarly, the Qur'an says about Prophet Solomon (peace be upon him) that he exercised control over wind and that he harnessed it for the journey to Syria. Whereas the Qur'an specifically says that he held control over the wind, it does not even hint at his flying. As long as the above point is not borne out by some historical study, the above verse should be explained only with reference to his control over the wind, which he employed for his ships. The Qur'an speaks of it as a great blessing for shipping:

> God it is Who enables you to traverse through land and sea so that you even board ships they sail with them with favourabe wind, and they rejoice in it.

(Yunus 10:22)

Another instance of loose translation of the Qur'an and of treating reports at par with the Qur'an text itself is that it is commonly believed that the knowledge related to *al-Ghyab* (the Unseen) is restricted to the following five points: a) the exact time of the Last Day, b) The exact time of rain, c) The identity of the gender in the foetus, d) No one knows what will happen tomorrow, and e) No one knows when he will die.

However, the Qur'an specifically mentions only three matters which lie outside the fold of the human knowledge:

> The knowledge of Hour is with Allah alone. It is He Who sends down rain, and it is He Who knows what is in the wombs. Nor does anyone know what he will earn on the morrow. Nor does anyone know in what land he is to die.

(Luqman 31:94)

Yet another example of this category is the interpretation of the following verse:

> And nearest among them in love to the believers will you find those who say: we are Christians; because among them are men devoted to learning and men who have renounced the world, and they are not arrogant.

(al-Maida 5:82)

The Qur'anic statement appears to be somewhat at variance with the actual experience. For centuries, the Christians have been the worst enemies of Islam and Muslims. Given this, it becomes somewhat difficult to appreciate the above statement. As a matter of fact, the Qur'an does not at all speak of the Christians whom we know, i.e. those of the West. Only such Christians are mentioned as the friends of Muslims, who abide by the teachings of Jesus Christ (peace be upon him). The above verse expressly describes them as the ones who take pride in being the followers of Jesus Christ (peace be upon him). As it is, the above reference does not cover the Americans or the Germans or the Italians, in sum, the inhabitants of the modern Western nation-states. This inability to adhere close to the Qur'anic text has misled many Orientalists and which lays bare also their lack of knowledge of the Qur'an. Noldeiki happens to be the most prominent Orientalist, who contributed the entry on the Qur'an to the *Encyclopedia Britannica.* In his piece, he says that since the author of the Qur'an (i.e. Prophet Muhammad) has had few opportunities to travel outside the Arabian Peninsula, he had little knowledge of geographical matters. To prove his point, he makes reference to this verse of Surah Yusuf in which the Prophet Joseph (peace be upon him) tells the Egyptians king that the seven-year-long famine will end with rainfall. In the above verse, Prophet Muhammad (peace be upon him) mistook Egypt as a tropical country, while the only source of water in Egypt is not rain water but flood caused by river Nile. The whole misunderstanding stems from Noldeiki misconstructing the Qur'anic word "Yughath." It might be a derivative of the root word "Ghyath" or "Ghauth." In Surah al-Kahf the Qur'an uses an identical expression derived from the latter root. So, in the above verse the more plausible meaning would be that all the people made supplication to God, not the Egyptians, in particular. Palestine and other countries had also been badly hit by the famine hence invocation to God by their inhabitants. Moreover, even if it relates to rain, obviously there must have been rainfall somewhere which caused flood in the river Nile. Noldeiki's carelessness accounts for his misperception and for his levelling a ridiculous charge against the Qur'an.

Finally, a word about miracles, without calling into question the significance of miracles, there is not much point in stretching the import of the Qur'anic verses to support the miracles narrated in certain reports. For example, the use of the same expression in the Surahs al-Sharah and al-Qamar. What is, however, regretful is that the Qur'anic allusions to the splitting of the moon have been explained by the classical *mufassirun* with reference to the incident in the fifth year of the Prophet Muhammad's career. In so far as the reported incident of the splitting of the moon into two, it was not hard to explain or justify a few centuries ago in that we knew little about the movement of the moon. Now since we have definite information about the law covering the movement of the moon, its temporary stoppage and its splitting into two parts poses difficult questions. And this reported incident cannot be ascribed to the Qur'an itself. If this extraordinary event had actually happened, it should have caused havoc in the universe and the whole solar system should have gone out of order. It is also worth reflecting that the unbelieving Quresh repeatedly asked the Prophet to produce more and more miracles, as reported at several places in the Qur'an. Yet the Qur'an nowhere refers to the above miracle in order to silence them.

In sum, a *mufassir* today owes a far greater responsibility in explaining more logically the meaning and message of the Qur'an by taking recourse to modern knowledge. Needless to say, it is not a plea, in the least, for a modernistic outlook.

Originally in Urdu, it is part of Daryabadi's work, *Mushkilat al-Quran ya Qurani Mutala Biswin Sadi Mein* Chennai, Islamic Research Foundation, 1977. Translated into English by Abdur Raheem Kidwai.

10

Jesus and Mary in the Quran

Abdul Majid Daryabadi

Jesus Christ

His birth, message and ministry:

يَٰٓأَهْلَ ٱلْكِتَٰبِ لَا تَغْلُوا۟ فِى دِينِكُمْ وَلَا تَقُولُوا۟ عَلَى ٱللَّهِ إِلَّا ٱلْحَقَّ ۚ إِنَّمَا ٱلْمَسِيحُ عِيسَى
ٱبْنُ مَرْيَمَ رَسُولُ ٱللَّهِ وَكَلِمَتُهُۥٓ أَلْقَىٰهَآ إِلَىٰ مَرْيَمَ وَرُوحٌ مِّنْهُ ۖ فَـَٔامِنُوا۟ بِٱللَّهِ وَرُسُلِهِۦ ۖ وَلَا
تَقُولُوا۟ ثَلَٰثَةٌ ۚ ٱنتَهُوا۟ خَيْرًا لَّكُمْ ۚ إِنَّمَا ٱللَّهُ إِلَٰهٌ وَٰحِدٌ ۖ سُبْحَٰنَهُۥٓ أَن يَكُونَ لَهُۥ وَلَدٌ ۘ لَّهُۥ مَا
فِى ٱلسَّمَٰوَٰتِ وَمَا فِى ٱلْأَرْضِ ۗ وَكَفَىٰ بِٱللَّهِ وَكِيلًا ﴿١٧١﴾

O people of the Book! In religion do not exceed the bounds,[1] and do not speak of Allah except what is truth. [2] and Jesus Christ is only a Messenger of Allah[3] and His word[4] which He conveyed to Mary and a spirit from Him. [5] Believe therefore, in Allah[6] and His Messengers[7] and do not say: "Three[8]" - Desist[9] that it may be well for you. Allah is but One God. [10] Hallowed be He that there should be a son for Himself[11]. His is all that is all that is in the heaven and all that is in the earth.[12] And Allah suffices as a Trustee. [13]

(al-Nisa 4: 171)

لَّن يَسْتَنكِفَ ٱلْمَسِيحُ أَن يَكُونَ عَبْدًا لِّلَّهِ وَلَا ٱلْمَلَٰٓئِكَةُ ٱلْمُقَرَّبُونَ ۚ وَمَن يَسْتَنكِفْ
عَنْ عِبَادَتِهِۦ وَيَسْتَكْبِرْ فَسَيَحْشُرُهُمْ إِلَيْهِ جَمِيعًا ﴿١٧٢﴾

Christ does not disdain that he should be a servant of Allah[14] , nor do the angles brought near [15] (to Him). And he who disdains serving Him and is stiff-necked, soon He shall gather them all unto Him. [16]

(al-Nisa 4: 172)

لَقَدْ كَفَرَ ٱلَّذِينَ قَالُوٓا۟ إِنَّ ٱللَّهَ هُوَ ٱلْمَسِيحُ ٱبْنُ مَرْيَمَ ۖ وَقَالَ ٱلْمَسِيحُ يَـٰبَنِىٓ إِسْرَٰٓءِيلَ
ٱعْبُدُوا۟ ٱللَّهَ رَبِّى وَرَبَّكُمْ ۖ إِنَّهُۥ مَن يُشْرِكْ بِٱللَّهِ فَقَدْ حَرَّمَ ٱللَّهُ عَلَيْهِ ٱلْجَنَّةَ وَمَأْوَىٰهُ ٱلنَّارُ ۖ وَمَا
لِلظَّـٰلِمِينَ مِنْ أَنصَارٍ ﴿٧٢﴾

Assuredly they have disbelieved who say: [17] Christ son of May is the very God, whereas Christ[18] had said: "O Children of Israel: worship Allah, my Lord and your Lord; [19] he who joins aught with Allah,[20]Allah shall surely forbid the Garden to him, and his resort is the Fire; and the ungodly shall have no helpers."

(al-Maida 5:72)

لَّقَدْ كَفَرَ ٱلَّذِينَ قَالُوٓا۟ إِنَّ ٱللَّهَ ثَالِثُ ثَلَـٰثَةٍ ۘ وَمَا مِنْ إِلَـٰهٍ إِلَّآ إِلَـٰهٌ وَٰحِدٌ ۚ وَإِن لَّمْ يَنتَهُوا۟ عَمَّا
يَقُولُونَ لَيَمَسَّنَّ ٱلَّذِينَ كَفَرُوا۟ مِنْهُمْ عَذَابٌ أَلِيمٌ ﴿٧٣﴾

Assuredly those have disbelieved who say: God is the third of the three[21], whereas there is no god except the One God[22] And if they do not desist from what they[23] say, there shall surely befall those of them who have disbelieved a torment afflictive.

(al-Maida 5:73)

وَقَفَّيْنَا عَلَىٰٓ ءَاثَـٰرِهِم بِعِيسَى ٱبْنِ مَرْيَمَ مُصَدِّقًا لِّمَا بَيْنَ يَدَيْهِ مِنَ ٱلتَّوْرَىٰةِ ۖ وَءَاتَيْنَـٰهُ
ٱلْإِنجِيلَ فِيهِ هُدًى وَنُورٌ وَمُصَدِّقًا لِّمَا بَيْنَ يَدَيْهِ مِنَ ٱلتَّوْرَىٰةِ وَهُدًى وَمَوْعِظَةً
لِّلْمُتَّقِينَ ﴿٤٦﴾

And in their footsteps We caused Jesus son of Mary to follow, confirming what had preceded him, the Torah, and We gave him the Gospels, in which there was guidance and light, confirming what had preceded him, the Torah and guidance and admonition[24] to the God-fearing.

(al-Maida 5: 46)

وَإِذْ قَالَ ٱللَّهُ يَـٰعِيسَى ٱبْنَ مَرْيَمَ ءَأَنتَ قُلْتَ لِلنَّاسِ ٱتَّخِذُونِى وَأُمِّىَ إِلَـٰهَيْنِ مِن دُونِ ٱللَّهِ ۖ قَالَ
سُبْحَـٰنَكَ مَا يَكُونُ لِىٓ أَنْ أَقُولَ مَا لَيْسَ لِى بِحَقٍّ ۚ إِن كُنتُ قُلْتُهُۥ فَقَدْ عَلِمْتَهُۥ ۚ تَعْلَمُ مَا فِى

نَفْسِي وَلَآ أَعْلَمُ مَا فِي نَفْسِكَ ۚ إِنَّكَ أَنتَ عَلَّٰمُ ٱلْغُيُوبِ ﴿١١٦﴾ مَا قُلْتُ لَهُمْ إِلَّا مَآ أَمَرْتَنِي بِهِۦٓ
أَنِ ٱعْبُدُوا۟ ٱللَّهَ رَبِّي وَرَبَّكُمْ ۚ وَكُنتُ عَلَيْهِمْ شَهِيدًا مَّا دُمْتُ فِيهِمْ ۖ فَلَمَّا تَوَفَّيْتَنِي كُنتَ أَنتَ
ٱلرَّقِيبَ عَلَيْهِمْ ۚ وَأَنتَ عَلَىٰ كُلِّ شَيْءٍ شَهِيدٌ ﴿١١٧﴾ إِن تُعَذِّبْهُمْ فَإِنَّهُمْ عِبَادُكَ ۖ وَإِن تَغْفِرْ لَهُمْ
فَإِنَّكَ أَنتَ ٱلْعَزِيزُ ٱلْحَكِيمُ ﴿١١٨﴾

And call to mind when Allah will say[25]: "Jesus son of Mary! Was it you who[26] had said to the people[27]: Take me and my mother as two gods besides Allah?"[28] "Hallowed be You![29] It was not for me to assert what I had no right; had I said it, You would surely have known it; You know whatever is in my mind while I do not know what is in Your mind. Surely You are the great knower of all secrets.

I did not say to them aught save what You bade me to say: worship Allah, my lord and your Lord. I was witness over them so long as I lived amongst them; then when You took me up, You have been the watcher, and You are a witness over everything. Should You punish them, then they are Your creatures and should You forgive them then You are the Mighty, the Wise.

(al-Maida 5: 116-118)

وَقَالَتِ ٱلْيَهُودُ عُزَيْرٌ ٱبْنُ ٱللَّهِ وَقَالَتِ ٱلنَّصَٰرَى ٱلْمَسِيحُ ٱبْنُ ٱللَّهِ ۖ ذَٰلِكَ قَوْلُهُم بِأَفْوَٰهِهِمْ ۖ
يُضَٰهِـُٔونَ قَوْلَ ٱلَّذِينَ كَفَرُوا۟ مِن قَبْلُ ۚ قَٰتَلَهُمُ ٱللَّهُ ۚ أَنَّىٰ يُؤْفَكُونَ ﴿٣٠﴾

And the Jews say: Ezra is a child of God. And the Christians say: Christ[30] is a child of God[31]. That is their saying with their mouths,[32] resembling the slaying of those who disbelieved aforetime.[33] Allah confounds them:[34] whither are they turning away:

(al-Tawbah 9: 30)

لَّقَدْ كَفَرَ ٱلَّذِينَ قَالُوٓا۟ إِنَّ ٱللَّهَ هُوَ ٱلْمَسِيحُ ٱبْنُ مَرْيَمَ ۚ قُلْ فَمَن يَمْلِكُ مِنَ ٱللَّهِ
شَيْـًٔا إِنْ أَرَادَ أَن يُهْلِكَ ٱلْمَسِيحَ ٱبْنَ مَرْيَمَ وَأُمَّهُۥ وَمَن فِي ٱلْأَرْضِ جَمِيعًا ۗ
وَلِلَّهِ مُلْكُ ٱلسَّمَٰوَٰتِ وَٱلْأَرْضِ وَمَا بَيْنَهُمَا ۚ يَخْلُقُ مَا يَشَآءُ ۚ وَٱللَّهُ عَلَىٰ كُلِّ شَيْءٍ
قَدِيرٌ ﴿١٧﴾

Certainly they are disbelievers who assert,[35] "Christ, son of Mary[36], is the very God himself." Say you:[37] who can avail in aught against Allah, if He meant to destroy Christ,[38] son of Mary,[39] and his mother,[40] and those on the earth[41] altogether? And Allah's is the kingdom of the heavens and the earth and what is in-between.[42] He creates whatever He will, and Allah is potent over everything.

(al-Maida 5: 17)

مَّا ٱلْمَسِيحُ ٱبْنُ مَرْيَمَ إِلَّا رَسُولٌ قَدْ خَلَتْ مِن قَبْلِهِ ٱلرُّسُلُ وَأُمُّهُۥ صِدِّيقَةٌ ۖ كَانَا
يَأْكُلَانِ ٱلطَّعَامَ ۗ ٱنظُرْ كَيْفَ نُبَيِّنُ لَهُمُ ٱلْءَايَٰتِ ثُمَّ ٱنظُرْ أَنَّىٰ يُؤْفَكُونَ ٧٥

The Christ,[43] son of Mary, was naught but a Messenger;[44] surely there passed away Messengers before him,[45] and his mother was a saintly[46] woman; they both[47] ate earthly food[48]. See how We explain to them Our evidence.[49] Then see whither they are deviating.[50]

(al-Maida 5: 75)

ٱتَّخَذُوٓا۟ أَحْبَارَهُمْ وَرُهْبَٰنَهُمْ أَرْبَابًا مِّن دُونِ ٱللَّهِ وَٱلْمَسِيحَ ٱبْنَ مَرْيَمَ وَمَآ أُمِرُوٓا۟ إِلَّا
لِيَعْبُدُوٓا۟ إِلَٰهًا وَٰحِدًا ۖ لَّآ إِلَٰهَ إِلَّا هُوَ ۚ سُبْحَٰنَهُۥ عَمَّا يُشْرِكُونَ ٣١

They have taken their priests[51] and their monks[52] for their Lords, besides Allah[53] and also the Masih, son of Maryam;[54] whereas they[55] were enjoined[56] that they should worship but One God;[57] no god is there but He. Hallowed be He from that which they associate with Him.[58]

(al-Tawbah 9: 31)

۞ يَوْمَ يَجْمَعُ ٱللَّهُ ٱلرُّسُلَ فَيَقُولُ مَاذَآ أُجِبْتُمْ ۖ قَالُوا۟ لَا عِلْمَ لَنَآ ۖ إِنَّكَ أَنتَ عَلَّٰمُ
ٱلْغُيُوبِ ١٠٩

Beware of the Day when Allah will assemble the Messengers and ask them[59]: "How were you answered"?[60] Then they will say: "No knowledge have we[61] and surely it, is You: You are the great knower of things hidden."

(al-Maida 5: 109)

إِذْ قَالَ ٱللَّهُ يَٰعِيسَى ٱبْنَ مَرْيَمَ ٱذْكُرْ نِعْمَتِى عَلَيْكَ وَعَلَىٰ وَٰلِدَتِكَ إِذْ أَيَّدتُّكَ بِرُوحِ ٱلْقُدُسِ
تُكَلِّمُ ٱلنَّاسَ فِى ٱلْمَهْدِ وَكَهْلًا ۖ وَإِذْ عَلَّمْتُكَ ٱلْكِتَٰبَ وَٱلْحِكْمَةَ وَٱلتَّوْرَىٰةَ وَٱلْإِنجِيلَ ۖ وَإِذْ

تَخْلُقُ مِنَ ٱلطِّينِ كَهَيْـَٔةِ ٱلطَّيْرِ بِإِذْنِى فَتَنفُخُ فِيهَا فَتَكُونُ طَيْرًۢا بِإِذْنِى ۖ وَتُبْرِئُ ٱلْأَكْمَهَ
وَٱلْأَبْرَصَ بِإِذْنِى ۖ وَإِذْ تُخْرِجُ ٱلْمَوْتَىٰ بِإِذْنِى ۖ وَإِذْ كَفَفْتُ بَنِىٓ إِسْرَٰٓءِيلَ عَنكَ إِذْ جِئْتَهُم
بِٱلْبَيِّنَٰتِ فَقَالَ ٱلَّذِينَ كَفَرُوا۟ مِنْهُمْ إِنْ هَٰذَآ إِلَّا سِحْرٌ مُّبِينٌ ﴿١١٠﴾

And call to mind when Allah will say, "O Jesus of Mary: Remember My favour to you and your mother[62] when I aided you with the holy spirit[63] so that you spoke to mankind in the cradle[64] and in maturity and when I taught you the Scripture[65] and wisdom and the Torah and the Gospels[66] and when[67] you formed out of clay the likeness of a bird[68] at My command and when you caused the dead to come forth by My command and you healed by My command those born blind and the leper. And when I restrained the children of Israel from you when you came to them with evidence, and those of them who disbelieved, they said: "This is but open magic."[69] Of them some are guided and many ungodly.

(al-Maida 5: 110)

وَلَقَدْ أَرْسَلْنَا نُوحًا وَإِبْرَٰهِيمَ وَجَعَلْنَا فِى ذُرِّيَّتِهِمَا ٱلنُّبُوَّةَ وَٱلْكِتَٰبَ ۖ فَمِنْهُم مُّهْتَدٍ ۖ وَكَثِيرٌ
مِّنْهُمْ فَٰسِقُونَ ﴿٢٦﴾ ثُمَّ قَفَّيْنَا عَلَىٰٓ ءَاثَٰرِهِم بِرُسُلِنَا وَقَفَّيْنَا بِعِيسَى ٱبْنِ مَرْيَمَ وَءَاتَيْنَٰهُ
ٱلْإِنجِيلَ وَجَعَلْنَا فِى قُلُوبِ ٱلَّذِينَ ٱتَّبَعُوهُ رَأْفَةً وَرَحْمَةً وَرَهْبَانِيَّةً ٱبْتَدَعُوهَا مَا كَتَبْنَٰهَا
عَلَيْهِمْ إِلَّا ٱبْتِغَآءَ رِضْوَٰنِ ٱللَّهِ فَمَا رَعَوْهَا حَقَّ رِعَايَتِهَا ۖ فَـَٔاتَيْنَا ٱلَّذِينَ ءَامَنُوا۟ مِنْهُمْ أَجْرَهُمْ ۖ
وَكَثِيرٌ مِّنْهُمْ فَٰسِقُونَ ﴿٢٧﴾

Thereafter, in their footsteps We caused Jesus, son of Mary, to follow them, and We vouchsafed to him the Gospels, and We placed in the hearts of those who truly followed him,[70] tenderness and mercy. And asceticism:[71] they innovated it - We prescribed it not for them, -- only seeking Allah's pleasure;[72] yet they tended it not with due tenderness.[73]So We vouchsafed to them such as believed their reward, and many of them are transgressors.

(al-Hadid 57: 26-27)

Mary

إِذْ قَالَتِ ٱمْرَأَتُ عِمْرَٰنَ رَبِّ إِنِّى نَذَرْتُ لَكَ مَا فِى بَطْنِى مُحَرَّرًا فَتَقَبَّلْ مِنِّىٓ ۖ إِنَّكَ أَنتَ
ٱلسَّمِيعُ ٱلْعَلِيمُ ﴿٣٥﴾

Re-call when the wife of Imran[74] said: "Lord: surely I have vowed to You what is in my belly (to be)[75] dedicated; Accept this of me, Surely You: only You are the Hearer,[76] the Knower.[77]"

(Al 'Imran 3: 35)

فَلَمَّا وَضَعَتْهَا قَالَتْ رَبِّ إِنِّى وَضَعْتُهَآ أُنثَىٰ وَٱللَّهُ أَعْلَمُ بِمَا وَضَعَتْ وَلَيْسَ ٱلذَّكَرُ كَٱلْأُنثَىٰ ۖ وَإِنِّى
سَمَّيْتُهَا مَرْيَمَ وَإِنِّىٓ أُعِيذُهَا بِكَ وَذُرِّيَّتَهَا مِنَ ٱلشَّيْطَٰنِ ٱلرَّجِيمِ ﴿٣٦﴾

Then when she bore her[78], she said[79]: "My Lord: Surely I bore a female[80] - And Allah knew best what she had borne[81] and the male is not as the female[82] - and surely I have named her Mary,[83] and I commit her and her progeny to You for protection[84] from Satan the accursed.[85]"

(Al 'Imran 3: 36)

فَتَقَبَّلَهَا رَبُّهَا بِقَبُولٍ حَسَنٍ وَأَنۢبَتَهَا نَبَاتًا حَسَنًا وَكَفَّلَهَا زَكَرِيَّا ۖ كُلَّمَا دَخَلَ عَلَيْهَا زَكَرِيَّا
ٱلْمِحْرَابَ وَجَدَ عِندَهَا رِزْقًا ۖ قَالَ يَٰمَرْيَمُ أَنَّىٰ لَكِ هَٰذَا ۖ قَالَتْ هُوَ مِنْ عِندِ ٱللَّهِ ۖ إِنَّ ٱللَّهَ
يَرْزُقُ مَن يَشَآءُ بِغَيْرِ حِسَابٍ ﴿٣٧﴾

Then her Lord accepted her[86] with goodly acceptance[87] and made her grow up with a goodly growth,[88] and He made Zechariah[89] take care of her.[90] Whenever Zechariah entered the apartment[91] to see her, he found provision[92] by her. He said: "Mary: whence[93] have you this?" She said: "This is from before Allah[94]" Surely Allah provides for whom He will without stint.[95]

(Al 'Imran 3: 37)

هُنَالِكَ دَعَا زَكَرِيَّا رَبَّهُۥ ۖ قَالَ رَبِّ هَبْ لِى مِن لَّدُنكَ ذُرِّيَّةً طَيِّبَةً ۖ إِنَّكَ سَمِيعُ ٱلدُّعَآءِ
﴿٣٨﴾ فَنَادَتْهُ ٱلْمَلَٰٓئِكَةُ وَهُوَ قَآئِمٌ يُصَلِّى فِى ٱلْمِحْرَابِ أَنَّ ٱللَّهَ يُبَشِّرُكَ بِيَحْيَىٰ مُصَدِّقًۢا بِكَلِمَةٍ
مِّنَ ٱللَّهِ وَسَيِّدًا وَحَصُورًا وَنَبِيًّا مِّنَ ٱلصَّٰلِحِينَ ﴿٣٩﴾

Immediately[96] did Zechariah[97] pray to his Lord: “My Lord! bestow on me[98] from Your presence a goodly offspring surely You! only You, are the Hearer of prayer. Then the angels[99] called to him while he stood praying in the apartment. Surely Allah announces to you, John![100] Confirming the word from Allah,[101] a leader[102], and chaste[103], and a Prophet, from among the righteous[104].

(Al 'Imran 3:38-39)

قَالَ رَبِّ أَنَّىٰ يَكُونُ لِى غُلَٰمٌ وَقَدْ بَلَغَنِىَ ٱلْكِبَرُ وَٱمْرَأَتِى عَاقِرٌ ۖ قَالَ كَذَٰلِكَ ٱللَّهُ يَفْعَلُ مَا
يَشَآءُ ﴿٤٠﴾ قَالَ رَبِّ ٱجْعَل لِّىٓ ءَايَةً ۖ قَالَ ءَايَتُكَ أَلَّا تُكَلِّمَ ٱلنَّاسَ ثَلَٰثَةَ أَيَّامٍ إِلَّا رَمْزًا ۗ
وَٱذْكُر رَّبَّكَ كَثِيرًا وَسَبِّحْ بِٱلْعَشِىِّ وَٱلْإِبْكَٰرِ ﴿٤١﴾

He said: "My Lord! How will there be unto me a son while old age has overtaken me and my wife is barren?[105]" Allah said: "So[106] it shall be, Allah does what He will.[107]" He said: "My Lord: appoint to me a sign.[108]" Allah said: "The sign is that you shall not speak to anyone[109] for three days[110] save by tokens,[111] and remember your Lord much,[112] and hallow Him in the evening[113] and morning.[114]"

(Al 'Imran 3: 40-41)

وَإِذْ قَالَتِ ٱلْمَلَٰٓئِكَةُ يَٰمَرْيَمُ إِنَّ ٱللَّهَ ٱصْطَفَىٰكِ وَطَهَّرَكِ وَٱصْطَفَىٰكِ عَلَىٰ نِسَآءِ ٱلْعَٰلَمِينَ
﴿٤٢﴾ يَٰمَرْيَمُ ٱقْنُتِى لِرَبِّكِ وَٱسْجُدِى وَٱرْكَعِى مَعَ ٱلرَّٰكِعِينَ ﴿٤٣﴾ ذَٰلِكَ مِنْ أَنۢبَآءِ ٱلْغَيْبِ
نُوحِيهِ إِلَيْكَ ۚ وَمَا كُنتَ لَدَيْهِمْ إِذْ يُلْقُونَ أَقْلَٰمَهُمْ أَيُّهُمْ يَكْفُلُ مَرْيَمَ وَمَا كُنتَ لَدَيْهِمْ
إِذْ يَخْتَصِمُونَ ﴿٤٤﴾

And recall when the angels[115] said: 'O Mary: Surely Allah chose you[116] and cleansed you[117] and chose you[118] above the women of the worlds. O Mary: "Be devout unto your Lord, prostrate yourself and bow down with those who bow down.[119] This is of the tidings of the Unseen which We reveal to you,[120] and you were not with them[121] when they cast their reeds[122] as to which of them should have charge of Mary.[123] Nor were you with them when they disputed".[124]

(Al 'Imran 3: 42-44)

إِذْ قَالَتِ ٱلْمَلَٰٓئِكَةُ يَٰمَرْيَمُ إِنَّ ٱللَّهَ يُبَشِّرُكِ بِكَلِمَةٍ مِّنْهُ ٱسْمُهُ ٱلْمَسِيحُ عِيسَى ٱبْنُ مَرْيَمَ وَجِيهًا
فِى ٱلدُّنْيَا وَٱلْءَاخِرَةِ وَمِنَ ٱلْمُقَرَّبِينَ ﴿٤٥﴾ وَيُكَلِّمُ ٱلنَّاسَ فِى ٱلْمَهْدِ وَكَهْلًا وَمِنَ
ٱلصَّٰلِحِينَ ﴿٤٦﴾ قَالَتْ رَبِّ أَنَّىٰ يَكُونُ لِى وَلَدٌ وَلَمْ يَمْسَسْنِى بَشَرٌ ۖ قَالَ كَذَٰلِكِ ٱللَّهُ
يَخْلُقُ مَا يَشَآءُ ۚ إِذَا قَضَىٰٓ أَمْرًا فَإِنَّمَا يَقُولُ لَهُۥ كُن فَيَكُونُ ﴿٤٧﴾

And recall when the angels[125] said: "O Mary! Surely Allah announces to you a word[126] from Him: his name[127] shall be the Christ[128], Jesus[129] son of Mary[130], illustrious in this world[131] and the Hereafter[132], and one of those brought nigh[133] and he will speak to mankind[134] in the cradle[135] and maturity[136] and be one of the righteous."[137]

She said: "My Lord: how will there be a son unto me while no man has touched me?"[138] Allah said[139]: "So[140] it shall be. Allah creates what He will.[141] When He decrees a thing, He only says to it: “Be[142]”, and it becomes."[143]

(Al 'Imran 3: 45-47)

فَأَتَتْ بِهِۦ قَوْمَهَا تَحْمِلُهُۥ ۖ قَالُوا۟ يَٰمَرْيَمُ لَقَدْ جِئْتِ شَيْـًٔا فَرِيًّا ﴿٢٧﴾ يَٰٓأُخْتَ هَٰرُونَ مَا كَانَ
أَبُوكِ ٱمْرَأَ سَوْءٍ وَمَا كَانَتْ أُمُّكِ بَغِيًّا ﴿٢٨﴾ فَأَشَارَتْ إِلَيْهِ ۖ قَالُوا۟ كَيْفَ نُكَلِّمُ مَن كَانَ فِى
ٱلْمَهْدِ صَبِيًّا ﴿٢٩﴾ قَالَ إِنِّى عَبْدُ ٱللَّهِ ءَاتَىٰنِىَ ٱلْكِتَٰبَ وَجَعَلَنِى نَبِيًّا ﴿٣٠﴾ وَجَعَلَنِى مُبَارَكًا أَيْنَ
مَا كُنتُ وَأَوْصَٰنِى بِٱلصَّلَوٰةِ وَٱلزَّكَوٰةِ مَا دُمْتُ حَيًّا ﴿٣١﴾ وَبَرًّۢا بِوَٰلِدَتِى وَلَمْ يَجْعَلْنِى جَبَّارًا
شَقِيًّا ﴿٣٢﴾ وَٱلسَّلَٰمُ عَلَىَّ يَوْمَ وُلِدتُّ وَيَوْمَ أَمُوتُ وَيَوْمَ أُبْعَثُ حَيًّا ﴿٣٣﴾ ذَٰلِكَ عِيسَى ٱبْنُ
مَرْيَمَ ۚ قَوْلَ ٱلْحَقِّ ٱلَّذِى فِيهِ يَمْتَرُونَ ﴿٣٤﴾ مَا كَانَ لِلَّهِ أَن يَتَّخِذَ مِن وَلَدٍ ۖ سُبْحَٰنَهُۥٓ ۚ إِذَا
قَضَىٰٓ أَمْرًا فَإِنَّمَا يَقُولُ لَهُۥ كُن فَيَكُونُ ﴿٣٥﴾ وَإِنَّ ٱللَّهَ رَبِّى وَرَبُّكُمْ فَٱعْبُدُوهُ ۚ هَٰذَا صِرَٰطٌ
مُّسْتَقِيمٌ ﴿٣٦﴾

Then she[144] brought him[145] to the people carrying him.[146] They said: "Mary, you have surely brought a thing unheard of.[147] Sister of Aaron![148] Your father was not a man of evil, nor was your mother a harlot."[149] Then she pointed out to him.[150] They said: "How shall we speak to him who is in a cradle[151], a child?" (Jesus) said: "I am a bondman of Allah:[152] He has vouchsafed me the Book and made me a Prophet.[153] And He has made me blessed wherever I may be and enjoined on me prayer and purity as long as I am alive.[154] And dutiful unto my mother,[155] and has not made me high-handed and unblest.[156] And peace be on me the day I was born and the day I die and the day I shall be raised up alive."[157] Such is Jesus, son of Mary. This is the word of truth in which they[158] are doubting.[159] Allah is not one to take (to Himself) a son.[160] Hallowed be He. Whenever He decrees an affair, He only says to it "Be" and it[161] becomes.[162] And[163] surely Allah is my Lord[164] and your Lord, so worship Him. This is a way straight."

(Maryam 19: 27-36)

Notes

1. (by ascribing Godhead to Jesus). Paganization of Christianity was complete by the time of the revelation of the Holy Quran. Lamentable, indeed, is the reflection that so small a portion of the fair form of Christianity was disclosed by the ecclesiastics and monks of Syria to the earnest inquirer; and that little how altered and distorted. (Muir, *Life of Mohammad,* pp. 21-22)
2. and the first truth regarding God is that He is One, without a second.
3. (and not His son or Incarnation).
4. i.e. born out of His Word.
5. i.e. a being receiving the soul direct from God without any human agency.
6. (i.e. the One, the Unique; the Eternal).
7. (as taught by them).
8. i.e. three really distinct persons; the Father, the Son and the Holy Ghost - co-equal, co-eternal and consubstantial.
9. (from holding a doctrine as flagrantly blasphemous and preposterous).
10. (with no second or third person to share His substance and attributes).
11. The term 'Son of God', even if used by Christ at all meant no more than one who subordinates himself and his own will to God (Schmiedel, *Jesus and Modern Criticism*, p.40). In the original Christianity, Jesus was the Christ or an anointed man not as the incarnate, Angel - Messiah born by a virgin (Bunsen: *Islam or True Christianity*, 4, 148).
12. That is the only true relationship that exists between all the creatures and their Creator.
13. i.e. the sole Arbiter, the Disposer of all affairs, needing no redeemer or Mediator.
14. i.e. a true worshipper and obedient servant of God. Cf. Christ's own words as recorded in the Christian Gospels: 'My job is to do the will of him that sent me and to finish his work' (Jn. 4:34) 'If ye keep my commandments, ye shall

abide in my love; even as I kept my father's commandments, and abide in his love.' (15:30). And Peter, an apostle, has in the course of a long address used the following words: 'Jesus of Nazareth, a man approved of God among you.....' (Ac.2:22). These words, according to the best Biblical scholars, 'describe Jesus as He was known and regarded by his contemporaries. He was "found in fashion as a man", that is, in all particulars which presented themselves to outward observation. He appeared and behaved as one of the human race. He 'was made man". The Gospels leave no room for doubt as to the completeness with which these statements are to be accepted. He not only made no claim to omniscience: He distinctly waived it. There is still less reason to predicate the omnipotence of Jesus. There is no indication that He ever acted independently of God, or as an independent God, by his habit of prayer and in such words as "this kind goeth not forth save by prayer." He even repudiates the ascription to himself of godness in the absolute sense in which it belongs to God alone." (*EBr*, XIII, p. 24)

15. This knocks the bottom out of the Christian angelolatry. In the Catholic Catechism one comes across the following daily prayer addressed to 'Our Angel Guardian; O Angel of God, to whose care I am committed. Enlighten and direct me, defend and govern me this day, and during my whole life: Amen'. 'This adoration of the angels 'can be traced to the earliest ages of the Church. We venerate their excellence and petition their ministrations. The month of October is specially dedicated to them and the feast of all the angles is celebrated in common with that of Michael, 29th Sept.' (*CD*. p. 44)
16. (to answer for their misdeeds) 'Mariolatry is probably now more prevalent in the Church of Rome than at any former time. (p. 291). In the Orient there did not exist, in the early centuries, certain Christian sects who worshipped Mary. The Colyridians, says St. Epiphany, offered little cakes (collysis) as sacrifices to the virgin like those offered to Ceres by the pagans. (Darmingham). The title of Thotokos, or 'Mother of God' as enforced on the Virgin Mary by the Ecumenical Council of Ephesus in 431. According to the Roman Catholic Church, God, without ceasing to be God, in the characteristic pharase of St. Paul "implied Himself" and was born in the human form of Mary's womb and she became Virgin Mother, the Virgin Mother of God.' (Ptoserpie, *The Council of Ephesus and the Divine Motherhood,* p. 4) To Catholics the Council of Ephesus is above all, the Council of "Thotokos," Mother of God. From it dates the rise of that intimate and personal devotion to Our Blessed Lady which ever since has found one of the most beautiful and distinguishing features of the Catholic Church, Mother of God: It is the form and centre and explanation of the worship we pay to her." (p. 25)
17. (with whom Jesus is on a par in the attribute of powerlessness)
18. i.e. He is the sole Creator, the sole Author, the sole Ruler of the universe, undivided into several 'persons'.
19. (and believe). To the Orthodox Christian "Jesus is without qualification God, and the greater the contradiction to the mind, the more the heart responds to the wonder of the mystery" (*HJ* Oct. 1934, p. 6).
20. 'Thou shalt worship the Lord thy God, and him alone shalt thou serve. '(Mt. 4:10; Lk.4:8).' And Jesus said unto him why callest thou me god? None is god

save one, that "Son of God", and the title when bestowed upon Him by others probably involves no more than the acknowledgement that he was the Messiah.' (*EBr.* XIII, p. 23). 'That the trinitarian baptismal formula does not go back to Jesus himself is evident and recognized by all independent critics. (*EBi.* c.4689). 'A critical study of the synoptical material leads invariably to the conclusion that Jesus never called himself the 'son of God" and never was addressed by that title.' (*EBi.*c. 4701)

21. (either in His Person or His Attributes, as the Christian do). That the Christians are proud of their Christolatry is a fact self-evident. It is noted in their books with self-adulation that the Church in the course of its long history has never ceased to offer prayer to Christ with the Father.' (*ERE.* I, p.104)

    'These are three that bear record in heaven - the Father, the Word, and the Holy Ghost: and these three are one.' The Athanasian Creed runs: - 'There is one person of the Father, another of the Son and another of the Holy Ghost: the Father is God and Lord; and the Holy Ghost is God and Lord.' These words of the Creed, says Swedenborg, make it 'as clear as water in a crystal cup, that three persons, each of whom is God and Lord. '(Du Bunsen, *The True Christian Religion*, p.244). This central doctrine of the Christian religion can only mean that God 'is three really distinct Persons, the Father, the Son, and the Holy Ghost ... Three persons are co-equal, co-eternal, and consubstantial, and deserve co-equal glory and adoration.' (*CD.* p.973) 'The dogma of the 'Trinity", which still comprises three of the chief articles of faith in the creed of Christian peoples, culminates is the notion that the one God of Christianity is really made up of three different persons: (1) God the Father (2) Jesus Christ; and (3) Holy Ghost, a mystical being over whose incomprehensible relation to the Father and the Son millions of Christian theologians have racked their brains in vain for the last 1900 years.' (Haeckel, *The Riddle of The Universe*, p. 227)

22. (with no divisibility of Person). And thus the Christians are as much steeped in polytheism as are the Pagans. The Christians 'acknowledge one God indeed with the lips, but in three persons, each of whom simply or by himself was God.' (Swedenborg)
23. i,e., from ascribing 'trinity' to God.
24. (for right conduct).
25. (on the day of Judgement).
26. (whilst living on the earth).
27. i.e. the so-called Christians.
28. i.e. the objects, worship are adoration. The clear allusion is to the cult of Mary or Madonna common to the vast bulk of Christian community.

    Compare the Angelical salutation: "Holy Mother of God! Pray for us sinners, now and at the time of our death. Amen!" And their Angeleo Domini: 'Pray for us, O Holy Mother of God!, *ERE* IX p.908) ' Popular devotion gradually developed the entire system of devotion and practice which Protestant controversialists are accustomed to call by the name of Mariolatry." (*EBr.* XIV, p. 1000, 14th Ed).
29. (greatly hurt at the attributes of his adherents).

30. literally 'wiped over with some such thing as oil', and (with the definite article) is 'the Anointed, the Christ,' Note that the Quran never disputes the title of Jesus to Messiahship.
31. 'Children of God' and Sons of God' are both Biblical phrases. In the former, the favourite phrase of St. John, the idea of origin is most prominent'; while the latter, so frequently used by St. Paul, emphasizes 'rather the notion of relation and privilege' (DB.II. p.215). The doctrine of Jesus being 'a child of God' is distinct from his sonship, though the two ideas later on coalesced into one. Both are equally blasphemous and derogatory to the dignity of God.
32. (void of all substance). i.e. unsupported by their own Prophets.
33. Pagan mythologies and polytheistic theologies are full of the underlying notion of the fatherhood of God, man's genetic relationship with Him, and community of nature between man and God. 'The idea of divine Fatherhood had not failed to make its appearance in the Jewish scriptures, canonical and uncanonical, as it indeed appears in many religions.' (*EBr.* XIII, p.21) There may be a special reference to great influence on the Christian theology of Greece which 'supplied the philosophy of the Christian religions' and of Rome of which 'the stubborn local traditions survive in Catholic Europe to this day.' (*UHW*. IV, p. 2083).
34. An expression of reproach at the willful blindness and perversity of the Jews and Christians.
35. (and believe). 'Those who asserted that their God was a man, and that a crucified man was their God, laid themselves open to the accusation that they were idolaters and blasphemers.'(Denison, *Emotion and the Basis of Civilization*, p. 286)
36. The reference here is mainly to certain less well-known varieties of Christianity, such as Docetism, Monarchianism and Sabellianism, which rest on some such propositions as the following: 'That one and the same God is the Creator and Father of all things ; and that when it pleased Him, He appeared.' 'When the Father had not been born, He yet was justly styled Father and when it pleased Him, to undergo generations having been begotten, He himself become His own Son, not another's.' 'Father and Son, so called, are one and the same substance, not an individual produced from a different one, but Himself for Himself.' (*ERE*. VIII, p. 779) 'Modalistic monarchianism conceiving that the whole fullness of the Godhead, dwelt in Christ.....maintained that the names Father and son were only different designations of the same subject, the One God.' (*EBr.* XI. p. 686) But hardly distinguishable from these 'heresies' and equally bewildering to the Muslim mind is the accepted central doctrine of the orthodox Christianity: 'Jesus is very God of very God, Who for us men and for our salvation came down form haven and was made Man.' His nature is 'consubstantial' with God.' 'He is not inferior to the Father, nor posterior, nor merely like unto Him, but identical in substance and in essence with Him, He is truly God, God of very God, consubstantial with the Father, as the Nicene Creed has its, having, or rather, being, the Godhead no less that the Father.' (*CD*.p.252)
37. (to these Christolators, O Prophet).

38. (a mere mortal, by death)
39. i.e. son of a frail, mortal woman.
40. (who also is adored and worshipped as divinity by a very large number of the Christians). ' In the most widely distributed form of Christianity the "virgin" mother of Christ plays an important part as the fourth deity; in many Catholic countries she is practically taken to be much more powerful and influential than the three male persons of the celestial administration.' (Haeckel, *op. cit.*, p. 232) Even as early as the 3rd century, the titles of Mary as the 'Mother of God' and as the 'Queen of Heaven', 'were demanded by the more fanatical Christians who claimed Divine honours for the ideal and prototype of virginity' *(DB.* III, p. 289).
41. All the creatures.
42. Allah Who is Supreme.
43. (himself a mortal and born of a frail, mortal woman)
44. (and neither God, nor His Son, nor His Incarnation). Some of the most ancient Christians were not slow to perceive the humanity of Christ, as contradistinguished from his divinity, The Ebionites regarded him ' as an ordinary man though superior to other men.' (*ERE.* I, p. 103). Paul of Samosata held that ' Christ was a human person, who possessed the Logos as an attribute. Finally he becomes God; i.e., he was united to God in the only way in which unity between persons is possible, by absolute harmony of will.... His miracles manifested the harmony of his will with the will of God.' (XI.p.171) And Justin has remarked: ' There are of our number some who admit that he is Christ but declare that he was man born of man' (*EBI.* c. 2963). Similarly the inquiries of the most modern of the Christian inquirers are once again approximating the Islamic view: 'The picture of Jesus' as Loisy sees him, 'is purely human... Jesus did not offer himself to his contemporaries as a sage or a moralist, or as a Prophet pure and simple, but as one sent from God who claims, in relation to the kingdom, the position of Grand Ambassador.' (*The Hibbert Journal*, Oct. 1934, p. 30) on purely historical grounds all that can be affirmed of Jesus Christ is that he was a man in a certain environment. The Christ of the Gospels is the product of faith.' (*The Hibbert Journal, April,* 1935, p. 374)
45. (now surely no apostle, however great and eminent, and however superior to his fellow-beings can, in any sense, be God or part of God, or one of the 'Triad'). The familiar companions of Jesus of Nazareth conversed with their friend and countryman, who, in all the actions or rational and animal life, appeared of the same species with themselves. His progress from infancy to youth and manhood was marked by a regular increase in stature and wisdom.' (*GRE.*V p.97)
46. This refutes the outrageous calumny of the Jews who held her guilty of misconduct, and reinstates her in her pure, saintly character. 'The feminine as used in the Koran means superlative in *al-Sidq* and *al-Tasreef.*' (LL)
47. mere mortals and mere human beings as they were.

48. (and needed it). i.e. obliged to support their lives by the same means, and subject to the same necessities and infirmities as the rest of mankind, they could be gods or godlings.
49. (to expose the hollowness of the so-called Christians' position). That the Holy Qur'an did, to some extent, assert modifying influence on certain Christian sects is now an admitted truth. The opposition of Islam also partly determined the forms of men's views on the doctrine of Christ's person.' (*EBr.* I, p. 177)
50. (from the truth; and how they cling to error and falsehood).
51. i.e. men learned in religious lore.
52. i.e., men devoted to religious penances.
53. (by considering them infallible as the very Lord God.) Among the Jews, the ancient rabbis claimed 'under certain circumstances even to suspend and to abrogate a Biblical law... There are cases mentioned in the Talmud, in which a Biblical law was entirely abrogated.' (*JE.* I, p. 131). 'The distinguished rank of the high priest is apparent from the fact that his sins are regarded as belonging also to the people' (VI. p. 390). Among the Christians, the Church of Christ and the Pope are salvation. It is under the abiding influence of the Holy Ghost, and therefore cannot err in the matters of faith.' (*EBr.* XVI. p. 940) 'The Church and the Pope cannot err when solemnly enunciating as binding on all the faithful, a decision on a question of faith or morals.' (XII. p. 318) 'Catholicism maintains that the Church alone with the assistance of the Holy Ghost promised her by Christ can tell us with infallible certainly what truth God has actually revealed, whether these be found in the Bible or in tradition.' (*CD.* p. 358)
54. (whom the Christians have taken as their very Lord God). Inaudible as it may sound to the Muslim ears, the position of Jesus among the Christians is actually that of God. The Catholic Church holds: 'That her Founder and generator of her inerrancy, Jesus Christ is God.' (*CD.* p. 265). 'Christ is both God and man. As man He was the Ambassador of His Eternal Father: as God, He and the Father are equal in all things' (p. 824). 'God the Son, made man and named Jesus Christ, is worshipped in His Divinity and in His Humanity.' (p. 1027)
55. i.e. both the Jews and Christians.
56. (by God through their prophets)
57. In the *OT*: 'I am the Lord God. Thou shalt have no other gods before me.' (Ex. 20:1-2). Also Dt. 5:6-7; 6:4, 14. And in the *NT*: 'The first of all the commandments is, Hear, O Israel; the Lord our God is one Lord.' (Mk. 12:29) Also Mt. 4:10; Lk. 4:8.
58. The truth emphasized by Islam.
59. The Messengers.
60. (your people when you preached to them)
61. Of what was in their minds in our life time nor of what they did in perverting and mutilating our teachings after us.
62. It is God Who as Creator and Ruler is conferring His favours on Jesus and Mary who as His creatures are mere recipients of them.
63. (in a special way as explained above)

64. i.e. while yet an infant. Even St. Luke tells of one happening during that time of the encounters with the doctors in the temple when he was twelve years old (*The Catholic Times* 14th Jan. 1946)
65. i.e. the Revealed Books in general. The word is used in a generic sense. Thus Jesus (peace be on him) was tangent of God, even as our holy Prophet was.
66. (in particular). There the man Jesus in all these matters stood in the need of the tutelage of God.
67. (in order to generate belief in the minds of their audience)
68. i.e. the form of a bird; a counterfeit bird. 'He also made figures of birds which could fly and of animals which could work' (Buoge, *Legends of our Lady Mary*).
69. i.e. a real live bird. On another occasion Jesus was said to have been playing with some boys on the Sabbath, modeling birds, oxen, camels, out of clay, a Pharisee passed by and after rebuking them for profaning the Sabbath proceeded, to their great grief, to destroy their handiwork with his foot, When Jesus saw this, He clapped His hands over the sparrow He had made and cried: 'Go. Fly through all the world and live. Immediately the clay sparrow became alive and to the astonishment of the bystanders spread her wings and soared up into the sky.' (*The Catholic Times*, London, 14th December 1945)
70. i.e., his true and real followers and not the so-called Christians. Mark the implication of the phrase instead of the single word.
71. Or monkery, monasticism.
72. (for their spiritual benefit under the influence of false devotions).
73. 'With the passing of the concubine, the nuns in the convents provided them: "holy men" with the means of satisfying their sexual cravings.' (Scott, *History of Prostitution,* p.112).
74. i.e. Mary's mother, or Jesus's maternal grand-mother, was known as Hanna or Anne. 'It has been generally imagined by Christian writers that the Quran here confounds Mary the mother of Jesus with Mary or Miriam, the sister of Moses and Aaron. Yet I do not see how it can be made out from the words of the Koran.' (Sale) Muslim historians have traced the genealogies of both. The Christians admit that in their own record and genealogies nothing of any historical value is recorded of parentage of Mary. (*EBR*. XIII. p. 811)
75. (to Your sole service). 'He set apart a child for the worship of God and the service of the mosque: or he devoted him to the service of the Church as long as he should live.' (*LL*) The phrase thus means: 'I will not occupy him with anything else, he shall be freed from all worldly occupations and wholly devoted to the service of Your Sanctuary.' The Protestant Christian version, based on 'legends,' is: An angel comforted her by the news that Joachim was returning, and that who could bear him a child, who, she at once vowed to dedicate to the service of the temple.' (*DB*.II. p. 258) The Catholic Church holds, on the authority of the apocryphal literature: "Anne and Joachim had reached old age and still remained childless; their prayers were answered, an angel of the Lord announced to Anne that the fruit of her womb would be blessed by all the world.' (*CD*. p. 48) and according to the tradition of the Coptic Church: "And Hannah said, 'My Lord and My God: If it is to be that You have given me a son, I will give him to God and I will dedicate him to

the service of Sanctuary all the days of him.' (Budge, *Legends of Our Lady Mary*, p. 124).

76. (of my Prayer)
77. (of the sincerity of my motives)
78. i.e., a daughter, Mary (of blessed memory)
79. (in her great disappointment)
80. (and not a son as I had desired and expected). The birth of a daughter naturally seemed to Hannah to be a disappointment, since a girl could not be very suitable for the service of the sanctuary.
81. A parenthetical proposition directly from God, intended to glorify the child and to show that the mother knew nothing of its worth.
82. i.e., in this particular instance. No male child (such as Hannah desired) could be like this female child in worth (Th). The principle, though enunciated only incidentally, is also of general application, and emphasizes the fundamental biological differences between the sexes. From the moment of fertilization onwards, man and woman differ in every cell of their body in regard to the number of their chromosomes - those bodies which, for all the world's unfamiliarity, have been shown by the best decades' work to be the bearers of heredity the determiners of our characters and qualities. The differences then are considerable; so considerable that they can never permit of the simple equivalence of the sexes... It is temperament which in the long run decrees what was we shall make our intellects, and in temperament there is and will be - not for centuries but for biological periods - a fundamental average difference between the sexes,' (Julian Huxley, *Essays in Popular Science*, pp. 64-65)
83. i.e., Mary of the Bible.
84. i.e., I commit her and her descendants to God's care and protection. Hannah intercedes with her Lord and begs that He will protect the child and let her prosper.
85. The 'accursed' is simply one lying under a curse execrable, driven away from the Divine grace, and has, in this connection, nothing whatever to do with the 'pelting of stones' so ineptly alluded to by the Christian translators of the Quran.
86. (and was satisfied with her in place of the male for the fulfillment of the vow).
87. 'And when the maiden was three years old, Iyakem called his pure, Hebrew maid-servants…and brought her into the house of the sanctuary … and the priest, and the elders, and all the children of Israel blessed her and God made great joy to come upon her.' (Budge, op. cit. p. 127)
88. Note that it is the Quran, not the Bible, that makes mention in terms of high honour and glory, of Mary's birth and upbringing; 'goodly growth' may either be of her body and physique, or of her righteousness and virtue, or of both.
89. i.e., Zacharias of the *NT*: commended as blameless before God. 'There was in the days of Herod, the king of Judea, a certain priest named Zacharias, of house of Abijah: and his wife was of the daughters of Aaron, and her name was Elizabeth. And they were both righteous before God walking in all the commandments and ordinances of the Lord blameless.' (*Lk.* 1:5,6) He was Mary's maternal uncle, i.e., husband of Hannah's sister.

90. (and to act as her guardian after 'Imran or Iyakem, the grandfather of Mary, and the chief priest at the sanctuary, who was dead by now).
91. i.e., the loneliest part of the sanctuary to which she had retired out of the way of the people.
92. This naturally excited wonder in him, since none could enter her apartment except himself, and he used to lock doors upon her.
93. i.e., from what direction or quarter.
94. i.e. from God direct, so do not be surprised.
95. (miraculously, without the intervention of any physical agency).
96. i.e., at that time, or at that place. Originally an adverb of place, is also used as an adverb of time.
97. (moved at the sight of the miraculous supply of provision to Mary).
98. (as You bestowed on the old and barren Hannah).
99. i.e., some of the class of angels : like the expression, 'he rides horses,' i.e., certain of them.
100. i.e., a son so named. 'John the Baptist' of the Bible. Cf. the NT: But the angel said unto him: "Fear not, Zechariah : for thy prayer is heard ; and thy wife Elisabeth shall bear thee a son, and thou shalt call his name John. And thou shalt have joy and gladness; and many shall rejoice at his birth," (*Lk*. 1:13).
101. 'A word from Allah' is the Prophet Jesus (peace be on him!). He is called 'a word' because he came into existence by His command, without the ordianary instrumentality of a father. (Bdh)
102. (i.e., a leader of men in matters religious and spiritual). 'Large crowds flocked to his teaching'. (*EBr*. XIII. p. 17). 'It is clear that very large numbers came to him, and he was generally accepted as a prophet' (*DB*. II. p. 679).
103. i.e., continent: one who preserves his soul from all worldly pleasures and enjoyments, is 'Very fearful or cautious, who abstains, or refrains, from a thing through fear.' (LL) 'And the child grew, and waxed strong in spirit.' (Lk. 1:80). John was man of austere ascetic life, symbolizing the severity of his attitude as a moral critic of his time; preaching to all classes the necessity of repentance.' (EBi. C. 2437)
104. Note that the Qur'an distinctly affirms John's prophethood as well as righteousness.
105. i.e., in what particular way shall it come about? The expression is not of wonder, much less of incredulity, but merely a request for further enlightenment.
106. 'For I am an old man, and my wife well-stricken in years.' (*Lk*. I:18) Their union was not blessed with offspring. It was due to Elizabeth's barrenness; and she keenly felt the reproach which is occasioned. for it was a common opinion among the Jews that childlessness was God's punishment for guilt.' (Hastings, *Dictionary of Christ and the Gospels*, II. p. 844) According to the Muslim computation, he was 99 and his wife 98 years old.
107. i.e., it would happen to you whilst you are of this very age, without the restoration of youth.
108. 'For with God nothing shall be impossible.' (*Lk*. 1:36).
109. (whereby I may know that my wife has conceived, and in order that I may prepare some special offering to God).

110. (but shall remember and hallow God). Cf. the *NT*: 'And behold you shall be dumb, and not able to speak, until the day that these things shall be performed... And when he came out, he could not speak unto them.' (*Lk.* 1:20-22)
111. (and three nights)
112. (with the hands or the head)/ 'And he beckoned unto them, and remained speechless.' (*Lk.* 1:22) 'Silence, as an aid to worship or as a method of preparing the soul for spiritual experiences, has been practised among larger or smaller groups in almost all periods of religious history and in almost all parts of the world... The *OT* contains many references to the value of silence as a preparation for spiritual vision or revelation... The voice in the stillness was felt to be a clearer revelation of God than earthquake, fire, or storm.' (*ERE*. XI, 512)
113. i.e., both in your heart and by word of mouth during the period.
114. i.e., from the afternoon until sunset.
115. i.e., from dawn until midday.
116. (as a true servant of God)
117. (in the childhood, inasmuch as no other female had been accepted before her for Divine service in the Sanctuary). This 'Choice' may also have reference to her being supplied with sustenance in a miraculous way.
118. (of sins and moral impurities)
119. (once again, on your attaining maturity, by certain privileges such as conception without a male agency, and the like). *Cf.* the *NT*: 'And the angel came in unto her, and said: Hail you that are highly favoured, the Lord is with thee: blessed are you among women.'(*Lk.* 1:28)
120. With all her great gifts Mary is a mere mortal, and has no share of Divinity in her whatsoever, She is, like all true and devout servants of God, specially enjoined to pray, and the cannons of Prayer are mentioned in detail in order to lay stress on their accurate observance. She is neither a goddess, nor a semi-goddess, nor yet a Mother-God.
121. (O Prophet) i.e., this is among those events of which the accurate records are now obliterated altogether, and there is no means of ascertaining its full and exact details except by Revelation.
122. i.e., the priests at the sanctuary.
123. (in the river Jordan, as lots).
124. (as his ward). Mary being the orphan-daughter of the chief priest lyakem, the priests discussed and disputed as to who should have her in his charge. Zacharias (peace be on him). an elderly kinsman, put forward his claim; other demurred. Recourse was eventually taken to the casting of lots. All of them threw their reed-pens with certain passages of the Torah written upon them into the River Jordan. The reeds of all, except the reed of Zacharias, either sank down or drifted with the current; his alone swam against it. Thus he had the charge of her.
125. (among themselves on the point of her guardianship). The reminder is not superfluous. It is to emphasize that nobody could narrate these details with truth unless by Revelation.
126. Those who brought her the glad tidings of the birth of her son.

127. The announcement of a son, who being without a father, would be known as a Word from Him.
128. The Quranic expression in Arabic denotes surname as well as name.
129. i.e., Messiah of the Bible. Messiah, the surname of Jesus, is a title of honour, literally meaning 'the anointed'. Notice that the Quran fully concedes the Messiahship of Jesus; it is only his Divinity, his Sonship, his Godhead that it is so unsparing in assailing.
130. i.e., Jesus of the NT and Arabicized form of Ishu.
131. Himself a mere mortal, Jesus was also the son of a frail, ordinary woman, and not the son of God. The epithet calls attention to, and emphasizes, the fact of his humanity. It is one of the miracles of the Quran that in speaking of Jesus it refutes both the Jewish and the Christian misconceptions simultaneously, and constantly uses a language that implies answer both to the Christian deification and to the Jewish denunciation.
132. i.e., above the ridicule and vilification of his enemies the Jewish literally is, 'worthy of regard.' The Quran affirms the honour and glory of Jesus (peace be on him) chiefly in answer to the calumnies of the Jews who remember him 'as the man who had chiefly brought dissension to Israel, and as one who practised magic and deceived and led astray Israel, with coarse allusions to his birth.'(*ERE*. VII, p. 551). The few allusions to him contained in the Talmud and the contemporary literature are, for the most part, contemptuous references to one who deceived Israel, and who owed his birth to the unfruitfulness of his mother;' (Hastings, op. cit. II, p. 877). Even they before long have learnt to speak of his person and character in terms of respect and appreciation. Witness recent books on Jesus by Jewish writers.
133. (like other Prophets).
134. (unto God). Notice the form of the words 'one of those brought nigh;' one of the many. Not even in this respect was Jesus unique or without parallel.
135. (and discourse on serious subjects).
136. i.e, while yet he shall be a mere boy. There would be no sense in recording the fact if it meant nothing more than 'the ordinary experience of every child who is not dumb.' A truism like that could hardly merit mention in the Quran. Compare the account in the *GB*: 'Jesus having come to the age of twelve years went up with Mary and Joseph to Jerusalem... The third day they found the child in the temple in the midst of the doctors disputing with them concerning the law. And everyone was amazed at his questions and answer, saying: How can there be such doctrine in him, seeing he is so small and hath not learned to read?' (p.15) And also the *NT*: 'And when he was twelve years old, they went up to Jerusalem... And it came to pass, that after three days they found him in the temple, sitting in the midst of the doctors, both hearing them, and asking them questions. And all that heard him were astonished at his understanding and answers.' (*Lk*. 2, 42, 46, 47)
137. is "of mature age," of any age between 30 and 50, and not necessarily "old age". The mention of the infancy of Jesus and then of his maturity emphasizes the obvious fact that he lived and grew like all human beings, there being no meaning in a God-man or man-God 'growing'.

138. Note that Jesus (peace be on him) in his great attributes is not spoken of singly but as one of a company of good souls. He is 'of the righteous." "of those right," that is to say that he one of the many chosen by God.
139. (by way of intercourse). 'Then said Mary unto the angel, How shall this be, seeing I know not a man?' (*Lk*. 1:34) Mary is naturally amazed and puzzled at the announcement of the birth of a son when she was a virgin. The story is related in the *GB* at greater length.
140. (through an angel).
141. i.e., without the touch of a man; out of the ordinary course of nature.
142. His will alone is sufficient to bring anything into being. He can create anything out of His mere will. He is not bound in His creative activities by His usual methods – the so-called 'law of nature.'
143. (whether attended or not with the circumstances generally associated with it). This explains the nature of His 'willing'. Just as He creates things in stages and by intermediary cause, equally able is He to create them immediately, directly, and without intermediary causes.
144. i.e., Mary
145. i.e., the infant Jesus.
146. (in her arms).
147. Literally, a thing forged or fabricated, hence unknown, unheard of.
148. i.e., like him in piety, or comparable to him in virtue. This epithet is all the more apt, since she was a descendant of Aaron, and through him belonged to the tribe of Levi, noted for piety or virtue.
149. So how shameful of you to have gone wrong and to have brought his disgrace to your illustrious family.
150. (for an answer).
151. till recently
152. (and not a Son or Incarnation of God). A refutation of the Christian position.
153. (and not a charlton or magician). A refutation of the Jewish position.
154. *Cf.* I am Jesus, son of Mary, of the seed of David, a man that is mortal and feareth God, and I seek that to God be given honour and glory.' (*OBh*. 1211).
155. This rejects and contradicts the position implied in various prayers of the NT that the attitude of Jesus towards his mother was cold and indifferent. (See *Mt* 12; 46-50, *Mk* 3:31-35, *Lk*. 8:19-21)
156. *Cf.* I am weak and lowly in body and heart (*Mt* 11:29). By the use of the two words *Jabbar* and *Shaqi* the Quran denies exactly the two charges – of sedition and blasphemy brought against Jesus by the Jews in the Roman court. The charges were two in number, one sedition, the other blasphemy (Rosadi, *Trial of Jesus*, p. 198)
157. (like all mortals) see these facts of birth, death and resurrection serve to emphasize the absurdity of ascribing Godhead to Jesus.
158. i.e. the Christians and Jews.
159. (and wrangling among themselves).
160. i.e. this is not all in keeping with the nature of divinity.
161. (from all such derogatory imputations).
162. So in this way He brought Jesus into being.
163. (Say, O Prophet)

164. (O Christians and non-Christians!)

Abbreviations

Ac	-	Acts of Apostles
Bdh		Commentary by Baidhawi.
CD	-	Allen and Wynne's *New Catholic Dictionary.*
Dt	-	Deuteronomy.
DB	-	Hastings's *Dictionary of the Bible* (5 Volumes).
EBi	-	Cheyne and Black's *Encyclopedia Biblica.*
EBr	-	*The Encyclopedia Britannica* (24 Volumes, 14th Edition)
ERE	-	Hastings's *Encyclopedia of Religion and Ethics*(13 Volumes)
Ex	-	Exodus.
GB	-	Ragg's *Gospel of the Barnabas.*
GRE	-	Gibbon's *Decline and Fall of the Roman Empire* (7 Volumes)
Hj	-	*The Hibbert Journal* (London)
Jn	-	*The Gospel according to St. John.*
JE	-	*The Jewish Encyclopedia* (12 Volumes).
Lk	-	*The Gospel according to St. Luke*
LL	-	Lane's *Arabic-English Lexicon.*
Mk	-	*The Gospel according to St Mark.*
Mt	-	*The Gospel according to St Matthew.*
NT	-	*New Testament.*
OT	-	*Old Testament.*
Th	-	The Quran commentary by Ashraf Ali Thanvi.
UHW	-	Hammerton's *Universal History of the World.* (8 Volumes)

11

Maulana Daryabadi as a Quranic Scholar

Syed Abdul Hasan Ali Nadvi

The Qur'ānic *i'jāz*, variously interpreted as its inimitable ellipticism, miraculous elegance, grandiose cadence and emotive and evocative force, is so multilateral that Imām Suyūtī has in his work, enumerated 35 distinctive features of the Divine Scripture, all of which pertain to its literary excellence alone. These, by no means, exhaust the marvellous super-excellence of the Holy Qur'ān: some have been discussed by other writers while others are yet to be expounded, but these are so self-evident that not even the most inveterate enemy of Islam can deny them. One of these is that writers like T. Noldeke, Friedrich Schwally, Charles Francis Potter, Philip K. Hitti and several other Orientalists, none of whom are known for their sympathetic approach to Islam, had to acknowledge the fact that the Qur'ān is 'the most widely read book in existence,'[1], and the Prophet to whom it was revealed was 'the most successful of all the Prophets.'[2] They had, willy-nilly, to admit this undeniable fact for they had noticed that Christian missionary societies, financed by affluent Western countries, had succeeded in rendering the Christian Bible into about seven hundred languages,[3] making finely printed copies of it available to nearly all urban centers or placing it in every high class hotel the world over, yet the numbers who go through these in ten years is just a fraction of those who recite the Qur'ān every day.[4] Another notable aspect of the *i'jāz* of the Qur'ān is that notwithstanding the persistent campaign launched against it since the beginning of the thirteenth century to the present and which sees the Holy Qur'ān as a product of the human mind, drawing the material contained in it indiscriminately from the apocryphal books of Judaism and Christianity, hundreds of its translations, commentaries and glossaries have been brought out, even in Europe. Nor has the political and industrial ascendancy of the West, coupled with its intellectual and educational supremacy and its control over the world's mass media, been able to shake the faith of the Muslims in Holy Qur'ān as the Word of God. This conviction has increased with the passage of time, rather than being eroded by these deliberate misrepresentations: the denigrators of the Qur'ān have, on the other hand, been forced to put themselves on their guard. Professor

R.B, Serjeant writes in his introduction to the *Dictionary and Glossary of the Kuran* by John Penrice that readers of the Qur'ān ought to understand the Book directly from it since the Arab and Muslim countries which are now forsaking conservatism in favour of modernism still take the Scripture as a divine revelation and the people are still accustomed to saying, "God Exalted has said" before quoting any passage from it and ending the citation with the words, "God Almighty has truly spoken".

European scholars of Islam, whether they be Serjeant or Sale or contributors to the *Encyclopedia Britannica,* cannot be expected to express anything beyond their own impression of the Holy Qur'ān. They, even if not inspired by a malicious prejudice, cannot shake off their mistaken notions about Islam that have become a part of their intangible heritage of thought and feeling. But, for us, Muslims, it is an apparent fact that God Almighty Himself has taken the responsibility of preserving the Holy Qur'ān in its absolute purity. 'Verily We, it is We Who have revealed the Admonitions, and verily We are its Guardian'. [15:9].

This prophecy has been strikingly confirmed by the fact that the Qur'ān has remained free from all alterations, accretions and deletions ever since it was sent down to the Holy Prophet (peace be upon him). The purity of the Qur'ān text, maintained through fourteen centuries, has already been acknowledged by all, friend and foe alike. I should better cite here the comment of Maulana Daryabadi on the above verse. He writes: "Islam knows no such thing as "redactions" of its Holy Text. Even those who have most stoutly denied its being the Word of God are unanimous in testifying to its being exactly the same "work of Muhammad" as it was thirteen centuries ago. Let us have the testimony of a few such unwilling witnesses:

(i) "The text of the Qur'ān is the purest of all works of a like antiquity". (Wherry: *Commentary on the Koran* I, p. 349).

(ii) "Othman's recension has remained the authorized text, from the time it was made until the present day." (Palmer: *The Quran*, p. liv).

(iii) "The text of this recension substantially corresponds to the actual utterances of Muhammed himself". (Arnold: *Islamic Faith*, p.9).

(iv) "All sects and parties have the same text of the Qur'ān". (Hurgroneje: *Mohammedanism*, p.18)

(v) "It is an immense merit in the Kuran that there is no doubt as to its genuineness. That very word we can now read with full confidence that it has remained unchanged through nearly thirteen hundred years". (Lane-Poole: *Selections from the Kuran,* p. 3)

(vi) "The recension of Othman has been handed down to us unaltered.... There is probably in the world no other work which has remained twelve centuries with so pure a text". (Muir: *Life of Muhammad,* pp. xxii-xxiii).

(vii) "In the Koran we have, beyond all reasonable doubt, the exact words of Mohammad without subtraction and without addition". (Bosworth Smith: *Mohammed and Mohammedanism*, p. 22)

(viii) "The Koran was his own creation; and it lies before us practically unchanged from the form which he himself gave it". (Torrey: *Jewish Foundations of Islam*, p. 2)."

In addition to these testimonies from European Orientalists about the purity of the text of the Holy Qur'ān, Daryabadi goes on to substantiate the claim of the Qur'ān to be a Divine Revelation which is undisputed and unique among all the religious Scriptures. He writes: 'Not only is the meaning of the Holy Book therefore inspired but every word, every letter dictated through the angel Gabriel to the Holy Prophet from an Archetype preserved in the heaven. That is the distinctive claim of the Holy Qur'ān shared by no other "revealed Book" in the world. The Bible, in particular makes no such claim. The Bible is the work of a large number of poets, prophets, statesmen, and lawgivers, extending over a vast period of time, and incorporates with itself other and earlier, and often conflicting documents'. (Bosworth Smith: *Mohammed and Mohammedanism* p. 19)

The Divine care to preserve the purity of the Holy Qur'ān provided the impulse to put dots on alphabets of similar shape in order to distinguish between their pronunciation, to develop the twin sciences of philology and lexicography, and to lay down the rules of Arabic grammar and the criteria for rhetoric and the style of prose writing. This literary activity has never ceased for a day since the second century of the Islamic era. Additionally, the etymological structure of the Arabic language has saved its dialects, like a strong cementing force, from falling apart into distinct languages and thus, the Divine Revelation has remained intelligible to succeeding generations. The providential arrangement of writing of commentaries on the Holy Qur'ān started as early as the third century AH, is also noteworthy. At the outset, the exegesis of the Qur'ān formed a part of the science of *Hadīth* since it was generally thought that Divine Revelation could only be understood in light of the Holy Prophet's Traditions, especially those handed down by 'Abdullāh Ibn 'Abbās. However, the exegesis of the Qur'ān became an independent science with the *Tafsīr al-Tabarī* of Abū Ja'far Muhammad Ibn Jarīr al-Tabarī (d. 310 AH) and it has ever since been vigorously cultivated by Muslim scholars. The commentaries on the Holy Qur'ān written from time to time are in fact a mine of historical information shedding light on the way the Qur'ān was understood during different periods.

Arabists and Orientalists, on the other hand, started to translate the Holy Qur'ān from the thirteenth century and rendered it into almost all European languages, of which the largest numbers of translations have been brought out in French, German and English. A list of such translations is given by Professor Hamidullah in the introduction to his own French rendering of the Holy Qur'ān published in 1961. His other work entitled *Al-Qur'ān fī-Kull Lisān*, now out of print, contains a complete list of all the translations of the Holy Qur'ān brought out up to 1922. The list, I believe, would now be two-fold in volume if Professor Hamidullah were to bring it up to date.[5]

Translations of the Holy Qur'ān in English can be divided into two categories. Firstly, there are those penned either by non-Muslim Orientalists or by those Muslim apologists who were unduly impressed by the political ascendancy and industrial advancement of the West, such as the Qadiyani exegetes, Shaikh Muhammad 'Abduh of Egypt, Sir Syed Ahmad Khan of India and Muhammad Asad of Austria, but their writings never met with the approval of the Muslims. Secondly, there are Muslim translators and commentators who mostly belong, excepting Marmaduke Pickthall, to the Indo-Pak subcontinent. Pickthall was an English Muslim, a journalist and a literary man of standing but he, too, was commissioned by the then Nizām of Hyderabad to undertake an explanatory translation of the Holy Qur'ān and he also wrote that work in India.

Among those belonging to the second group, the translation and commentary on the Holy Qur'ān by Abdullah Yusuf Ali was received well. His rendering of the Qur'ānic verse which, according to him, is more suited to conveying something of the Qur'ān's inimitable symphony to its readers. The requirements of prosody, however, made it inevitable that he alter the word order of the sacred text. He had also occasionally to deviate from a literal rendering. Pickthall's explanatory translation, on the other hand, is most readable. Although it too is not free from mistakes, it has an edge over other translations because of its fluency and gracefulness of style.

There was, however, the need for another English translation of the Holy Qur'ān, complete with explanatory notes, which could be recommended with confidence to Muslims and non-Muslims whose mother tongue was English or who found it easy, owing to their cultural background or educational upbringing, to understand it better in the English language. The author of such an exegesis inevitably had to expound the Qur'ānic text in terms acceptable to scholars of the *Ahl al-Sunnahwa al-Jamā'ah;* to avoid putting forward his own views and ideas in the exegesis; to be fully conversant with Arabic lexicon and rules of grammar; to avoid an apologetic approach in expounding Qur'ānic injunctions and institutions; to have firm faith in Life-After-Death and the rewards and retributions promised in the Qur'ān as Divine pronouncements instead of taking them merely as symbolical expressions; to have studied all the classical and modern commentaries in depth; to expound the significance of Qur'ānic injunctions in regard to polygamy, slavery, dowry, the execution of apostates, blood-wit etc,; to hold the same belief about the throne (*'arsh and kursī*), the preserved tablet (*lawh al-Mahfūz*), jinn, angels, prophethood (*nubuwwah*), Revelation (*wahī*), and the earlier and final Divine Scriptures as entertained by the earliest Muslims; and to have no qualms about the bodily lifting of Jesus Christ to the higher regions. Taking all these factors into account, Abdul Majid Daryabadi's translation and commentary is undoubtedly unique and most acceptable among all the exegetical renderings of the Holy Qur'ān attempted so far in the English language.

The exegesis by Daryabadi throws ample light on all those communities who have been mentioned in the Holy Qur'ān along with their geographical locations and the eras in which they flourished. One can find all the necessary details about the earlier Prophets who find a mention in the Holy Qur'ān, since Daryabadi's exegesis provides answers to such questions as what was the time of their advent, who were the peoples to whom they disseminated the Message vouchsafed to them, who were the 'Ādites and Thamūdites and the people of Prophet Sālih, where did those live, where were Babil and Madyan located and similar other questions that arise in one's mind while reading the Holy Qur'ān. His exegesis also demonstrates, in the light of human experience and researches made in the field of anthropology and sociology, the superiority of the Islamic social order and its legislations pertaining to marriage, divorce, inheritance etc., over all other social laws and systems. It shows how Islamic injunctions represent the most refined and elaborate system of social existence known to the civilized world. In addition to these, a distinguishing feature of Daryabadi's exegesis is that it provides a conclusive answer to those Jewish and Christian critics of Islam who claim that the Holy Qur'ān draws its material from the Scriptures and apocryphal writings of Judaism and Christianity. It demonstrates how these critics are unable to appreciate the fact that the Holy Qur'ān has been revealed to confirm the Scriptures of old and to restate and uphold the spirit of their true teachings, which, by itself, involves the refutation of such accretions, alterations and additions as have found a place in the Scriptures of Judaism and Christianity.

> "And when there came unto them a Book from before Allah confirming that which was with them - and aforetime they were entreating God for victory over those who disbelieved - then when there came unto them that which they recognised, they disbelieved therein".

(al-Baqarah 2: 89)

earlier Scriptures is an article of faith for Muslims, but it was necessary to bring out those teachings of the Torah and the Gospels which were confirmed by the Holy Qur'ān in order to distinguish them from the spurious matter inserted into these Scriptures by their scribes, translators and commentators. For whatever in these Books finds confirmation by the Holy Qur'ān is undoubtedly correct; everything else is a later addition mixed up with Divine Revelation. The learned author has taken great pains to make a thorough, comparative analysis of Biblical and Qur'ānic teachings and the narratives of events common to both, in order to show how the Holy Qur'ān upholds only the correct and original teachings of the Old and New Testaments. He also provides food for thought to those Orientalists and students of comparative religion who prefer not to talk about the systematic refusal of the Holy Qur'ān to confirm numerous accretions to the existing Bible. His exegesis pinpoints all such differences showing that the Biblical version of many an incident is nothing but a product of human imagination. His treatment of such matters makes it amply clear that if there had been any parallelism in the Bible and the Qur'ān, as asserted by almost all European scholars, there would not have been the differences, indicated by him, in the narration of the same event by the Scriptures. To give an example we may refer to the following verse in the Holy Qur'ān:

> "O people of the Book; do not exceed the bounds in your Religion, and say not of Allah save what is the truth. The Messiah 'Īsā, son of Maryam, is but a Messenger of Allah and His Word. He cast it upon Maryam and a Spirit from Him. Believe therefore in Allah and His Messengers, and do not say: three".

(al-Nisa 4: 171)

Commenting on the Christian belief in Trinity, Daryabadi says:

> Trinity denotes the central doctrine of Christian religion. It means that God is three really distinctive Persons - the Father, the Son, and the Holy Ghost. Each of these persons is truly the same God, and has all His infinite perfections. Yet He is really distinct from each of the three Persons. These Persons are co-equal, co-eternal and consubstantial, and deserve co-equal glory and adoration, which the Church expresses in the oft-repeated prayer: "Glory be to the Father, and to the Son, and to the Holy Ghost". (Allen and Wynne: *New Catholic Dictionary,* New York, p. 973.) The book of Islam 'found in the dogma of Trinity whatever emancipated thinker finds on impartial reflection - an absurd legend, which is neither reconcilable with first principles of reason, nor of any value whatever for our religious

advancement. In the Brahmanic religion the Trimurti is also conceived as a "divine unity" made up of three persons - Brahma (the creator), Vishnu (the sustainer) and Shiva (the destroyer)'. (Haeckal: *Riddle of the Universe*, pp. 226, 233). 'The Divine trinity has been considered a tripersonal trinity, each person being God and Lord. Men's minds have been brought by this into such a state of bewilderment that they do not know whether there is one God or whether there are three; one is on their lips, but three in their thoughts.' (Swedenborg: *The True Christian Religion,* p. 5). The Nicene Creed really teaches three Divine Persons and denies three Gods, and leaves us to guess what else is a Divine Person but a God or a God but a Divine Person".

(Newman: *Phases of Faith,* p. 23)

The Jews and Christians generally charge Islam with preaching fanaticism and intolerance, as for example, its prohibition of marriage between a believing and disbelieving couple. The author has, in his commentary on the relevant verse, quoted the other Scriptures to show that the criticism actually applies to these religions rather than to Islam. In like manner, he has demonstrated the superiority of Islamic legislation in regard to divorce and marriage *vis-a-vis* the ruptured family relationships of the Christian West.

Classical commentators of the Holy Qur'ān occasionally had to take the help of Israelite traditions, though cautiously, for elucidating a certain event of which only a particular aspect of the happening finds a mention in the Qur'ān and this to draw a moral from it. To cite an example here, the Qur'ān says about King Solomon in verse 102 or Sūrah al-Baqarah: 'And Sulaimān blasphemed not, but the satans blasphemed; teaching the people magic. And they follow also what was sent down unto the two angels in Babil, Hārūt and Mārūt.'

In the absence of any more detail about the incident, one may wonder how the charge of blasphemy came to be levelled against King Solomon, a Prophet of God, and which has been refuted by the Qur'ān. Like earlier exegetes, Daryabadi has also referred to the accusation of idolatry made against King Solomon in 1 *Ki.* 11: 4, 9, 10. He also mentions how the Jews unblushingly attributed to him the cult of crude occultism and witchcraft, and goes on to cite the findings of modern Biblical researches which support the Qur'ān in stoutly denying these charges. Similarly, he sets forth evidence to show that Babylonia was the strongest citadel of magic and witchcraft in all antiquity.

Another distinctive feature of Daryabadi's rendering of the Qur'ānic text is that he has always kept in view the most appropriate expression in English or the one which is nearest to the interpretation of a word used in the Holy Qur'ān. For example, the words (*ẓāhir*) and (*bātin*) in the passage

(6: 120) have been translated by him as outside and inside, and this conveys the literal sense of these words, which are normally adopted by other translators in rendering this passage into English, are given by him in the footnotes. This approach shows the author's painstaking diligence and reverential regard for the sacred text. Another example of the assiduous care taken by Daryabadi in this regard is to be found in rendering the verse 17: 29. This verse has been translated to read as follows:

'Let not your hand be chained to your neck, nor stretch it forth to the utmost of its extremity, lest you sit down reproached, impoverished.' The English rendering of the above verse is literal; an idiomatic translation would have better conveyed the sense but it would have meant a deviation from the text of the sacred Scripture. Unlike other translators of the Holy Qur'ān who prefer to give the derived meanings of an Arabic word or phrase, Daryabadi has chosen to give an exact translation of the text and then explained in a footnote that 'let not your hand be chained to your neck' means do not be niggardly. This, however, does not suggest that the renderings of other translators are incorrect, but it nevertheless evinces the regard and attachment of Daryabadi, as well as his preference for maintaining the original wordings, to the Divine Revelation. He goes on to explain the correct significance of the words and phrases according to Arabic usage and also points out, at several places, the incorrect renderings given by earlier translators, and thus acquaints the readers with the Arabic idiom.

Every student of the Holy Qur'ān knows that the Divine Scripture has its own distinctive vocabulary. As, for instance, the Qur'ān is not referred to by its proper name at all places; often it is alluded to as *(al-Dhikr),* or *(al-Kitāb)* or (*al-Furqān*). For Doomsday, it uses the words (*Yawm al-Qiyāmah*), (*Yawm al-Hisāb*), (*Yawm al-Taghābun*) and (*Yawm al-Ākhirah*). In addition to (*al-Salāt*), Prayers are also referred to as (*al-Dhikr*)and(*Qur'ān al-Fajr*)and similar other epithets. Classical commentators of the Qur'ān have explained the correct purport of each word in the context of particular verses so as to make it clear where a certain word with more than one connotation as, for example, (*al-Dhikr*) denotes the Qur'ān and where it implies Prayer. Legists of Islam have likewise indicated the significance of each word having more than one import in its particular context. In the verse (2: 4) the phrase اركعو امع الراكعين signifies offering congregational prayers as explained by Qurtubī, Baghawī, al-Nasafī, al-Baidāwī and al-Zamakhsharī. Instead of rendering this phrase "as bow down among those who bow" the author has interpreted it as 'bow down with those who bow down', and further elucidated it in the notes with the words, with Muslims in congregational prayer so that the correct significance of the phrase given by classical exegetes becomes clear to readers.

The Holy Qur'ān is, after all, the Word of God, perfect and faultless, while no man can make a claim to finality or impeccability. Every product of the human mind is likely to contain some deficiency, yet for all that, Abdul Majid Daryabadi has acquitted himself of this onerous task in a laudable manner. Throughout his life he preoccupied himself with the study of the Holy Qur'ān and wrote an exegesis in Urdu in addition to the English one. His translation and commentary is, to my mind, unique and the most reliable among all translations and commentaries of the Qur'ān so far attempted in the English language.

May Allah accept his praiseworthy endeavour and shower His choicest blessings on him. The Academy of Islamic Research and Publications deems it a favour from the Almighty that the heirs and successors of the late Abdul Majid Daryabadi agreed to transfer the publication rights of this commentary to it. The first edition of this work was brought out by the Taj Company of Lahore, in 1957, after which the author revised his earlier translation. The late author desired that a new edition be brought out with the revised translation but, as God had willed it, his wish could not be fulfilled during his lifetime. Now, the commentary is being published with the revised translation. Muhammad Rabey Nadwi took a keen interest in fulfilling the wishes of the departed author while Syed Mohiuddin, an associate scholar of the Academy, and Sher Mohammed Syed of Lahore took pains to check and correct the mistakes that had crept into the earlier edition by comparing almost all the quotations given in the notes with the original sources. Certain additions made by the author in his manuscript have also been incorporated into this edition. May Allah recompense all of them with goodly returns.

Notes

1. Charles Francis Potter, *The Faith Man Lives By,* Surrey, 1995, p.18; *Phillip* K. Hitti, *History of the Arabs,* London, 1953, p.426.
2. Lamartine, *Histoire de la Turquie,* Paris, 1854, 2, 277; D.G. Hogarth, A *HistoryofArabia,* Oxford, 1922, p.52.
3. Muhammad Mubārak, *Khasā' is al-Lughat al-'Arabīyah,* Beirut, p.6.
4. John Arnold, 'World Religions and Societies', *Readers' Digest* (June 1961).
5. For a comprehensive bibliography of the Qur'ān translations in world languages, see Ekmeleddin Ihsanoglu (ed.), *World Bibliography of Translations of the Meanings of the Holy Quran: Printed Translations 1515-1980,* Istanbul, OIC Research Centre for Islamic History, Art and Culture, 1986, pp.913.

Originally Syed Abul Hasan Ali Nadwi's "Introduction" to Daryabadi's English translation of and commentary on the Qur'ān published by the Academy of Islamic Research and Publications in 1981.

12

Maulana Daryabadi's Contribution to the Quranic and Islamic Studies

Amid Daryabadi's many works, standing out as valuable contributions to philosophy, Urdu literature and journalism and Islamic studies, his *magnum opus* is his English translation of the Quran, *The Holy Quran: Translated from the original Arabic, with lexical, grammatical, historical, geographical and eschatological comments, and explanations and sidelights on comparative religion* (1957). Its unusually long subtitle is fairly indicative of the wide range of material, especially comparative religion, covered in this feat of scholarship. On the genesis of this pious venture Daryabadi's own account is worth-noting:

> In 1933 while I had been staying for weeks at Maulana Thanwi's khanqah (spiritual training centre) I came into contact with the Maulana's disciple, Maulwi Sirajul Haq Machhlishahri, who was a teacher at Majidia Intermediate College, Allahabad. Our acquaintance soon grew into friendship. It was he who first suggested to me to embark upon the English translation of the Quran, arguing that no English version, representative of the mainstream Muslim viewpoint (*ahl al-Sunnah wa al-Jama*) was available. As I was fully aware of my inadequacies, especially of my command over English and Arabic, his suggestion took me by surprise. However, he kept insisting on the pressing need for this work. His sincere persuasion prevailed and I embarked upon this project, notwithstanding my inability.
>
> As I commenced the job, its enormity gradually dawned upon me … I temporarily closed down my Urdu weekly *Sach* (from 1933 until 1935), and cut down my other engagements. However, I realized that it was essential to go through a plethora of tomes on lexicon, geography, history, world religions, culture and civilizations, *tafsir,* Hadith, scholasticism and jurisprudence etc for writing the commentary on the Quran. The job of translation proved to be very tough, though the earlier translations by Pickthall, Sale, Bell and Syed Hussain Bilgrami's unpublished ones were helpful. The first draft was completed in less than two years. Then its typing took very long. Its pre-publication copy was sent to many for review and suggestions. However, there was hardly any response. Throughout, I missed these two stalwarts who

had by then passed away: i) Maulana Hamiduddin Farahi who would have resolved my queries about the Arabic usage and idiom, and ii) Maulana Muhammad Ali who would have improved much my English presentation. In 1939, Taj Company, Lahore signed the contract, promising that its thirty parts will be published in the next 30 months. In 1941 the first part came out, though it was highly defective. The second part appeared after a gap of two years in 1943. Despite numerous reminders and all possible efforts it was published in full only in 1957, some 18 years after signing its contract.[1]

It is indeed a pity that the publication of such a valuable work was so much delayed by the publisher's apathy. Its three reprints were issued in 1962, 1970 and 1971. During all these years Daryabadi kept on revising his *tafsir*, especially in terms of updating it with the latest archaeological studies having some bearing on the historical sites referred to in the Quran. After Daryabadi's demise in 1977, Maulana Abul Hasan Ali Nadwi took the initiative of acquiring the publishing rights of Daryabadi's both English and Urdu *tafasir* under the aegis of the Nadwatul Ulema's publishing house, the Academy of Islamic Research and Publications, Lucknow. Accordingly the revised edition of Daryabadi's English *tafsir* in four volumes came out between 1981- 1985.

Another significant development in the publication of Daryabadi's English *tafsir* was also at the behest of Maulana Nadwi. At the request of the leading publisher of books on Islam in the West, the Islamic Foundation, Leicester, UK, Maulana Nadwi granted it permission to bring out a single volume edition of this work. This abridged edition contains the full English translation by Daryabadi and an intelligent, careful selection of his explanatory notes. This edition has been re-issued several times by the Islamic Foundation. It is gratifying that its distribution at a large scale, especially among new Muslims in the West has been sponsored by some Arab philanthropists. Moreover, this edition has been reprinted by the Sidq Foundation, Lucknow, thanks to the laudable initiative and efforts of Hafiz Naimur Rahman Siddiqi. As a result, readers in the subcontinent now have easy access to this single volume abridged edition.

Daryabadi's work indeed filled a big gap in the then Quranic scholarship in English. For there was hardly any reliable, satisfactory English translation by a Muslim scholar in 1930s when he undertook it. The only translations were by Abul Fadl (1911), Hairat Dihlawi (1916), Ghulam Sarwar (1920), Muhammad Marmaduke Pickthall (1930) and Abdullah Yusuf Ali (1934-1937). The ones by Abul Fadl and Hairat Dihlawi are eminently forgettable. For they were not the scholars of Islam. They were fired by their pious zeal to vindicate the truth of Islam/the

Quran against the aggressive and menacing Christian missionary onslaught in the early twentieth century British India. Their presentation, however, leaves much to be desired. As to Ghulam Sarwar, he was a judge in Singapore. A remarkable feature of his work is his extensive, scathing critique on the Orientalists' forays, namely the English translations of George Sale (1734) J. M. Rodwell (1861) and E. H Palmer (1880). His critique is a testament to his sound, sterling scholarship, his discerning familiarity with the Orientalist discourse, his painstaking attention to detail and his sharp critical eye. However, all these qualities are not inexplicably reflected in his own translation of the Quran. Since he had his career in Malaya (present day Malaysia) as a civil servant, his translation did not receive attention in the subcontinent. Another reason could be his ambivalent position on Qadyanism. Although the Qadyani translator Muhammad Ali's work (1917) figures in his critique, he is all praise for the latter. Amid his glowing tribute he makes no mention of Muhammad Ali's Qadyani credentials. Nor does he say a word about the interpolation of Qadyani beliefs into Ali's explanatory notes on the Quran which misguide the unsuspecting readers. Muhammad Marmaduke Pickthall's is a translation only, with almost no explanatory note about the Quranic allusions or any background to the Quranic Surahs. For those new to Islam this translation is not helpful. Abdullah Yusuf Ali's, no doubt, contains copious notes, illustrating his wide range of scholarship. However, his is a pseudo- rational, apologetic account of the Quranic description of *al-ghayb* (all that which lies beyond the domain of man's sense perception). His branding of miracles and of the joys and punishments of the Hereafter as symbolic or allegorical is discordant with the basic articles of Islamic faith.[(2)] Little wonder then that the Ministry of Religious Affairs, Saudi Arabia which used to distribute thousands of free copies of Abdullah Yusuf Ali's work discontinued this practice and got his work thoroughly revised by an expert committee. Since 1989 this revised and considerably abrogated edition has been in circulation.[3] The two other English translations, bearing Muslim names as translators – Muhammad Abdul Hakim Khan (1905)[4] and Muhammad Ali (1917) were by Qadyanis and hence patently unreliable.

Maulwi Sirajul Haq was not off the mark in his significant observation about the non-existence of a credible English translation by a Muslim scholar. Armed with his mastery over English, his thorough familiarity with the Western thought patterns, his first hand knowledge of comparative religion, and his Islamic fervour after his return to Islam and his knowledge of the finer details of the meaning and message of Islam which he gained at the feet of Maulana Thanwi, Daryabadi was suited best for taking up this formidable task. As he set out, he received much encouragement from

Maulana Thanwi, Maulana Hussain Ahmad Madni, Maulana Manazir Ahsan Gilani, Syed Suleman Nadwi, Saiyyid Abul Ala Mawdudi and others. Let us first recount Maulana Thanwi's advice to him, as reported by Daryabadi as part of his correspondence with the Maulana:

> **Daryabadi:** I seek your blessings and advice about a highly important matter. For the last some weeks I have been thinking seriously of translating the Quran into English.
>
> **Thanwi:** I have felt its need for years. However, it calls for these two requisites: i) competent translators, and ii) ample funds for its production. For these constraints it remained so far my wish only. May be it is time for the actualization of this dream.
>
> **Daryabadi**: Maulana Hussain Ahmad Madni too, had asked me to undertake this work. However, I told him about my incompetence for this undertaking. Although I am still aware of my inadequacies, I strongly realize the urgent need for this work. During this period I have supplicated many times after prayers that I be blessed with guidance and ability by Allah.
>
> **Thanwi:** You should embark upon it, taking Allah's name. Allah may provide you with all that is required for it. The most important requirement is that a responsible person should undertake this job. Who is better suited than you for this? More importantly, this will give us the peace of mind. In your case we will have the satisfaction that you would keep consulting us. In other words, it would be our collaborative effort.
>
> **Daryabadi**: Your encouragement about undertaking the English translation has indeed inspired me much. Inshallah I will commence it in Ramadan.
>
> **Thanwi**: This news is so delightful for me like celebrating Idd in Ramadan itself.[5]

Another significant piece is by Sayyid Abul Ala Mawdudi. On learning about Daryabadi's venture he wrote this editorial note:

> I have gone through the special number of *Sach* (Daryabadi's weekly) in which Abdul Majid Daryabadi has spelled out the need for an authentic English translation and *tafsir* of the Quran. He has mentioned the efforts he has already undertaken for accomplishing this task. We endorse the view that a standard, reliable English translation is the need of the hour for not only non-Muslim English readership, but also for another very large constituency comprising modern educated Muslims. They need it for gaining the correct understanding

> of Islam. It is an accepted fact that among our modern educated group, the best person to take up this job is Maulana Abdul Majid Daryabadi. For he has already passed through the stages in which most of the Western educated persons find themselves entangled. He is fully alive to the fact how skepticism and atheism make their inroads into the hearts and minds. By Allah's grace he is equipped well with the knowledge and resources to counter the challenges posed by skepticism and atheism. Since he is the most suitable person, it is likely that he would accomplish this job.[6]

Let us now turn to some of the distinctive features of Daryabadi's venture. First, he holds the distinction of being the pioneer in the Indian subcontinent to have authored his *tafsir* in English which is perfectly in accordance with the primary Islamic sources. Moreover, far from being a loose, lax paraphrase of the original Quran as in the case of Abdullah Yusuf Ali's work, his is faithful to the original to the extent possible. His *tafsir* abounds in material on comparative religion, gleaned from primary sources. Moreover, his elucidation of eschatology, polygamy, *jihad* and miracles etc does not smack of apologia. Rather, his cogent *tafsir*, drawing at places on the Bible and modern Western thought, succeeds largely in establishing and highlighting the eternal message and truth of the Quran. It goes a long way in allaying the doubts agitating the minds of the Muslims exposed to Western thought patterns. Gifted with a deep insight into the nuances of the Quranic idiom and a thorough, first-hand knowledge of the latest anthropological, archaeological and sociological studies, he explicates the meaning and significance of some enigmatic Quranic expressions. The Quranic term *Nasara* (al-Baqarah 2: 62) is usually translated carelessly as Christians, even by Muslim translators. Daryabadi, however, renders it as "Nazarene" on the ground that the "Nazarenes or the primitive Christians were the followers of the pre-Pauline Church, not quite like the present-day Christians of the Pauline variety."[7] At another place Daryabadi vindicates the veracity of the Quranic description (al-Baqarah 2: 60) of the twelve springs gushing forth miraculously from a rock in Sinai, as Prophet Moses (peace and blessings be upon him) struck it with his rod: "This wonderful rock, real, not fictitious, exists even to this day. It stands in the wide valley of Leja, under the Rass of Sufsafeh."[8] Significantly enough, while the Qadyani translator Muhammad Ali denies this incident altogether, Abdullah Yusuf Ali plays it down as some local tradition which should be better interpreted as a parable. While elucidating the Quranic statement: "And Sulaiman did not blaspheme" (al-Baqarah 2: 102), Daryabadi contributes this insightful explanatory note:

> The Jews, true to their traditions of ingratitude and malevolence have not hesitated to malign their own hero and national benefactor,

> Prophet Solomon (peace and blessings be upon him) and to accuse him of the most heinous of all offences – idolatry (The Bible, *The First Book of Kings*, ii, iv, ix and x)… The Quran upholds the honour of all Prophets of God, to whatever race or age they may belong.[9]

Among the Muslim English translators of the day it was thus Daryabadi alone who explained the above enigma, as blasphemy is unthinkable in the context of a Messenger of Allah. He adds that the Quranic assertion about Prophet Solomon's unblemished conduct is corroborated by modern Biblical studies which show that "Solomon was a sincere worshipper of Yahwe."[10] It is common knowledge that the Quran addresses in particular the children of Israel, repeatedly mentions their history and confers upon them the coveted title of being Allah's favourites (al-Baqarah 2: 40 and 47). This special attention to them is explained thus by Daryabadi:

> The children of Israel had been the nation of priests, patriarchs and prophets, blessed of their Lord and … were in the early days of Islam, in effect intellectually, the dominating masters of the country. In matters religious and divine they were the trusted advisors of the unlettered pagans and their acknowledged superiors. It helps to explain the extent of attention they receive in the Quran and the long series of admonitions, warnings and exhortations addressed to them.[11]

In al-Baqarah 2: 102 the Quran designates Harut and Marut as the two angels sent down by Allah, who taught magic to men. Unnerved by this apparently anomalous Quranic statement, Abdullah Yusuf Ali resorts to pleading: "The word" angels "as applied to Harut and Marut is figurative. It means good men, of knowledge, science (or wisdom), and power."[12] Without any streak of apologia, Daryabadi explains away that these angels were sent in order that its nature [i.e. of magic and witch craft] be explained and its mischief be demonstrated in full, and people may be weaned from the engulfing superstitions, just as a physician acquires an intimate knowledge of diseases not of course to propagate but to combat these…[13]

For pressing home Allah's Omnipresence and the pre-requisites for piety the Quran says:

> The east and the west belong to Allah. To whichever direction you turn, you will turn to Allah. Surely Allah is All Embracing, All Knowing.
>
> (al-Baqarah 2: 115)
>
> It is not virtue that you turn your faces to the east or west. Virtue is to believe in Allah…
>
> (al-Baqarah 2:177)

Insightfully Daryabadi points out that the above verses aim also at denouncing the prevalent practice of "Direction Worship", a popular form of polytheism:

> To the East the Christians, in common with the sun-worshippers and many other polytheists attach special sanctity. From the very early times and in more than one ethnic religion, the direction towards which the worshipper made his prayer was considered of great importance. The Essenes prayed in the direction of the rising sun and the Syrian Christians also turned eastward at prayer. To the Christians again the West is full of meaning: "In the rite of baptism... the catechumen was placed with the face toward the west." (Taylor, *Primitive Culture*, p. 428) "In Greek religion, deities were classified as Olympians and Chthonians. The East was the abode of the Olympian gods ... while the West was the direction which the worshippers of the Chthonian gods faced" (Hastings, *Dictionary of the Bible*, Vol. 5, p. 143). According to Hindus, the direction of south-east was to Manu ..."(Hastings, *Encyclopedia of Religion and Ethics*, Vol. 12, p. 618).
>
> It was the belief of the early Church that the evil entered from the north. The above quoted Quranic verse (al-Baqarah 2: 177) strikes at the root of the "Direction Worship" and says in effect that there is no merit at all in turning towards any particular direction. Islamic worship, it must be manifest to the reader, is not directed towards *any direction as such* – east west, north or south, but towards Ka'ba, a particular House, on whatever side of the worshipper it may happen to be.[14]

Daryabadi achieved another distinction of bringing into sharper light the excellence of the Quran by comparing and contrasting several Quranic and Biblical passages. Apart from reinforcing the conviction of Muslim readers, this feature of his *tafsir* is of immense appeal to the new Muslims. A weighty testimony to this contention is afforded by the avowal of a leading new Muslim lady of our time, Maryam Jameelah. In her piece "How I Discovered the Quran" she states:

> ... my immature mind regarded the Quran as nothing more than distorted and garbled versions of the former stories from the Bible. ...I found his (Daryabadi's) commentary excellent, particularly the parts dealing with comparative religion and learned much from it.[15]

Apart from hundreds of quotations from the Authorized Version of the Bible, as part of his comparative study, Daryabadi draws also upon these prestigious Western sources on comparative religion: Pallen and Wyne's *New Catholic Dictionary*; Josephus's *Antiquities of the Jews;* Hastings's *Dictionary of the Bible*; Smith's and Cheetham's *Dictionary of Christian Antiquities*; Hastings's *Encyclopedia of Religion and Ethics*; Cohen's *Everyman's Talmud*; and Valentine's *Jewish Encyclopedia.*

Instances illustrative of Daryabadi's comparative strain are as follows:

1) In explaining the Quranic expressions *al-sama* (heavens) occurring in al-Baqarah 2: 22, Daryabadi is quick to "refute the Biblical notion of heaven as the dwelling place of God as mentioned in *The Book of Psalms* 11: 4 and 33: 13 and 14. In a sharp contrast to this, Islam looks upon the idea of God occupying a certain space as preposterous."[16]

2) While elucidating al-Baqarah 2: 48, which states the concept of Allah's forgiveness, Daryabadi points out that it aims to "repudiate the Rabbinical doctrine that 'grace is to be given to some because of the merits of their ancestors, to others because of the merits of their descendants' (*The Jewish Encyclopedia*, Vol. 6, p. 61).[17]

3) That the Quranic concept of God, as outlined in al-Baqarah 2:160, is radically different from the Biblical one is brought into sharper focus by Daryabadi thus: "The God of Islam, unlike the God of so many religions, is neither jealous nor vindictive. This requires frequent reiteration not only in view of the doctrines of the pagans but also of the teachings of the Bible (See *Joshua* 24: 19)."[18]

4) In spelling out the Quranic laws of war laid down in al-Baqarah 2: 190, Daryabadi compares these with the laws of war in the Bible by citing *2 Kings* 3: 25, *1 Kings* 11:16 and *1 Samuel* 15: 3, which brings out the ethical superiority of the Quranic laws of war. [19]

5) In elaborating the Quranic directive that a believer should seek good in both this and the Next world, as mentioned in al-Baqarah 2: 201, Daryabadi contrasts it with the Biblical directive in *John* 18: 36 and informs readers that the Bible is concerned only with the Next Life. Daryabadi's exposition is indeed gratifying and reassuring for one engaged in lawful worldly activities. For, according to the Quran he is one who performs a religious duty and is assured of divine reward in the Hereafter.[20]

6) While discussing the Quranic observation about the menstruating women in al-Baqarah 2: 222 Daryabadi demonstrates that the Biblical regulations in this respect, as recorded in *Leviticus* 15:19-21, are far more rigid.[21]

7) Daryabadi's note on al-Baqarah 2: 228 compares the Quranic and Biblical stances on divorce. It conclusively shows Islam as the natural way, representing the middle path. He maintains:

The course of divorce, or dissolution of the marriage tie, among ancient nations has been erratic, some making it too loose, others making it too tight ...The Jewish law allows it as a matter of no great concern (See *Deuteronomy* 24: 1 and 2). Christianity, on the other hand, taking its stand on the reported saying of Prophet Jesus (See *Mark* 10:9 and 11) and also upon the dictum of Paul (See 1 *Corinthinians* 7: 10) has interdicted divorce altogether... The climax was reached in the rules of the Roman Catholic Church... It treats marriage as a sacrament and demands indissolubility and unchanging fidelity. Islam has steered the course midway between the two, avoiding the extremes of either making divorce too rigid and banning it altogether, or of making it too loose and frivolous.[22]

8) Likewise, on comparing the status of women in the Quran (al-Baqarah 2: 228) and the Bible, Daryabadi points to the lead taken by Islam in according rights and honour to woman:

> According to the Quran, women have rights quite similar to those of men. This bold and explicit declaration of the rights of women centuries before a Mill dreamt of writing on the "Subjection of women" has no parallel in the pages of other Scriptures. Contrast this with the attitude of the Bible which as a punishment of the sin of Eve makes wife a subject to her husband who is to rule over her. According to the Old Testament, woman is responsible for the fall of man, and this became the cornerstone of Christian teachings ... It is a remarkable fact that the Gospels (barring *Matthew* 19: 9) contain not a word in favour of woman... *The Epistles of St. Paul* definitely insist that no change be permitted in the position of woman ... St. Jerome has taught but good to say of woman:" Woman is the gate of devil, the road of evil, the string of the scorpion." Canon Law declares: "Man only is created in the image of God, not woman; therefore woman shall serve him and be his handmaid." Kraft Ebing, *Psychopathia Sexualis*).[23]

9) In explaining the Quranic injunction prohibiting usury (al-Baqarah 2:275) Daryabadi, once again, points to the ethical superiority of the Quran:

> The devastating propensities of usury are visible to every eye... Yet it is Islam alone that has the unique distinction of declaring this pernicious practice illegal absolutely and unconditionally. The Bible... forbade the usurious loans to the Israelites (see *Exodus* 22: 25 and *Deuteronomy* 23: 19). But even the Biblical prohibition did not include usurious loans to non-

> Israelites. It is the Holy Quran, which to its everlasting glory has forbidden usury in all its forms categorically.[24]

To sum up, Daryabadi set in motion the trend of the English translations of the Quran by Muslim scholars. It is gratifying that after 1980 some presentable translations by Muslim scholars have appeared which cater to the needs of those who have access to the meaning of the Quran only in English. Some notable additions to the field after Daryabadi are by Muhammad Muhsin Khan and Taqi al- Din al- Hilali (1977), M. M. Khatib (1986), the English version of *Tafsir-i Usmani by* Mahmudul Hasan and Shabbir Ahmad Usmani (1991), and of *Tafhim al-Quran* by Saiyyid Abul Ala Mawdudi (1967-1988), Ali Ozek and others (1992), M.A.S. Abdel Haleem (2004), Unal Ali (2006), Ahmad Zaki Hammad (2007) and Tarif Khalidi (2008).[25]

Daryabadi's *Tafsir-i Majidi* (Urdu)

Among all the *mufassirun* perhaps Daryabadi alone holds the unique distinction of having written his *tafsir* in two languages – English and Urdu. It must be clarified at once that both the *tafasir* are independent of each other and addressed to two different mindsets of readers. The English one is directed at the Western educated Muslims exposed to Western thought patterns. They were vulnerable to skepticism, mistaking the Quran as a dated work, of which the message and teachings were no longer relevant, particularly in the post-Industrial, modern, scientific world of the twentieth century. While drawing upon the sources of modern knowledge, as detailed above, Daryabadi brought home the eternal truth and meaningfulness of the Quran in our time.

His Urdu *tafsir* is, however, aimed at average, practicing Muslims and seeks to convey to them the eternal guidance of the Quran in charming, forceful Urdu. About the background of his Urdu *tafsir* Daryabadi states:

> After having completed my English translation and *tafsir*, I embarked on my Urdu *tafsir*, which is far more extensive than the former. In writing this Maulana Thanwi's *Bayan al –Quran* was of immense help to me. There have appeared, no doubt, some excellent Urdu *tafasir*. For example, Shah Abdul Qadir's translation is unique. However, Maulana Thanwi's *tafsir* has many merits, which are not found in any other *tafsir*. As to my Urdu translation, it is mostly borrowed from *Bayan al-Quran*. Same holds true for my *tafsir* notes on juristic issues, which are again taken, in a large measure, from it. I was fortunate to interact regularly with Maulana Thanwi while writing my *tafsir* and often sought his guidance.

> My Urdu *tafsir* is much wider in its coverage than the English one. Numerous quotations from lexicon and classical *tafasir* account partly for this. I was able to finish this job in four years. In 1944 I dispatched it to Taj Company, Lahore for printing. The publisher took some years to bring it out. Worse, they opted for such a format (interlinear translation and commentary on the margins of the page), which hampered its presentation.[26]

Daryabadi kept revising his work and was able to revise and enlarge considerably his *tafsir* by late 1960s. It is a great pity that he could not find any publisher for bringing out the revised edition. Since he did not belong to any organized group or sect, no one came forward to publish his *tafsir*. With his own meagre resources he managed to publish only two parts of his grand work up to Surah Yunus. It was his ardent desire to see its publication in full. However, he passed away in January 1977, with this unfulfilled wish. The above speaks volumes about the regrettable sectarianism, group politics, personality cult and apathy towards good quality academic work in the Muslim society, especially of the subcontinent. After his demise, at Maulana Abul Hasan Ali Nadwi's behest the Academy of Islamic Research and Publications, Nadwatul Ulema, Lucknow, acquired its publication rights. It is another sad story that since 1977 up to 2013, in thirty-five long years the Academy has been able to publish only 6 volumes up to Surah al-Hujurat. At least two more volumes are yet to come out. It must be, however, at once said that the Academy has printed it very well, containing all the scholarly apparatus.

Daryabadi's "Preface" stands out as an insightful piece, throwing valuable light on the text and context of the Quran, issues and challenges in its translation, and more importantly, how readers should approach the Quran for gaining its understanding:

> It is quite a task to translate any literary masterpiece. For, a translator finds himself at a loss to convey faithfully the syntax, idiom, collactions, grammatical and rhetorical features and nuances of expressions into another language. If one renders text into chaste, idiomatic target language, it is, at best, a paraphrase or adaptation, not translation. At the other end of the scale, however, a strictly literal translation turns out to be dull, soulless, and uninspiring, having no appeal for readers. The poetical works of Ghalib and Iqbal, Sadi's *Gulistan* and Rumi's *Mathnawi* have been translated into English and Urdu by eminently competent persons. However, these have none of the literary charms of the original. Since this is true for the products of human minds, the Word of God, which is supreme in every respect, cannot be translated while retaining any of its numerous hallmarks. It is

simply beyond man's ability to capture its inimitable beauty and eloquence. However, out of His boundless mercy Allah has promised His reward for a sincere effort in this direction.

Let this be borne in mind that the Quran is a timeless, universal book of guidance for everyone of all time and place. At the same time, it has its time-place context in that it was revealed at a particular point of time addressed to a particular people of a certain place. This twin role of the Quran is something amazing.

Likewise, the Quran is no doubt universal in its message yet its presentation is in only the Arabic language. If one judges it by standards of any other language, it would betray sheer foolishness on his part. Moreover, the Arabs of the early seventh century were its immediate addressees. It therefore takes into account their mental level and their ethos. Had the Quran talked about such historical or scientific facts with which they were unfamiliar, it would not have served any purpose. The Quranic statements are nonetheless flexible enough to accommodate later developments in man's knowledge. This miraculous aspect of the Quran itself proves that it is the Word of God. The Quran is essentially a book of guidance. Piety and sincerity of the heart are the key to fathoming its message. One's linguistic competence alone does not suffice. Abu Jahl and Abu Lahab being members of the Quraysh had no language barrier yet they never turned to the Quran. As a result, they could not derive any guidance from it.

The Quran imparts ample guidance about *al-ghayb* (all that which lies beyond the ken of man's sense perception), as for example, about Allah, the soul, revelation, angels, Messengership, Paradise, Hell and divine recompense. For no other source of knowledge can enlighten man about these. However, the Quran says very little even about the body of knowledge which is accessible to man's mind and other faculties. It has only some passing references to what is now called science. It is done in view of the fact that consequent upon the development of the human intellect man himself will discover and harness the laws of nature. The miracle of the Quran consists in it that no scientific fact unravelled at any time can contradict the Quranic statements. Rather, all later day scientific discoveries do and will vindicate its veracity.[27]

Daryabadi's sources in writing his *tafsir* point to his predilections and approach. Some of his oft-quoted sources are:

- Ibn Jarir, *Tafsir Tabari*
- Ibn Abbas, *Tanwir al-Miqyas*

- Ibn al-Arabi, *Ahkam al-Quran*
- Ibn Qutaibiya, *Mushkilat al-Quran*
- Abu Hayyan al- Gharnati, *al-Bahr al-Muhit*
- al- Zarkashi, *al-Burhan fi Ulum al-Quran*
- al- Baydawi, *Anwar al-Tanzil*
- Ashraf Ali Thanwi, *Bayan al-Quran*
- al- Razi, *Mafatih al-Ghayb*
- al-Alusi, *Ruh al-Mani*
- Qurtubi, *Ahkam al-Quran*
- al- Zamakhshari, *al- Kashshaf*
- al- Nasfi, *Madarik al- Tanzil*
- al- Baghwi, *Ma'alim al-Tanzil*
- al- Nishapuri, *Gharaib al-Quran*

Besides these standard Arabic *tafasir,* he consulted a host of works on the Arabic/ Quranic lexicon and some Urdu *tafsir.*[28] As Daryabadi himself acknowledges, Maulana Thanwi's *Bayan al-Quran,* (published first in 1916), was his first and foremost source. More importantly, he derived more guidance on specific *tafsir* issues from Maulana Thanwi through correspondence, which is documented in Daryabadi's *Hakim al-Ummat: Nuqush wa Tathurat* (Azamgarh, Darul Musaniffin, 1953). This correspondence served many purposes: a) It resolved many of Daryabadi's *tafsir* queries, thanks to Maulana Thanwi's sterling Quranic scholarship. b) In the course of writing his *tafsir,* Daryabadi closely studied Thanwi's *Bayan al- Quran* and noted in it some inadvertent lapses which he brought to the latter's notice. In most of the instances Maulana Thanwi magnamaniously acknowledged and corrected these in the next edition of *Bayanal-Quran.* In some cases, however, he justified his stance, by citing classical authorities or by advancing some arguments. This led to Daryabadi's recanting of his observations. c) On some issues, especially related to establishing the Quranic place fixities in the light of the latest historical, geographical or archaeological findings, Daryabadi could not persuade the Maulana to alter his stance, and he therefore followed what he deemed to be more tenable. This correspondence between the two is thus full of lessons for the students of the Quran – how to raise and formulate questions, how to present these while expressing and maintaining utmost respect for a senior, elderly figure, how to advance and defend one's stance, how to differ without any rancour and how to exert oneself with all his mental faculties in the cause of advancing and propagating the message and truth of the Quran. This discourse stands out as an unprecedented, valuable addition to *tafsir* studies. The discussion between the two is mostly on: choice of a more suitable Urdu expression as equivalent to the Arabic original; some inadvertent inaccuracy or omission in Thanwi's translation; some ambiguity or confusion in Thanwi's translated version; authenticity of certain reports and norms in writing *tafsir* and some broader principles of interpreting the Quran.[29]

Daryabadi's *Tafsir-i Majidi* is studded with several distinctions. What sets it apart from other Urdu *tafasir* is brought out eloquently by Maulana Abul Hasan Ali Nadwi in his "Foreword" to its, revised edition published by the Academy of Islamic Research and Publications, Nadwatul Ulema Lucknow:

> Since the Quran is the explanation of the divine intent *par excellence* and as Allah Himself has guaranteed its presentation in its pristine purity, it is not surprising that in every age some providential arrangements are made for affirming and highlighting its truth. With the advancements in knowledge and the emergence of new facts as a result of discoveries and inventions, new questions and challenges also arise. Allah has ensured that in all such instances the believers in the Quran, who are devoted heart and soul to it, rise to the occasion in addressing and resolving all the new challenges. Equipped with their expertise, insights into the Quran, familiarity with the latest sources of knowledge and by dint of their hard work and dedication they keep bringing into sharper light the veracity of the Quran. They point to the yawning gap between its eternally valid, life-giving principles and message and the shallowness and inadequacies of human knowledge and reason. They thus present in every age the Quran as the everlasting source of guidance.
>
> In their respective eras illustrious *mufassirun* such as Baqillani, Rumman, Jurjani, Zamakhshari, Baydawi and Razi etc responded effectively to the challenges of the day.
>
> In our time, there was a pressing need for unravelling the truth of the Quranic message in the light of the latest developments in experimental and empirical sciences, history, geography, economics, sociology, law and archaeology. For accomplishing this difficult job Maulana Abdul Majid Daryabadi came forward. He achieved this in his English and Urdu *tafasir*. To the best of my knowledge, he was the most suitable person for this enterprise. For he possessed enviable insights into modern knowledge. He was a voracious reader and his vision was characterized by exceptional breadth. He was fully alive to the psyche of the modern educated class and always kept himself abreast of new developments in the scholarly field. During the long period of his writing *tafasir* he ensured a regular supply of such books

which would amplify the Quranic statements. His English and Urdu *tafasir* stand out as a testimony to his wide and deep study and his painstaking efforts to affirm energetically and forcefully the truth of the Quran.

Notwithstanding my limitations, let me state that from the beginning of my career *tafsir* has been the field of my special interest and study. For ten years I taught *tafsir* at Darul Ulum Nadwatul Ulema. Thus Allah enabled me to serve this noble cause. As part of this, I have gone through every classical *tafsir* which is worth-mentioning. During my frequent travel to the Arab world I have a clear idea of the latest publications in the field. On the basis of this wide ranging and first-hand experience I testify that *Tafsir-i Majidi* is unique in certain respects. There was a need for such a *tafsir* notwithstanding the availability of so many good *tafasir*. Many Quranic passages cannot be fathomed well without having a clear idea about their circumstantial setting and historical context. Likewise, the Quranic refutation of certain fallacious notions becomes comprehensible once we learn first what these false beliefs are. Maulana Daryabadi is to be complimented in particular by all those who do not have first-hand access to Western learning. Daryabadi has culled from numerous sources valuable material on the Quranic allusions to persons, places, communities and sects. Again, to the best of my knowledge, he never deviates from the orthodox viewpoint in his interpretations. There was the need for the study of comparative religion, for proficiency in English, and above all for conviction in the inimitability and purity of the Quran in a *mufassir* of our time. In the light of my knowledge of the current scholarly activities in the field of the Quran, based on my visits to the Arab world, Europe and the US, I affirm that Allah enabled an Indian scholar serving admirably the cause of Islam, Maulana Daryabadi to undertake an extensive, systematic study of comparative religion and of the earlier Scriptures. His *tafsir* is a testament to his ambition and sincerity. I cannot think of anyone equal to him in today's India, rather in the entire Muslim world.[30]

In his critique, Professor Yasin Mazhar Siddiqi, one of the eminent living authorities on Islam/the Quran in the subcontinent, identifies the following distinctive features of Daryabadi's *tafsir*.

- His Urdu rendering is remarkable for being in consonance with the Quranic syntax and idiom.
- He has done well in listing in his "Preface" some of the problems in translating the Arabic Quran into Urdu. More significantly, he

has spelled out certain norms and principles, of which the observance helps resolve these problems.

- In this translation he has been faithful to the Quranic syntax and word order. It is quite a task to accomplish this.
- He is the first among the Urdu *mufassirun* to have drawn upon such a variety and large number of sources on the Quran.
- His *tafsir* notes provide the quintessence of his deep and wide study of important sources.
- His taking recourse to modern academic studies, including the Western ones, is breathtaking. Both the classical Muslim and modern Western sources are represented well in his *tafsir.*
- While dealing with the Orientalists' writings, he does not reject these out of hand. Rather, he acknowledges the valid points made by them.
- Likewise, he both endorses and refutes the Biblical statements in the Quranic terms of reference.
- His interpretation is both academic and Islamic, as it happens to be in accordance with the Quran and Sunnah.
- He does not betray blind conformity to his predecessors. Rather, he cites them as long as their stance fits in with the tenor of the Quran.
- Daryabadi was a stylist of Urdu prose. No Urdu *mufassir* matches him on this count. His translation and *tafsir* are characterized by distinct literary charms.[31]

Professor Abdullah Abbas Nadwi, (d.2006) who was an accomplished Quran scholar in his own right, has paid this glowing tribute to Daryabadi's genius:

> Some of the features are common to both English and Urdu *tafasir* of Daryabadi. However, some appear in their full glory only in his Urdu *Tafsir-i Majidi.* For example, the stylistic charms and citing the classical sources in original Arabic are special to his *tafsir* in Urdu. To me, its other hallmarks are:
>
> 1. A *mufassir* should first and foremost be sincere. For conveying the meaning and message of the Book of Allah to others, one must necessarily be a person of utmost integrity.

2. Next to integrity is his level of knowledge. Competence is an essential prerequisite.

3. Besides sincerity of purpose and excellent knowledge, one should be enlightened by a gifted mentor. Such guidance is of immense help for a *mufassir*.

Fortunately enough, Daryabadi fulfilled all the above requisites. He embarked upon *tafsir* for the sake of winning only Allah's pleasure. He was grounded well in *tafsir* corpus. His objective was to produce a *tafsir* which may affirm the truth of Islam, rather than offer its apologetic defence. His other goal was to enable the seekers of truth to obtain guidance from the Quran. Above all, he was guided all along in writing his *tafsir* by Maulana Thanwi, an acclaimed authority on *tafsir*. Daryabadi does not deviate from the stance of classical *mufassirun*. He does not use his *tafsir* as a pretext for parading his own whimsical views.

Another great contribution of his is his critical analysis of the Bible. So doing, he excels both his predecessors, and contemporaries. The classical authorities used to draw upon the Israelite reports. Illustrative of this trend are al-Tabari, Ibn Kathir, Razi, Baghwi and Alusi. They followed the dictum: "We do not endorse or refute such reports." A small group of writers on the Quran went to the other extreme in rejecting altogether Israelite reports and in projecting their own whimsical interpretations. To this group belong Muhammad Abduh, his disciple Rashid Rida, and their follower Muhammad Asad, and the Qadyani translator, Muhammad Ali. Daryabadi's contribution consists in his critical study of the Bible, the Jewish and Biblical encyclopedias, and other authentic works on comparative religion. He thus removes the doubts created by the unreliable Israelite reports. Moreover, he established the tampering and shallowness in the Bible. By comparing Surah al-Fatihah with the Lord's Prayer in the Bible and by contrasting the Quranic description of Prophets Joesph, Jonah and Solomon (peace and blessings be upon them) with their Biblical account, he presses home the excellence of the Quran. Reading his *tafsir* one readily recognizes that the divine revelation is embodied only in the Quran, not in other Scriptures.

His *tafsir* is a compendium of the viewpoints of both classical *mufassirun* and recent scholarship, as he quotes these sources profusely. His *tafsir* is largely successful in conveying the glory, greatness of the Quran, its eloquence and effectiveness, the note of Allah's overflowing mercy as well as His wrath in the Quranic verses. Of course, it is impossible to capture the spirit of the original Quran in any translation.

> Nonetheless, Daryabadi's *tafsir* helps one perceive a glimpse of the force of the Arabic original. Yet another distinction of his *tafsir* is that without indulging in polemics, it exposes the fallacious notions of certain Muslim sects and schools of thought. For example, his apt translation of al-Anam 6: 59 demolishes the flawed premise of Qadyanism.
>
> In sum, this conspectus has many merits of both conception and execution. His *tafsir* being the quintessence of the entire *tafsir* corpus entitles it to the same acclaim which is enjoyed by the *tafasir* of Razi, Zamakhshari, Suyuti, Qurtubi, Baydawi and Alusi.[32]

Maulana Syed Rabey Hasani Nadwi, Rector Nadwatul Ulema, Lucknow and President, Muslim Personal Law Board, makes the following observations about *Tafsir-i Majidi.*

> The Quran is the book of guidance, showing man the way which is prescribed by his Creator. Notwithstanding the changing times this role of the Quran has remained constant. *Tafsir* scholars have identified the Quranic guidance applicable to various eras. Among such scholars Daryabadi occupies an eminent position. For he had obtained modern education and drew upon the latest Western scholarship. He then turned to the Islamic sources and made his mark as a scholar of Islam. He devoted himself to vindicating the Islamic faith and gained specialized knowledge of the Quran. While benefitting from both the classical Muslim authorities and modern knowledge, he came out with his *tafsir* which was greeted by both Ulema and modern educated people.
>
> In his *tafsir* Daryabadi has not deviated from the consensus opinion of Muslim authorities. More importantly, he makes full use of his knowledge of the sources in Arabic, Urdu and English in writing his *tafsir.* For example, his account of Prophet Jesus's crucifixion, which is based on his extensive study, goes a very long way in grasping better the import of this Quranic verse: "And they claimed: 'We killed the Messiah, Jesus the son of Mary, the Messenger of Allah.' However, they could not kill or crucify him. But the matter was made dubious to them."
>
> (al-Nisa 4:157)
>
> His *tafsir* excels others in that its sources are not restricted to Arabic. For affirming the veracity of the Quranic assertions he has been remarkably successful in obtaining material from modern sources, including the Jewish history.[33]

Maulana Qari Muhammad Tayyab, (d. 1983), former Rector of Darul Ulum, Deoband speaks of the following features of *Tafsir-i Majidi* which struck him:

> This *tafsir* is indeed Maulana Daryabadi's masterpiece. For it caters to the needs of the modern educated class. I always look for these two components in a *tafsir*: i) Sufficient background information about the historical context of the Quranic verses describing the Jews and Christians. For, without this, those Quranic verses cannot be fully comprehended. ii) A comparison between the Quran and the Bible, which may highlight the excellence of the Quran. As soon as I opened *Tafsir-i Majidi* for study, to my great delight, both of the above constituents figured prominently in it. It fulfilled my long felt desire. Daryabadi has concisely covered the aspect of comparative religion in his *tafsir*. It was a distinctive feature of Waliullahi School that the teaching of *tafsir* included also the study of the relevant Biblical passages. This aimed at bringing home the excellence of the Quran, especially of its laws replacing the Biblical ones. No study of *tafsir*, for them, was complete, without some idea of comparative religion. Daryabadi appears to have assimilated this Waliullahi concern in his *tafsir*.[34]

Daryabadi has very generously acknowledged his indebtedness to his mentor Maulana Thanwi's *Bayan al-Quran* in writing his *tafsir*. This has left the impression on some minds that his is replica of his mentor's earlier work. This is far from true. As noted earlier, and pointedly acknowledged by many reviewers, *Tafsir-i Majidi* has much, which is not to be found in other *tafasir*, including *Bayan al-Quran*. Daryabadi's discourse on comparative religion, on vindicating the supremacy of Islam/the Quran on the basis of the material culled from the latest Western writings, and on addressing and resolving the concerns agitating the minds of modern educated Muslims are special to his *tafsir*. He, no doubt, drew heavily upon Maulana Thanwi, seeking his valuable guidance on the issues of translating and interpreting the Quran. Thanwi's profound comments on mysticism (*tasawwuf*), guiding the seekers of truth, do appear at places in *Tafsir-i Majidi*. However, in terms of his approach to the Quran, his own well trained inquiring, rational mind and his objective of pressing home the excellence of the Quran by comparing it with the earlier Scriptures and by pointing to the flaws inherent in the Western way of life, Daryabadi's *tafsir* displays originality and ingenuity. Take his commentary on Surah al-Fatihah as illustrative. Apart from explaining the Quranic terms, concepts and articles of faith featuring in it, he goes a step forward in inserting the Urdu translation of the Biblical Lord's Prayer (*New Testament,* Mathew 6:9-14) and offers these faith-enriching comments in the strain of comparative religion:

1. Surah al-Fatihah speaks of the all-embracing, boundless Lord of the worlds. In contrast, the Lord's Prayer locates Him in the limited, specific heavens only: "Our Father who are in heaven". Moreover, He is designated as father, which instantly brings to mind some material, biological relationship between man and God.
2. Surah al-Fatihah asserts the absolute lordship, compassion, mercy and mastership of God whereas the Lord's Prayer refers only to the kingdom of God on earth.
3. The note of pure, unadulterated monotheism is to the fore in Surah al-Fatihah in its prohibition of not turning to anyone other than Allah for worship or help. The Lord's Prayer is devoid of all this.
4. The pointed reference to "daily bread" in the Biblical Prayer underscores the importance of material things in its outlook.
5. The supplication for deliverance from evil, as in the Biblical Prayer, is not so comprehensive as the Quranic prayer for showing and following the straight way.[35]

That Daryabadi's *Tafsir-i Majidi* represents an amazing amalgam of the classical and the modern, tradition and modernity and faith and reason is illustrated, as for example, by his commentary on Surah al-Fatihah, especially in the light of the range of the sources consulted by him. Amid his sources are *tafasir* and Quranic studies of Qurtubi, Razi, Ibn Kathir, Ibn Qayyim, Ibn Abbas, Baydwai, Zamakhashari and Alusi; Ahadith recorded by Bukhari, Muslim and Tirmidhi; Hanafi and Maliki *fiqh* writings and Arabic lexicographers and grammarians such as Raghib al-Isfahani, Zabidi Bilgrami, Abu al-Baqar, and the standard lexicons, *al-Qamus* and *Lisan al-Arab.* More strikingly, alongside the above there are quotations from the Bible, *the Encyclopedia Britannica,* and some Orientalist writings.[36]

Notwithstanding Daryabadi's dabbling with Sufism on only Maulana Thanwi's authority, his *tafsir* is highly valuable in that it admirably meets the needs of modern educated Muslims. For it presents before them cogently Islam as the natural way which instructs man how to lead life in a way which may bring him every happiness and success in both the worlds – this and the Next one. Furthermore, it interprets the Quran essentially as the book of guidance from Allah. This, in turn, enables readers to grasp and appreciate the articles of Islamic faith and practices, modes of worship in Islam and the Islamic stance on man's entire life in a rational, convincing way. The comparative note, of the Quran in relation to the Bible and modern Western thought, which is to the fore in *Tafsir-i Majidi* blesses readers with conviction in the eternal, excellent message of Islam and the Quran. In all this resides the relevance, validity and uniqueness of Daryabadi's Urdu *tafsir*.

Daryabadi's other Works on the Quran

By authoring several reference or companion works on the Quran, Daryabadi enriched much the Quranic corpus in Urdu. He was engaged for decades in writing his English and Urdu *tafasir*. Little wonder then that he was soaked in the Quranic scholarship. Some of the valuable material which he had collected during the course of writing his *tafasir* could not be included in these. For this material constituted partly background and partly supplementary stuff. It was nonetheless useful for acquainting readers better with the content and context of the Quran. Such reference/companion/ background works are fairly common in the Western scholarship. For these prepare readers mentally to appreciate better the larger picture. In the early twentieth century Urdu academic tradition such works were almost non-existent. Daryabadi, nonetheless, set in motion this trend by producing a triology of works related to the Quran – i) *Arz al-Quran* (the Quranic geography), *Aalam al-Quran* (Proper names in the Quran) and *Haywanat-i Qurani* (Animals in the Quran). Essentially all these three works seek to explain in detail and situate in a broader context the Quranic allusions to persons, places and animals. Some of the material figuring in these features in Daryabadi's *tafsir,* though in brief. Constraints of space did not allow him to include all this material. Moreover, too much focus on this material in *tafsir* would have diverted readers' attention from the basic meaning and message of the Quran. Quite intelligently therefore Daryabadi published this material as independent works for those interested in an in-depth study of all the historical and geographical references in the Quran. In bringing out these works Daryabadi's objective, as ever, was to bring into sharper light the soundness and accuracy of the Quranic account of even those things which are incidental to its main narrative. Daryabadi's description of things Quranic is endorsed by the latest scientific information. What the Quran said about these matters some fourteen hundred years ago, of which much was incomprehensible to the largely illiterate seventh century Arabs, has stood all along the test of time. In the light of current knowledge explosion readers can appreciate better the painstaking attention to detail and correctness which characterize the Quranic allusions.

Take as illustrative the following Biblical account of rivers:

> A river flowed out of Eden to water the garden, and there it divided and became four rivers. The name of the first is Pishon; it is the one which flows round the land of Havilah, where there is gold;

> and the gold of that land is good; bdellium and onyx stones are there. The name of the second river is Gihon; it is the one which flows round the whole land of Cush. And the name of the third river is Tigris, which flows east of Assyria. And the fourth river is Euphrates.
>
> (*Old Testament*, Genesis2:10-14)[37]

The above Biblical description contains many unanswered questions, leaving readers confused and perplexed: How did the river of Eden

- descend to earth and get divided into four rivers?
- Where is the Pishon river?

The *New Compact Bible Dictionary* vaguely states:

> The first of the four rivers of Eden, flowed around the whole land of Havilah. Conjectures as to its identification are almost as numerous as the rivers of south western Asia, and include the Persian gulf thought of as a river, and even the Nile.[38]

Likewise, there is this convoluted description of Havilah, another key word in the above:

> A land encompassed by the river Pishon which flowed from a source in the Garden of Eden.[39]

Nothing concrete or specific emerges even from this otherwise helpful Biblical reference work. One is only left bewildered, trying to figure out how the rivers of Eden made their way into our planet.

In contrast, the Quran mostly uses general, rather generic words. At several places it refers to *al-yam* (a sea), *al-nahr* (a river) or *majma al-bahrayn* (the meeting point of the two rivers in Prophet Moses's account). As to its proper nouns, their identification is not taxing. Classical *mufassirun* have thrown light on these, based on the then available information. Being a twentieth century Quranic scholar, enjoying the first-hand access to Western scholarly treasures, Daryabadi updates information in his three reference works on the Quran.

Amid Daryabadi's triology, *Arz al-Quran ya Jughrafiya-i Qurani* (Lucknow, Sidq Jadid Book Agency, 1955) came out first. The countries, towns, mountains, structures, fields and other sites referred to in the Quran are listed alphabetically in this slim work. 119 Quranic allusions to geography are annotated. Daryabadi's work is distinct from Maulana Syed Suleman Nadvi's earlier magisterial work on this subject, with an almost identical title *Arz al-Quran* (1915). Maulana Nadwi's coverage is far more extensive. For he discusses the culture and civilization of the past communities mentioned in the Quran. So doing, he corrects the mistakes or inaccuracies which occasionally mar some classical *mufassirun's* description. Being a gifted and trained historian, Maulana Nadwi explores energetically even such issues as trade, languages and religions in the pre-Islamic Arabia. Daryabadi, nonetheless, goes a step forward in culling information from both the Bible and Western sources in order to elucidate the Quranic geographical allusions. For example, the entries on the twelve springs which had gushed forth as Prophet Moses (peace and blessings be upon him) struck his rod (al-Baqarah 2: 60); the blessed land (al-Maidah 5: 21), the people of Aykah (al-Hijr 15:78 and other verses); Babylon (al-Baqarah 2:102); Judi (Hud 11:44), Corah (al-Qasas 28:81); Saul (al-Baqarah 2:246) Mary (al-Muminun 23:50), Tur (al-Baqarah 2: 63 and other verses); Sodom and Gomorrah (al-Anbiya 21:74) and. People of the Cave (al-Kahf 18:10 and other verses) are explained in the light of relevant passages from the Bible. As a result, readers get a clearer picture of the Quranic geography.

The second title of Daryabadi's triology *Haywanat-i Qurani* (Benaras, Nadwatul Ma'arif, 1955) represents his thorough familiarity with the Quranic text. For he has identified and elucidated 176 entries in the Quran related to animals and insects. Apart from providing accurate, concise information about them, Daryabadi explains well the context in which the Quran refers to them. As a result, his annotations help readers appreciate all the more the ingenuity of the Quranic text. For example, in explaining the Quranic reference to the camel (al-Ghashiyah 88:17), his focus is on projecting it as a living testament to Allah's creative wonders. Since the immediate addressees of the Quran were quite familiar with it, Daryabadi points to the effective communicativeness of the Quran. Likewise, his annotation on several Quranic references to cattle is in a similar vein. That man is much dependent upon cattle should persuade him of Allah' superb creation plan and His amazing arrangement for making cattle meet man's many needs. He is, however, quick to add that at places those men who are blind to truth, leading a materialistic life, are likened by the Quran to cattle in view of their disregard for anything other than meeting their own immediate needs. Being conversant with the history of world religions and polytheism, Daryabadi points also to the incredibly foolish practice of man venerating and worshipping animals, which the Quran denounces. While making his call Prophet Moses (peace and blessings be upon him) tells: "Allah sends down water from the heavens and produces with it many different plants which you eat yourselves and give it to your cattle" (Ta Ha 20: 53-34). Aptly Daryabadi remarks: "Cattle had a very important role in the Egyptian culture and economy and hence this part of his call was quite meaningful for his audience." Likewise, the Quranic reference to honey and milk which man gets from the belly of the honey bee and cattle respectively is elaborated by him as yet another sign of Allah's creative power. Even the highly advanced chemical laborarties cannot produce these items which Allah has provided for man in return for nothing. A little reflection on these natural products should persuade man of Allah's merciful and amazing dispensation. The Quranic declaration: "All four-footed animals are lawful for you, except those mentioned to you later" (al-Maida 5:1) is interpreted by Daryabadi thus:

> Polytheistic religions venerated animals. The Quranic assertion that animals are man's food strikes at the roots of such false notions. This underscores also man's exalted status as the supreme creature in the world. Animal worship has been an important manifestation of polytheism. Many animals, be these the cow, ass or snake, have been worshipped in various parts of the world.[40]

The Quran contains this graphic account of the Resurrection:

> On the Day of Judgement when the angel will call them to something terrible, they will come out from their graves, looking down like locusts spread everywhere.
>
> (al-Qamar 54: 6-7)

Daryabadi draws readers' attention to the apt use of the simile of locusts in the above:

> There could not be a better similitude than the swarms of locusts for the rising of the multitudes of human beings from their graves on the Day of Judgement. With the help of this simile the addressees of the Quran could and did form a clear idea of the sudden emergence of the thronging multitude.[41]

The Quran mentions the ritual of animal sacrifice, followed by this observation:

> Their meat or blood does not reach Allah. It is only your good intention that reaches Him.
>
> (al-Hajj 22: 37)

The above Quranic message is loud and clear. Nonetheless, Daryabadi delves into world history and provides the following background information, which throws further light on the above-quoted verse:

> This verse removes a common misconception held by the polytheists. They believed that their idols eat the sacrificial meat. For example, the Babylonians held that the animal sacrifice comes as a feast for their gods in the heaven. They eat its meat. Even the Bible affirms the relationship between the shedding of the animal's blood and forgiveness of sin: "Indeed, under the law almost everything is purified

with blood, and without the shedding of blood there is no forgiveness of sins."

(*Hebrews* 9:22)[42]

Aa'lam al-Quran ya Qurani Shakhsiyat (The Quranic personalities):

It is the last in the series, published in 1959 by Sidq Jadid Book Agency, Lucknow. The subtitle appropriately clarifies that it covers all the persons, jinn and angels mentioned by name in the Quran. However, on browsing the work, it emerges that Daryabadi has meticulously discussed even those who are alluded to by their pronouns as, for example, someone's mother, wife, son or father, or the persons or group with a specific trait as mentioned in the Quran. This speaks volumes about Daryabadi's in-depth study of the Quranic text and his keen desire to explicate all that which occurs in the Quranic text even implicitly or in passing. Apart from paraphrasing the Quranic description of 158 proper nouns, he supplements and complements the account with the relevant information painstakingly gathered by him from the Bible and modern Western/Biblical scholarship. In many instances his valuable comments contribute to a better understanding of the Quran and bring into sharper light the excellence of the Quranic version.

While discussing Prophet Lot (peace and blessings be upon him), Daryabadi painfully refers to some outrageous Biblical allegations against his moral conduct. About Iblis (Satan) his extensive note clarifies that unlike the Bible, the Quran does not speak of him as a "fallen angel" who had led the revolt against God. In the Quranic parlance Satan is not an angel at all; he is a jinn. (al-Kahf 18:50) Nor is he akin to Ahriman, the Zoroastrian god of evil. According to the Quran, far from being a god, Satan is a created being who can at most prompt man to commit evil; he does not enjoy any power over man. Likewise, about Prophet Adam (peace and blessings be upon him), the first man and Prophet, Daryabadi informs that both the Bible and the Quran designate him as the progenitor of all mankind. However, the Bible inextricably links him with the original sin and divine punishment. The Quran, however, absolves him of his lapse and depicts him as a pious figure. In Surahs al-Anam 6:84, al-Anbiya 21:72 and al-Saffat 37:112 the Quran designates Prophet Isaac (peace and blessings be upon him) as a pious, guided person, which apparently seems to be stating the obvious. For he was a Prophet. However, Daryabadi explains that the Quranic emphasis on his unblemished conduct is in view of his character assassination in the Bible (see *Genesis* 26: 7-11). Prophet Elias is found in the Quran censuring his community for worshipping Baal and for turning away from Allah, the best Creator. (al-Saffat 37: 124-125). Besides providing precise, substantial information about this idol worshipped by the Phoenicians in the 9th century BC, Daryabadi makes this insightful tribute to the miraculous veracity of the Quran:

> Bible scholars have demonstrated that Baal was not the name of a particular deity; there were Baals in every region. This explains why the Quran uses the generic word, Baal, rather than al-Baal, a proper noun standing for a particular deity.[43]

Equally meaningful is Daryabadi's comment on the Quranic expression, *banati* (my daughters) used by Prophet Lot (peace and blessings be upon him). When the wicked people of his community rushed to his house, bent on sodomising his guests, he tried to reason with them: "O my people, here are my daughters. They are better for you. Fear God and do not put me to shame about my guests." (Hud 11: 77). Since Prophet Lot (peace and blessings be upon him), according to the Bible, had only two daughters, the Quran uses the plural, not the dual form in the above instance. His allusion to "my daughters" included all females of his community. Being an elderly and fatherly figure he spoke of all them as his daughters. About Gabriel, Daryabadi points to the error of the Jewish scholars who misconstrue him as the angel of death and destruction, referred to in 2 *Samuel* 24: 15-17. *Ruh al-quds* (the holy spirit) is mentioned thrice in the Quran (al-Baqarah 2: 87 and 253, al-Maidah 5: 110, and al-Nahl 16: 102) as Gabriel's appellation. Daryabadi does well to alert readers not to mix up this Quranic term with the Christian notion of the Holy Spirit, which is part of their doctrine of the Trinity. About Samiri who had brazenly misguided the Israelites to indulge in the calf worship during Prophet Moses's absence, Daryabadi provides this helpful information:

> The Torah audaciously accuses Prophet Aaron (peace and blessings be upon him) of having introduced calf worship among the Israelites. Unabashedly the Bible says: "When the people saw that Moses delayed to come down from the mountain, the people gathered themselves together to Aaron and said to him, 'Up, make us gods…' And Aaron made a molten calf… and they worshipped it and sacrificed to it." (*Exodus* 32: 1-8).
>
> It is clear that the Quran specifically describes Samiri guilty of the above sacrilege, in order to exonerate Prophet Aaron (peace and blessings be upon him) from the Biblical calumny.[44]

In its account of the Israelite history the Quran reports that when Prophet Moses (peace and blessings be upon him) asked his people to fight in Allah's cause, they timorously refused, saying: "O Moses, very strong people live there. We will not enter unless they leave it… O Moses,… Go you, and your Lord and fight. We will sit here." (al Maida 5:22 and 24).

Equipped with his first hand knowledge of the Bible, Daryabadi does well to identify these people as the Amelikites, while citing the relevant Biblical passage, *Numbers* 13: 28 and 32. About Prophet Abraham (peace and blessings be upon him) the Quran reports that as he successfully passed his Lord's test in certain matters, Allah gave him the good news: "I will appoint you a leader of all people." (al-Baqarah 2: 124). Daryabadi amplifies the above Quranic statement with reference to the Bible which too, recognizes him as the patriarch. True to the Quranic assertion, Prophet Abraham (peace and blessings be upon him) is held in great esteem by the adherents of all the three major world faiths – Judaism, Christianity and Islam.

In sum, Daryabadi's triology on the Quranic studies enables readers to fathom better the plethora of historical, geographical and civilizational allusions in the Quran. These works also set a new trend of the Quranic scholarship in Urdu, as in addition to *tafsir,* other works on the Quranic studies started appearing in Urdu.

Daryabadi's *Qasas wa Masail* (Hyderabad, Deccan, Idara Ishat-i Urdu, 1944) is his other *tafsir* related work. This work grew out of his two lectures: i) "Baz Qadim Masail Jadid Roshni Mein" (Some Quranic issues in the light of recent scholarship) delivered at Raza Academy, Rampur on 20 December 1941, and ii) "Jadid Qasas al-Anbiya" (A new version of the Quranic account of Prophets) delivered on 10 January 1942 at Majlis-i Islamiyat, Peshawar, Pakistan. As is evident from the titles of these lectures, Daryabadi's aim was to enlighten his audience about the truth and accuracy of several Quranic statements in the light of the latest Western scholarship. He had collected such material in the course of writing his *tafasir.* In illustrating the Quranic allusions, mainly historical, geographical and cultural ones, his other objective was to let the Western educated Muslims realize that modern knowledge, including science, far from posing any threat, endorses the eternal truth of Islam and the Quran. For achieving this end, he takes up several Quranic allusions. Regarding the Flood in Prophet Noah's day pseudo-rationalists had serious reservations, dismissing it something utterly fanciful. However, on the authority of the following twentieth century Western studies, Daryabadi illustrates how the Quranic account of the Flood has been reiterated by these archaeologists: a) Charles Marston, *The Bible is True* (London, 1934), and b) Leonard Woolley, *Abraham* (London, 1935).[45] In a similar vein some Quranic descriptions about the Israelite history, the New Testament, Sabians, Pharaoh's drowning, sending down of *mann* and *salwa* for the wandering Israelites, Sabbath, the Jews' killing of Prophets, the beheading of Prophet John (peace and blessings be upon him), Jesus's crucifixion, sonship of God, and also about Prophets Adam, Noah and Abraham (peace and blessings be upon them) are elucidated, citing the pieces of Western scholarship which corroborate the Quranic account. Daryabadi thus facilitated a better understanding of some brief, allusive Quranic passages.

Mushkilat al-Quran ya Qurani Mutala Biswin Sadi Mein (Study of some difficult Quranic passages in the twentieth century)

It is another substantial *tafsir* based work of Daryabadi, which originated from the series of five lectures delivered by him at New College, Madras (now known as Chennai, Tamil Nadu, India) from 28 July 1970 to 5 August 1970. Maulana Syed Abul Hasan Ali Nadwi had chaired this lecture series. In his opening words, Maulana Nadwi states:

> It was my great privilege to be in chair. Educated Muslims from both Madrasas and universities of Madras, Banglaore and Mysore thronged to the lecture hall as they had heard of Maulana Daryabadi's towering personality. Ulema owe the obligation of resolving the questions and queries of readers of the Quran in every age. With their extensive and intensive study, their reflections upon the Quran, their awareness of the new intellectual challenges and with their hard work they should keep bringing into sharper light the eternal, timeless quality of the Quran... In our times Maulana Daryabadi has risen to the occasion. I am sure his observations would be highly informative and instructive for the students of the Quran.[46]

As many as 66 enigmatic Quranic passages are elucidated in Daryabadi's work under discussion, with the following objectives, as indicated by Daryabadi himself:

> An effort has been made to allay, to the extent possible, the doubts or mental reservations or queries which the twentieth century readers of the Quran may have. It will help them maintain, rather increase their conviction in the Quran. The cause of the Quran has been served in a variety of ways. Numerous *tafasir* have appeared, focussing on its literary, philological, philosophical, juristic and other aspects. Yet there is a need for fresh studies, and this will hold true until the Last Day. For it is beyond any individual to grasp all the hallmarks of the Quran which is the very Word of God.
>
> Imam Fakhr al-Din Razi (d. 606H) drew upon the knowledge of the day for highlighting the excellence of the Quran. May Allah enable someone today to follow in his footsteps by way of bringing out the glory of the Quran with reference to modern knowledge.[47]

Daryabadi's other work on Quranic studies is exceptionally original and unique. His *Bashariyat-i Anbiya* (Humanness of Allah's Messengers), with its self suggestive title, was published in 1959 (Lucknow, Sidq Jadid Book Agency). This study, firmly rooted in the Quranic text, inaugurates a new approach to both the Quranic and Muslim theological discourse. On the freshness of the tenor of his study, Daryabadi informs:

> In the face of the plethora of writings on the virtues and excellence of the Messengers of Allah, it is hard to think of making any original contribution to the field. More importantly, this aspect has been unintentionally so much overblown that the Quranic insistence on professing and practising unadulterated monotheism has been somewhat eclipsed. As a result, some tend to elevate the Messengers to almost Godhead. Out of the same adulatory stance, even every saint, spiritual master or religious scholar is regarded as superhuman, having none of the human needs and failings.
>
> Such excessive exaltation is patently discordant with the teachings of the Quran and Shariah commands. Furthermore, it is often at the expense of devoting oneself fully to Allah alone. Let this be clearly realized by all that the Quran portrays even the outstanding Messengers as mere human beings. It focusses on various strands of their humanness. As I noted Ulema's lack of attention to this aspect in their writings on Messengers, which has resulted in the spawning of false, pernicious notions, I gathered courage to address this issue, notwithstanding my incompetence. The Quranic viewpoint on the humanness of the Messengers constitutes the crux of this study, as I have cited relevant verses, with brief notes.[48]

In other words, it is Daryabadi's plea for the return to the original message of the Quran. For its revivalistic and reformist tenor this work deserves special attention. It represents an authentic, reasoned voice against popular Islam which venerates every pious figure. This syncretic tendency is more marked in the faith and practice of ordinary Muslims in the Indian subcontinent. Most of the Ulema had not thought about the root cause of this malaise. Once people tend to form a superheroic image of religious leaders, it is generally at the expense of their belief in the Most Glorious One True God, Allah Who alone deserves all respect and obedience. In the light of his study of world religions Daryabadi was alive to the danger how excessive veneration gives way to polytheism and idolatry. Christians' elevation of Prophet Jesus (peace and blessings be upon him) is a glaring example of this dangerous tendency. In his *Bashariyat-i Anbiya* Daryabadi delves deep into the Quranic text and persuades his readers that Allah alone is worthy of all praise and veneration. A note of balance, however, should characterize our attitude towards fellow beings, even if they happen to be the best human beings whom Allah chose to be His Messengers.

There should not, however, be a mix up between the Creator and the creature. It was nonetheless Allah Who granted them special faculties of the mind and body, let them perform miracles and achieve what is beyond the ability of other human beings. Messengers selflessly served the cause of faith and faced the worst opposition and persecution, including assassination. Yet, according to the Quran they were after all human beings. Allah, no doubt, rendered them infallible, as none of them ever committed any sin. However, they shared with all other human beings the same human traits, aspirations and emotions. They too, were wholly dependent upon Allah for everything --- resources, children, victory over the unbelievers etc. They faced, like all other human beings, bereavement in the family. They feared certain things as we all do. They, no doubt, possessed special knowledge, which was granted to them by no one other than Allah. About worldly matters their level of knowledge was almost the same as of other human beings. Occasionally did they commit some inadvertent lapses, which are documented in the Quran. Notwithstanding enjoying their special relationship with Allah and His help and support, they were subject to stiff opposition from their own community including, at times, even members of their own families. For years and years they preached true faith yet only few believed in them. Some of them were unjustly killed and they were helpless, at times, against their enemies. Like anyone else, they turned to Allah, invoking His help and support. For, on their own they could not achieve anything. Most importantly, they were, like anyone else, mortals. So doing, Daryabadi, of course, did not intend showing even the slightest disrespect to the Messengers. His concern was to impress upon the minds and hearts of readers the much neglected message that Allah alone, not some respectable religious figure who is after all human, should be the only object of their adoration, devotion and submission. For, his study of world religions had made him acutely aware of this bitter reality:

> The main stumbling block for polytheistic people of all time is their acceptance of the humanness of the Messengers. They generally mistook them as incarnation or manifestation of God Himself and readily venerated or worshipped them. However, they could not reconcile to the worship of the unseen One True God. Their fallacious logic ran thus: "If Jesus is truthful and it is an article of faith to believe in him, he must be worshipped as well." The Quran refutes this colossal error in its characteristic varied ways:
>
> "It does not befit a man whom God grants the Book and wisdom, to ask people: "Be my worshippers, rather than God's."
>
> (Ali Imran 3:79)

"God never asks you to take angels and Prophet as the lords. Will He ask you to disbelieve after you have submitted yourselves to God?"
(Ali Imran 3:80).[49]

Daryabadi has cited around 640 Quranic passages/verses which point to the Messengers' humanness – their accountability to Allah, their limited powers, their subjection to sorrows and grief, their occasional proneness to anger, their fear of certain things, their momentary forgetfulness, their vulnerability to death, their limited knowledge, their human feelings and emotions, their need for wives and their invocation to Allah for blessing them with children, their inadvertent lapses, their fervent and humble supplications to Allah, including seeking His forgiveness, and facing severe opposition, rejection and torture.

In sum, *Bashariyat-i Anbiya* testifies to Daryabadi's study of Quranic text from a fresh angle which seeks to emphasize the belief in and practice of the Islamic faith in its pristine purity, free of such ignoble accretion as saint worship or even personality cult.

Daryabadi's another publication arising out of his *tafsir* writing career is the posthumous publication in English, *Jesus and Mary in the Holy Quran* (Lucknow, Sidq Foundation, 2009). He had compiled this material related to comparative religion, primarily for inclusion in his English *tafsir*. Since all of this could not be incorporated into it, he planned to publish as a separate, independent monograph for the benefit of his Muslim readers who were mostly unfamiliar with this valuable strain of the Quran—-its sound critique on the earlier communities, especially how they had tampered with the Scriptures sent down to them.

Daryabadi has to his credit two substantial works on Prophet Muhammad's *Sira*(the Prophet's exemplary life and career) in Urdu. The first one *Sirat Nabawi Qurani* (Lucknow, Sidq Jadid Book Agency, 1963) like his above–mentioned work, is anchored deep into the Quranic text. It represents one of the earliest attempts in *Sira* corpus in Urdu to trace out the Prophet's illustrious life and mission with a specific reference to the Quran. Otherwise, there already existed several scholarly, comprehensive works on *Sira* in Urdu, especially by Maulana Suleman Mansurpuri, Maulana Thanwi, Maulana Manazir Ahsan Gilani, and the masterly multi–volume *Sirat al-Nabi* initiated by Shibli and concluded after his demise by Maulana Syed Suleman Nadwi.

Daryabadi's *Sirat Nabawi Qurani* is actually the book form of the nine lectures delivered by him in January 1958 at the New College, Madras (present day Chennai, Tamil Nadu, India). He has covered *Sira* under these nine headings. i) the Prophet's advent, ii) his name, family, birth place and era, iii) his outstanding qualities and mission, iv) his Messengership and humanness, v) his migration to Madina, vi) his battles, vii) the polytheists, Jews, Christian, Hypocrites and Muslims of his day, viii) his miracles and ix) his domestic and marital life. Although it appears at the first glance asa conventional account of *Sira,* Daryabadi's uniqueness consists in interlacing his description with many related Quranic verses. Even the chapter on the Prophet's domestic and marital life contains more than 25 Quranic passages. His work thus enables readers to appreciate how the Quran represents its bearer and more importantly, to realize that Prophet Muhammad's life was constantly under Allah's guidance and hence the numerous Quranic directives to him about his conduct and his mission.

His other work is a collection of his sixteen Urdu articles on various aspects of *Sira*, which has been issued under three different tittles: a) *Murdon ki Masihai* (Hyderabad Deccan, Idara Ishat-i Islam, 1943); *Zikr–i Rasul* (Calcutta, Idara Insha–i Majidi, 1996) and iii) *Sultan ma Muhammad,* (Lahore Makkah Books, 1982). In 1992 Dr. Tehsin Firaqi, a highly competent Pakistani, Islamic scholar, who has specialized in the study of Daryabadi,[50] brought out a much improved edition of *Sultan ma Muhammad* with his valuable editorial inputs. Daryabadi's pieces are remarkable mainly for bringing home some striking, original points about *Sira* and also for their stylistic charms. For instance, his piece "Zikr-e Rasul ki Bulandi" (The Prophet's ever- lasting fame) constitutes his elaboration of the Quranic assertion about the Prophet's renown, alluded to in verse 94 of al-Sharah: "Did Allah not increase your (the Prophet's) fame?" To substantiate the above, he draws attention to the tremendous love and respect for the Prophet (peace and blessings be upon him) by billions of Muslims down the ages and the devotion of the best minds of the Muslim community who spent their lives documenting and elucidating the Prophet's life and career (*Sira*), his conduct (*Sunna*) and his sayings and actions (*Hadith*). Then, there are numerous books in all major world languages, which extol his exemplary character and his astounding achievements. For jurists, men of letters, thinkers, and scholars too, the Prophet's role model has been the object of emulation throughout Muslim history. Such fame and love has not been earned by any other person, no matter how great, other than Prophet Muhammad (peace and blessings be upon him). More remarkably, as the Quran foretold it, the Prophet's renown has been ever-lasting. Even today, more than 1400 years after his demise, he continues to inspire, guide and teach more than one billion strong Muslim community. He commands such love and respect that every Muslim takes it as his highest privilege imaginable to lay down willingly his life for protecting the Prophet's honour.

As in his *tafasir*, his work on *Sira* indicates his wide, discerning familiarity with the recent Western scholarship. And he points to both their laudation of and their hostility towards the Prophet (peace and blessings be upon him). Throughout, his objectives is to persuade readers of the Prophet's greatness and glory on the basis of factual evidence and cogent arguments, couched in his chaste, idiomatic Urdu. More importantly, he presents the Prophet (peace and blessings be upon him) all along as a role model, to be emulated to the extent possible. This explains Daryabadi's greater focus on what the Prophet (peace and blessings be upon him) did for mankind and his eternally valid teachings which ensure the best for man in both the worlds.

Daryabadi's ardent desire to depict and promote an image of Islam being the best world religion and a complete way of life is reflected at its sharpest in his two other general works: a) *Tamaddun-i Islam* (Islamic culture) (Aligarh, Anjuman Islami Tarikh wa Tamaddun, 1941), and b) *Tasawwuf-i Islam* (Islamic mysticism) (Azamgarh, Darul Musaniffin, 1925). The former comprises his two lectures on the above subject delivered in August 1938 and October 1941 at the Aligarh Muslim University, Aligarh as part of the Islamic week programme under the auspices of Anjuman Islami Tarikh wa Tamaddun. In his Foreword, Maulana Qari Tayyab, former Rector, Darul Ulum, Deoband states:

> Addressed to the educated Muslims, these lectures present a living picture of the all–embracing, vibrant Islamic culture. His characteristic comparative note, at times in the satiric, sarcastic vein, is to the fore. As a result, one easily notes the deformities of other cultures and gains conviction about the comprehensiveness and excellence of the Islamic culture.
>
> He does well to point out that Islamic culture envelopes all that a Muslim does individually or collectively, ranging from his birth to death, from his worship to his personal habits, and from his social to political life. The Islamic culture rests on such life-sustaining virtues and valves as God-consciousness, honesty, trustworthiness, chastity, truthfulness, piety and cleanliness. He contrasts this to the non-Islamic way of life, disfigured by lust for power, drinking, unlawful earning, illicit sex and a staggering number of crimes, suicide, public disorder and other evils. In the face of all this readers are inevitably drawn towards the natural Islamic way of life.
>
> The merits of the work are enhanced by Maulana Daryabadi's stylistic and rhetorical embellishments. Some reflection on our part would help us get rid of the corruption which has crept into our culture, and which brings a bad name to Islam.

> Once we adhere to the Islamic conduct as detailed in this work, in accordance with the Prophet's promise, Islam would regain its lost glory. It would deliver us from the psychological inferiority from which we presently suffer. Maulana Daryabadi deserves credit for having renewed the call for our return to the truly Islamic way of life. He has reminded us of the important lesson which we had almost forgotten.[51]

As to his other work, *Tasawwuf-i Islam,* it is reflective of Daryabadi's life-long interest in the pure, unadulterated variety of Islamic mysticism, to which he had been introduced first by his study of Rumi's *Mathnawi* and Shaykh Ahmad Sirhindi's *Maktubat.* At a later stage, his interest in the subject was both reinforced and refined under his mentor Maulana Thanwi's influence. It was again Maulana Thanwi's training and teachings which convinced Daryabadi that self purification and self development, rather than any organized movement or political campaigns are more important and beneficial for the Muslim community as a whole. That mysticism is central to attaining self development is a truism which hardly calls for any further elaboration. Daryabadi, nonetheless, was wedded unflinchingly to the belief that popular practices under the pretext of Sufism have nothing to do with Islam. He therefore professed and practised only Shariah-oriented Sufism. His first notable writing on Sufism is his article, "Hukma-i Maghrib awr Falsafa-i Tasawwuf" (Western sages and the philosophy of Sufism), published in the prestigious Urdu academic journal, *Maa'rif* (February 1921). On the basis of his first-hand access to the Western philosophical corpus Daryabadi states that rationalism is the highest goal imaginable for Western sages. For they insist that sense perception, observation and all mental faculties should be geared only for harnessing, and manipulating the objects of nature. In contrast, the cornerstones of the Eastern thought are: divine revelation, meditation, intuition and self purgation. He, nonetheless, identifies some Western sages, particularly McTaggart, who do affirm the nexus between psychology, intuition and mysticism. Then he compares and contrasts the thought patterns of the Western psychologists and Sufi masters, and cites several authentic works on Sufism. At a later stage, he developed his thesis into a full length book, *Tasawwuf-i Islam.* It won a wide acclaim from the Ulema and scholars in the subcontinent. Professor R. A. Nicholson, University of Cambridge, too, felicitated Daryabadi on having produced a highly useful work on Sufism for the lay readers. According to Daryabadi's definition, Sufism is not something independent of Islam. Rather it is the pure form of Islam. He concedes the intrusion of patently un-Islamic beliefs and practices into popular Sufism, which has only traces of Islam. For him the representative Sufi figures are Ali, Salman Farsi, Abu Zar Ghifari, Junaid Baghdadi, Rabia Basri, Shaykh Abdul Qadir Jilani, Shaykh

Suhrawardi, Muinuddin Chishti, Khawaja Nizamuddin, Khawaja Naqshbandi and Shaykh Ahmad Sirhindi. To substantiate his stance he has quoted extensively from the select writings of these masters. His criticism against the popular variety of Sufism is trenchant. For him true Sufism which is anchored in Islam represents *ihsan* and its outcome should be one's wholesale devotion to the Quran and Sunnah. In sum, his *Tasawwuf-i Islam* being a brief introduction to Sufism and its worthy practitioners serves well as a short history of this Islamic trope.

Daryabadi's *Khutbat-i Majid* (Calcutta, Idara Insha-i Majid, 1978) is basically a collection of the four marriage sermons delivered by him on the occasion of the wedding of his daughters and niece. Originally published in his weekly *Sidq,* these were compiled and brought out soon after Daryabadi's demise. These sermons elucidate the institution of marriage in Islam, its significance and sanctity, and the norms to be observed by the spouses for ensuring a happy, long lasting marriage. Throughout, it cites Prophet Muhammad (peace and blessings be upon him) as the role model for being the best husband and excellent head of the family. Contained in it are some highly valuable pieces of advice. Take the following as illustrative, about treating wife well:

> Today, under the evil influence of non-Arab and Hindu cultures we proudly assert that we do not regard our wives as our equal. Rather, we are given to dominating and subjugating them. However, Prophet Muhammad (peace and blessings be upon him) never looked upon his wife as someone inferior. On the contrary, he labelled her as the best blessing bestowed by Allah: The Prophet's Companion, Abu Umama reports that the Prophet (peace and blessings be upon him) used to say: "For a believer, a wife with a good conduct is next only to piety in importance and as a blessing"(Ibn Majah).
>
> Abdullah Ibn Amr reports the Prophet (peace and blessings be upon him) saying: "This worldly life is no doubt brief. However, there is nothing better than a wife with good conduct in this short life. The best thing in life is to have a good, pious wife."
>
> (Muslim)

It is thus a laudable effort on Daryabadi's part to urge Muslim to practise the Islamic teachings in day to day life which alone would bring about their deliverance in the Next world and spiritual and emotional joy and happiness in this world.

His two edited works in the field of Hadith are: i) *Munajat-i Maqbul* (Everyday Supplications). Originally it is Maulana Thanwi's compilation of the Prophet's prayers. Daryabadi felt the need for its simpler, annotated updated version for the benefit of ordinary readers and hence his edited version (Lucknow, Sidq Jadid Book Agency, 1949). In all it contains 194 supplications, of which 40 are culled from the Quran and others from standard Hadith collections. Daryabadi's main contribution consists in providing extensive explanatory notes on the text of the supplications. These are in the vein of his *tafsir* notes, seeking to persuade readers of the excellence of Islam as the belief system, as the natural way of life and as all-encompassing moral code. His Urdu translation is fluent, as he had taken up this work after having already translated the Quran into Urdu. ii) *Chahal Hadith Waliullahi* (Lucknow, Sidq Jadid Book Agency, 1969). Shah Waliullah had compiled this collection before1760. Its two Urdu translations came out in 1838 and 1842, and another in the verse form in 1854. Daryabadi has simplified, revised and annotated the Urdu translation of 1842 by Muhammad Mustafa Khan.

There goes Abu al-Darda's report that the Prophet (peace and blessings be upon him) promised his intercession for one who records and propagates forty Ahadith. For attaining this felicity many selections of forty Ahadith have been compiled down the ages. Some have selected those Ahadith which specifically deal with monotheism and divine attributes, some with divine commands while others have opted for those forty Ahadith which have an impeccable chain of narrators. Shah Waliullah's selection is marked by these two distinctive features: i) All of these forty Ahadith are authentic and ii) these are brief yet pithy, with several layers of meaning. Accordingly, in his prefatory note Daryabadi affirms:

> In addition to his spiritual and other accomplishments, the Prophet (peace and blessings be upon him) had an exceptionally decent, refined literary taste. His sayings are pithy, packed with meaning. Their eloquence is next only to that of the Quran. This is noticeable in this selection of forty Ahadith. For each of these epigrammatic sayings encompasses concisely a whole range of truths. Little wonder then that some of these have become proverbs in Arabic.[52]

Daryabadi's revised translation in idiomatic Urdu and his helpful explanatory notes have enhanced the value of his new edition. Some of his comments are quite enlightening. On the Prophet's observation that *al-harb khada'* (In war resort is taken to deception), he clarifies:

> Since the objective of wars is to attain victory, by all means, both the parties openly resort to deception, without adhering to any moral code. Let this be clarified that the above observation is about an ordinary war with which we are quite familiar. However, the Prophet's remark is not about the Islamic concept and practice of *jihad* and *qital* (fighting) which is premised only on truth, and sincerity of purpose.[53]

Daryabadi's last work on Islam, though published as a book posthumously, is fittingly entitled *Shawq-i Watan* (Desire for the Hereafter). Essentially it is the simpler, annotated version of his mentor Maulana Thanwi's treatise bearing the same title. It projects the Islamic stance on death, instructing Muslims to be always ready for death and for their return to their eternal home, the Hereafter. Maulana Thanwi introduces this work thus:

> Out of our forgetfulness we have disregarded our real, abiding home – the Hereafter. This work seeks to draw attention to the Hereafter.[54]

Shawq-i Watan was serialized in Daryabadi's weekly *Sidq-i Jadid* between August 1969 and October 1972. Contained in it is an intelligent selection of Ahadith on health problems, distress in general, some mental, emotional, financial or spiritual crises, *barzakh* (the intermediate stage between one's death and his resurrection on the Day of Judgement), and death. In Daryabadi's words, these Ahadith serve as the best message for comfort, consolation and bereavement. These lend a soothing effect to those in condolence.

To recapitulate, with his more than a dozen substantial works on Islam, Daryabadi indeed enriched the field of the study of Islam. Some of his writings re-echo and extend the material which is special to his English and Urdu *tafasir*; others, more remarkably, present Islam in a fresh perspective. Generally speaking, his writings are informed by a comparative note, logical arguments and apt illustrations, testifying to his wide readings in Western thought and philosophy and comparative religion. His unique Urdu prose style added to the appeal and effect of his writings, as he enjoyed mastery over Urdu idiom. Many readers were drawn towards his writings mainly because of his stylistic charms. His only concern in authoring these and other works was to expound energetically and effectively the message of Islam and to enable readers to realize the excellence of Islam both as a faith and as the natural way of life. In doing so, he took into account the intellectual level, mental reservations and concerns, and even doubts of his readership, especially of the twentieth century modern educated Muslims. His mission was to persuade them of the adequacy and efficacy of Islam. Also, he was very keen on inculcating into the mind and heart of his readers the essential message of Islam and the Quran and to urge them to adhere fully to the guidance imparted to them by Allah through the Quran and Prophet Muhammad (peace and blessings be upon him). In this resides the contribution and greatness of Daryabadi as an author on Islam in both English and Urdu.

Notes

1. Abdul Majid Daryabadi, *Aap Biti,* Lucknow, 1998, p.p. 292-295 (abridged)
2. See the following for the serious flaws in Abdullah Yusuf Ali's approach to understanding the Quran:
    - Q. Arafat, *Incorrect Equivalents Chosen by Abdullah Yusuf Ali in his Translation of the Quran.* Leicester, UK.
    - *A Discussion on the Errors of Yusuf Ali.* By Majlisul Ulama, Transval, South Africa.
    - Abdur Raheem Kidwai, "Abdullah Yusuf Ali's Views on the Quranic Eschatology", *Muslim World League Journal,* Makkah, 12:5 February 1985, pp. 14-17.
    - S. A. H. Rizvi, "Some Errors in Abdullah Yusuf Ali's English Translation of the Quran", *Muslim and Arab Perspectives,* New Delhi. 1:1 October 1993, pp. 4-19.
3. Abdur Raheem Kidwai, "Review on Abdullah Yusuf Ali's Translation of the Quran", *Muslim World Book Review,* Leicester, UK, 12: 20, 1992, pp. 18-23.
4. Abdur Raheem Kidwai, "Mohammad Abdul Hakim Khan's *The Holy Quran* (1905): The First Muslim or the First Qadyani English translation?", *Insights,* Islamabad, Pakistan 2:1, 2009, pp. 57-75.
5. Abdul Majid Daryabadi, *Hakim al-Ummat,* Allahabad, 1990,pp. 317-321 (abridged)
6. Abu Ala Mawdudi, "Quran Majid ka Angrezi Tarjuma", *Tarjuman al-Quran,* Hyderabad, 4: 4, Rabi al-Thani 1353H.
7. Abdul Majid Daryabadi, *Tafsirul Quran: Translation and Commentary of the Holy Quran.* Lucknow, Academy of Islamic Research and Publications, 1981-1985, 1, 13A.
8. *Ibid.*, 1, 12B.
9. *Ibid.*, 1,18.
10. *EncyclopaediaBritannica*, London, 14th edition, 20, 952.
11. *TafsirulQuran,* 1, pp. 10A and 10B.
12. Abdullah Yusuf Ali, *The Meaning of the Glorious Quran*, Beirut, Dar al-Kitab, n.d., 1, 45.
13. *TafsirulQuran,* 1, 18B.
14. *Ibid.*, pp. 20A and 28A.
15. Maryam Jameelah, *Why I Embraced Islam,* New Delhi, Crescent Publishing, n.d., pp. 3 and 5.
16. *TafsirulQuran*, 1, 16.
17. *Ibid.*, 1, 31.
18. *Ibid.*, 1, 102.
19. *Ibid.*, 1, 123.
20. *Ibid.*, 1, 131.
21. *Ibid.*, 1, 148.
22. *Ibid.*, 1, 152-153.
23. *Ibid.*, 1, 154.
24. *Ibid.*, 1, 192.

25. For a critique on complete English translations of the Quran see the following:
    - Abdur Raheem Kidwai, *Bibliography of the Translations of the Meanings of the Glorious Quran into English: 1649-2002*. Madina, King Fahd Quran Printing Complex, 2007. 469 pages.
    - Abdur Raheem Kidwai, *Translating the Untranslatable, A Critical Guide to 60 English Translations of the Quran.* Delhi, Sarup Book, 2011, 345 pages.
    - Muhammad Mohar Ali, *The Quran and the Orientalists.* Norwich, UK,Jamiyat Ihya Minhaj al-Sunnah, 2004.
    - Basim Muflin Badr, "A Critique of Six English Translations of a Quranic Text", *Islamic Culture*, Hyderabad, India, 68: 3, July 1994, pp. 1-17.
    - Ahmad Zaki Hammad, "Representing the Quran in English," in *The Gracious Quran: A Modern Phrased Interpretation in English.* Lisle, LA, Lucent, 2007, pp. 67-87.
    - Khaleel Mohammad, "Assessing English Translations of the Quran," *Middle East Quarterly* 122, Spring 2005, pp. 58-71.
    - Neal Robinson, "Sectarian and Ideological Bias in Muslim Translations of the Quran," *Islam and Christian – Muslim Relations* 8: 3, 1997, pp. 261-278.
26. *Aap Biti,* pp. 296-297.
27. Abdul Majid Daryabadi, *Tafsir-i Majidi,* Lucknow, Majlis Tahqiqat wa Nashriyat-i Islam, 1995, Vol. 1, pp. 2 and 3.
28. *Ibid.*, 1, 15-19 (abridged).
29. Yasin Mazhar Siddiqi, "Hazrat Thanwi ke *Bayan al-Quran* par Istidarkat-i Daryabadi,"in *Tafsir-i Majidi: Naqd wa Nazr.* Edited by Naimur Rahman Siddiqi, Lucknow, Sidq Foundation, 2013, pp. 106-157. See also *Hakim al-Ummat, passim.*
30. *Tafsir-i Majidi*, Vol.1, pp. 1, 2 and 3.
31. Yasin Mazhar Siddiqi, "Maulana Daryabadi ki Qurani Basirat" in *Tafsir-i Majidi: Naqd wa Nazr*, pp. 101-102.
32. Abdullah Abbas Nadwi, "*Tafsir-i*-Majidi ki Khususiyat wa Infradiyat", in *Tafsir-i Majidi: Naqd wa Nazr,* pp. 57,58,64,66,67,68,71,72,73 and 74.
33. *Ibid.*, pp. 76,77 and 79.
34. Qari Muhammad Tayyab Qasimi, "*Tafsir-i Majidi*: Qadr Afzai," in *Tafsir-i Majidi: Naqd wa Nazr,* pp. 37 and 38.
35. *Tafsir-i Majidi,* 1, 44.
36. *Ibid.*, 1, 31-44 (abridged)
37. *The Bible: Revised Standard Version.* Swindon, The British and Foreign Bible Society, 1967, p. 2.
38. *The New Compact Bible Dictionary.* Minnesota, The Billy Graham Evangelistic Association, 1967, p. 461.
39. *Ibid.*, p. 218.
40. Abdul Majid Daryabadi, *Haywanat-i Qurani*, Delhi, New Crescent Publishing, 2000, p. 29.
41. *Ibid.*, p. 58.
42. *Ibid.*, p. 96.

43. Abdul Majid Daryabadi, *Aalam al-Quran,* Delhi, New Crescent Publishing, 1998, p. 61.
44. *Ibid.*, pp. 80-81.
45. Abdul Majid Daryabadi, *Qasas wa Masail,* Lucknow, Islamic Publishers, 1994, pp. 101-102.
46. Abdul Majid Daryabadi, *Mushkilat al-Quran,* Madras, T. Abdul Wahid Islamic Research Foundation, 1977, pp. 1-2.
47. *Ibid.*, pp. 5-6.
48. Abdul Majid Daryabadi, *Bashariyat-i Anbiya,* Lucknow, Maktaba-i Islam, n.d., pp. 5-6.
49. *Ibid.*, pp. 7-8.
50. See in particular his thorough, analytical study in Urdu of Daryabadi's thought and writings, *Abdul Majid Daryabadi: Ahwal wa Athar.* Lahore, Idara Thaqafat-i Islamia, 2006. Second edition. 568 pages.
51. Abdul Majid Daryabadi, *Tamaddun-i Islami,* Lucknow, Sidq Foundation, 2009, pp. 10-12.
52. *Chahl-i Hadith Waliullahi.* Edited by Abdul Majid Daryabadi. Lucknow, Sidq Jadid Book Agency, 1969, pp. 6 and 7.
53. *Ibid.*, p. 20.
54. Ashraf Ali Thanwi, *Shawq-i Watan,* Karachi, Kutubkhana Mazhari, n.d., p. 6.

Bibliography

The Quran, Sira and Islam

1. *Yatim ka Raj.* Lahore, Tahrik-i Sirat, 1938.
2. *Qasas wa Masail.* Hyderabad, Deccan, Idara Ishat-i, Urdu, 1944.
3. *Tafsir-i Majidi.* Karachi and Lahore, Taj Company, 1952
4. *Al Haiwanat fi al-Quran.*Varanasi, Maktaba Nadwatul Marif, 1955
5. *Arz-ul Quran Ya Jughrafiae Qurani.* Lucknow, Sidq Jadid Book Agency, 1955.
6. *Aalam-ul-Quran Ya Qurani Shakhsiyatein.* Lucknow, Sidq Jadid Book Agency, 1959
7. *Bashriyat-i Anbiya.* Lucknow, Sidq Jadid Book Agency, 1959.
8. *Sirat-i Nabwi Qurani.* Lucknow, Sidq Jadeed Book Agency, 1963.
9. *Tasawuf-i Islam.* Lucknow, Nasim Book Depot, 1965.
10. *Tafsir-i Majidi.* Revised edition. Lcknow, Sidq Jadid Book Agency, 1969 and Lucknow, Majlis-i Tahqiqat wa Nashriyat-i Islam, 2013.
11. *Mushkilatul Quran ya Qurani Mutala Biswin Sadi Mein.* Chennai, Islamic Research Foundation, 1977.
12. *Mashwiray aur Guzarishein.* Edited by Naimur Rahman Siddiqui. Lucknow, Al-Ilm Publishers, 1992.
13. *Sachchi Batein.* Edited by Naimur Rahman Siddiqui. Lucknow, Sidq Foundation, 2001.
14. *Murshid ki Talash.* Lucknow, Sidq Foundation, 2002.
15. *Zikr-i Rasul*, Lucknow, Sidq Foundation, 2004. Also published under these titles: *Murdon ki Masihai.* Hyderabad, Idara Ishat-i Islam, 1943 and *Sultan Ma Muhammad.* Edited by Tehsin Feraqi. Lahore, Makkah Books. 1981.
16. *Taqleed aur Hudood-i Taqleed.* Lucknow, Sidq Foundation, 2008.
17. *Yahydiyat wa Nasraniat* (A compilation of Daryabadi's critique on Judaism and Christianity in his writings, especially his *Tafsir-i Majidi*). Compiled by Muhammad Kamal Akhtar. Lucknow, al-Mahad li al-Dirasat al-Islamia, 2009.
18. *Qatl-i-Masih se Yahud ki Bariyat.* Lahore, Islami Mission, n. d.

Urdu Literature

19. *Zud-i Pasheman* (Drama). Lucknow, Al-Nazir Book Agency. 1917
20. *Mazamin-i Abdul Majid.* Edited by Ghulam Dastgir Rashid. Hyderabad, Idara Ishat-i Urdu, 1943
21. *Maqalat-i Majid.* Lahore, Ishrat Publishing House, 1954
22. *Iqbaliyat-i Majid.* Hyderabad, Iqbal Academy, 1979

Compiled by Naimur Rahman Siddiqui, Sidq Foundation, Lucknow

23. *Taghghazul-i Majidi.* Edited by Hakim Abdul Qawi Daryabadi. Lucknow, Maulana Abdul Majid Daryabadi Academy, 1979
24. *Zikr-o Fikr: Akbar Allahabadi.* Edited by Habib Ahmad Kidwai. Lucknow, Khatoon Manzil, 1988
25. *Insha-i Majid ya Lataif-i Adab.* Edited by Hakim Abdul Qawi Daryabadi. Calcutta, Idara Insha-i Majidi, 1991
26. *Akbarnama.* Edited by Abdul Aleem Qidwai. Calcutta, Idara Insha-i Majidi, 2008

Biography and Autobiography

27. *Mahmood Ghaznavi.* Amritsar, Wakeel Book Trading Agency, 1911
28. *Muhammad Ali: Zati Diary ke Chand Waraq.* Azamgarh, Darul Musaniffin, 1954.
29. *Hakim ul Ummat: Nuqush wa Tathurat.* Azamgarh, Darul Musaniffin, 1955.
30. *Wafiyat-i Majidi.* Edited by Hakim Abdul Qawi Daryabadi. Calcutta, Idara Insha-i Majidi, 1978.
31. *Muasirin.* Calcutta, Idara Insha-i Majidi, 1979
32. *Chand Sawanihi Tahrirein.* Lucknow, Maulana Abdul Majid Daryabadi Academy, Lucknow, 1985.
33. *Aap Biti.* Lucknow, Maktaba Firdaus, 2010

Philosophy and Psychology

34. *Ghiza-i Insani.* Amritsar, Wakeel Book Trading Agency, 1911
35. *Falsafa-i Jazbat.* New Delhi, Anjuman Taraqqi Urdu Hind, 1914.
36. *Faraiz-i Walidein.* Lucknow, Nawal Kishore Book Depot, 1914.
37. *Falsafa-i Ijtima.* New Delhi, Anjuman Taraqqi Urdu Hind, 1915.
38. *Falsafiyana Mazamin.* Lucknow, al-Nazir Book Agency, 1926.
39. *Mabadi Falsafa.* Azamgarh, Darul Musaniffin, 1931 and 1934. 2 volumes.
40. *Hum Aap.* Allahabad, Hindustani Academy, 1948.
41. *Falsafa ki Talim: Guzishta aur Maujuda.* Lucknow, al-Nazir Book Agency, n.d.

Lectures and Radio Talks

42. *Khutba Sadarat-i Majlis-i Istaqbaliya.* Lucknow, All India Khilafat Conference, 1927
43. *Tamaddun-i Islam.* Aligarh, Anjuman Islami Tarikh, 1941.
44. *Nashriyat-i Majid.* Edited by Abdul Aleem Kidwai. Lucknow, Khatoon Manzil, 1997.
45. *Khutbat-i Majid.* Lucknow, Sidq Foundation, 2005.
46. *Nadwatul Ulama ka Payam Farzandan-i Darul Ulum ke Nam.* Lucknow, Sidq Foundation, 2007.

Translated and Edited Works

47. *Tarikh-i Tamaddun.* Aligarh, Aligarh Institute College, 1918.

48. *Tarikh-i Akhlaq-i Europe* (2 volumes). New Delhi, Anjuman Taraqqi Urdu Hind, 1919.
49. *Mantaq Istikhraji wa Istaqrai.* Hyderabad, Dar al-Tarjuma Jamia Osmania, 1919.
50. *Tuhfa-i Khusrawi.* Barabanki, Awadh Book Agency, 1921.
51. *Tarikh-i Europe.* Hyderabad, Dar al Taba Jamia Osmania, 1922.
52. *Payam-i Aman.* Azamgarh, Darul Musaniffin, 1923.
53. *Namwaran-i Science.* Calcutta, Macmillan 1924.
54. *Makalmat-i Berkley.* Azamgarh, Darul Musaniffin, 1926.
55. *Masnawi Bahrul Muhabbat.* Azamgarh, Darul Musaniffin, 1928.
56. *Fih ma Fih.* Azamgarh, Darul Musaniffin, 1928.
57. *Munajat-i Maqbul*, Lucknow, Sidq Jadeed Book Agency, 1949.
58. *Chahal Hadith Waliullahi.* Lucknow, Sidq Jadid Book Agency, 1969.
59. *Shauq-e Akhrat.* Lahore, Idara Islamiyat, n.d.

Letters

60. *Makatib-i Akbar.* Delhi, 1924.
61. *Khutut-i Mashahir.* Lucknow, Nasim Book Depot, 1969.
62. *Maktubat-i Sulemani* (2 volumes). Lucknow, Sidq Jadeed Book Agency, 1963 and 1967.
63. *Ruqat-i Majidi.* Edited by Ghulam Muhammad. Karachi, Irfanul Kareem Ansari, 1981.
64. *Maktubat-i Majidi* (7 volumes). Edited by Dr Muhammad Hashim Kidwai. Kolkata, Idara Insha-i Majidi and New Delhi, Applied Books 2012.

Travelogues

65. *Dhai Hafta Pakistan mein Ya Mubarak Safar*, Lucknow, Sidq Jadid Book Agency, 1955.
66. *Safr-i Hijaz.* Lucknow, Nasim Book Depot, 1966.
67. *Tathurat-i Deccan*, Karachi, Bahadur Yar Jung Academy, 1977.
68. *Siyahat-i Majidi.* Edited by Muhammad Rashid Sheikh. Lucknow, Sidq Foundation, 2006.

Daryabadi's Books in English

69. *The Holy Quran.* Lahore, Taj Company, 1957.
70. *Quran-i Hakeem.* Lahore, Taj Company, 1962.
71. *Tafsirul Quran* (4 volumes). Lucknow, Academy of Research and Publication, 1981-1985.
72. *The Glorious Quran.* Leicester (UK), Islamic Foundation, 2001.
73. *The Glorious Quran*, Lucknow, Sidq Foundation, 2006.
74. *Jesus and Mary in the Holy Quran.* Lucknow, Sidq Foundation, 2009.
75. *The Psychology of Leadership.* London (UK), T. Fisher Unwin, n.d.

Compilations based on Daryabadi's writings

76. *Biswin Sadi ke Islamiat ke Mumtaz Sharih: Unki Fikr ka Tajziyati Mutala* (A compilation of Daryabadi's writings, mostly in his Urdu weekly, *Sach, Sidq* and *Sidq-i Jadid,* constituting his critique on these Muslim

scholars of his day — Iqbal, Muhammad Rafiuddin, Abul Kalam Azad, Hamiduddin Farahi, Manazir Ahsan Gilani, Obaidullah Sindhi, Mashriqi, Mawdudi and Ghulam Ahmad Parvez). Edited by Muhammad Musa Bhutto. Hyderabad, Sindh, Pakistan, Sindh National Academy Trust, 2005.

77. *Tabsarat-i Majidi.* Edited by Abdul Aleem Kidwai, New Delhi, National Council for the Promotion of Urdu Language, 2009.

Indexes of Daryabadi's weekly *Sach,Sidq* and *Sidq-i Jadid*

78. *Sach ka Wazahati Ishariya.* Compiled by Abdul Aleem Kidwai. Patna, Khuda Bakhsh Oriental Public Library, 2000.
79. *Sidq ka Wazahati Ishariya.* Compiled by Abdul Aleem Kidwai. Patna, Khuda Bakhsh Oriental Public Library, 2003.
80. *Sidq-i Jadid ka Tawzihi Ishariya.* Compiled by Abdul Aleem Kidwai. Patna, Khuda Bakhsh Oriental Public Library, 2013.

Books and Articles on Maulana Daryabadi

Books

1. *Abdul Majid Daryabadi: Ahwal wa* Athar by Tehsin Feraqi Athar. Lahore, Idara Thaqafat-i Islamia, 1993.
2. *Abdul Majid Daryabadi* by Saleem Kidwai, New Delhi, Sahitya Academy, 1998.
3. *Maulana Abdul Majid Daryabadi ki Kitab Zindagi ke Chand Waraq* by Naimur Rahman Siddiqui. Lucknow, Sidq Foundation, 2003.
4. *Maulana Abdul Majid Daryabadi: Khidmat wa Athar.* Edited by Ataur Rahman Qasmi. New Delhi, Shah Waliullah Institute, 2006.
5. *Maulana Abdul Majid Daryabadi: Hayat w Khidmat* by Abdul Aleem Kidwai. Lucknow, Sidq Foundation, 2009.
6. *Tafsir-i Majidi: Naqd wa Nazar.* Edited by Naimur Rahman Siddiqi. Lucknow, Sidq Foundation, 2013.
7. *Maulana Abdul Majid Daryabadi: Ek Bakamal Insha Pardaz* by Abdul Aleem Kidwai. Lucknow, Sidq Foundation, 2010.

Articles

8. Feraqi, Tehsin, 'Mustashiriqin ka Usloob-i Sirat Nigari awr Maulana Daryabadi", *Tahqiq Nama,* Lahore, (11) July 2012.
9. Feraqi, Tehsin, "Abdul Majid Daryabadi and the Orientalists' Biographies of the Holy Prophet (peace be upon him)," *Oriental College Magazine,* Lahore, 87:2, 2012.
10. Hussain, Muzaffar, "Maulana Daryabadi ki Urdu awr Angrezi Tafsiri Khidmat, *Tahqiqat-i Islami,* Aligarh, 10:2 April – June, 1991, pp. 70-80.
11. Khan, Muhammad Ajmal, "Tarjuma wa Tafsir-i Majidi par Ek Nazar", *Burhan*, Delhi, 60:1 January 1968, pp. 33-42.

12. Kidwai, Abdur Raheem, "The Quranic Exegesis and Maulana Daryabadi", *Hamdard Islamicus,* Karachi, 7: 2 (Summer 1985), pp. 63-70.
13. Kidwai, Abdur Raheem, "*Tafsir* in Modern Times: Pre-requisites and Challenges," *Muslim World League Journal*, Makkah 23:6 (November 1995), pp. 38-42.
14. Uthmani, Amir, "Tafsir-i Majidi", *Tajalli,* Rampur March-April 1974, pp. 117-124.
15. Zaid Homayra, "The Return of Gog: Politics and Pan-Islamism in the Haj Trvelogue of Abd al-Majid Daryabadi," in *Global Muslims in the Age of Steam and Print.* Eds . James L. Gelvin and Nile Green. Berkely, CA, University of California Press, 2014, pp. 227-248.

Ph.D.s on Maulana Daryabadi

1. *Abdul Majid Daryabadi: Hayat aur Adabi Khidmat* by Misbahul Islam, Ph. D., Lucknow University, 1976.
2. *Maulana Abdul Majid Daryabadi: Hayat aur Khidmat* by Muhammad Ateequr Rahman Khan, Ph. D., Patna University, 1977.
3. *Maulana Abdul Majid Daryabadi: Hayat aur Khidmat* by Aneequr Rahman Khan, Ph. D., Nagpur University, 1979.
4. *Abdul Majid Daryabadi: Ahwal wa Athar* by Manzoor Akhtar Tehsin Feraqi, Ph. D., Punjab University Lahore, Pakistan, 1985.
5. *Abdul Majid Daryabadi: Hayat aur Adabi Khidmat* by Tahir Muhammad Haleem Banarsi, Ph.D., Mumbai University, 1988.
6. *Abdul Majid Daryabadi Bahaisiyat Column Nigar* by Muhammad Arshad Suhail, M. Phil, University of Hyderabad, 2004.
7. *Maulana Abdul Majid Daryabadi ki Khud Nawisht Aap Biti ka Tanqeedi wa Tajziyati Mutala* by Muhammad Naseeruddin. M. Phil, Maulana Abul Kalam Azad National Urdu University, Hyderabad, 2008.
8. *Abdul Majid Daryabadi ke Nasri Marasi* by Abdul Mateen. M. Phil, University of Hyderabad, 2009.
9. *al-Mufassir Abdul Majid Daryabadi wa Tafsirihu* (Arabic) by Abdul Muheet al-Khateeb al Nadwi. Fazeelat, Darul Ulum Nadwatul Ulama, Lucknow, 2009.
10. *Maulana Abdul Majid Daryabadi ki Adabi Khidmat* by Dr Fauzia Khanam, Ph.D., Aligarh Muslim University, Aligarh, 2012.
11. *Maulana Abdul Majid Daryabadi ki Adabi Jihat* by Shaykh Salahuddin, University of Kolkata, 2013.
12. *Maulana Abdul Majid Daryabadi Bahaisiyat Sahafi* by Muzaffar Hussain. M. Phil, University of Delhi, n.d.
13. *Maulana Abdul Majid Daryabadi ki Adabi Tasaneef ka Tanqeedi Mutala* by Mujahid Ahmad. Ph. D., Rohilkhand University, Barielly, n.d.

Special Issues of Journals on Maulana Daryabadi

1. Mahnama *Farogh-e Urdu* Lucknow: Abdul Majid Daryabadi Number, August-October 1971.
2. Pandara Roza *Tameer-i Hyaat* Lucknow: Khususi Number (January-February 1977).
3. Mahnama *Naya Daur* Lucknow: Abdul Majid Daryabadi Number, April-May 1978.
4. Yadgari Mujalla: *Maulana Abdul Majid Daryabadi– Hayat wa Khidmat*, January 1978.
5. Yadgari Mujalla: *Zikr-i Majid*, January 1981.
6. *Sidq-i Jadid* Lucknow, Maulana Abdul Majid Daryabadi Number, January 1982
7. *Sidq-i Jadid* Lucknow, Maulana Abdul Majid Daryabadi Number, January 1983
8. *Sidq-i Jadid* Lucknow, Maulana Abdul Majid Daryabadi Number, January 1984
9. *Sidq-i Jadid* Lucknow, Maulana Abdul Majid Daryabadi Number, January 1985
10. *Sidq-i Jadid* Lucknow, Maulana Abdul Majid Daryabadi Number, January 1986
11. *Sidq-i Jadid* Lucknow, Maulana Abdul Majid Daryabadi Number, January 1987
12. Domahi *Academy* Lucknow: Uttar Pradesh Urdu Academy, Lucknow, November 1990-February 1991.

Works containing some material on Maulana Daryabadi

1. *Tarikh-i Daryabad* by Munshi Brij Bhokan Lal Muhib. Lucknow, Nami Press, 1925.
2. *Ifadat-i Mehdi.* Edited by Mehdi Begum. Lahore, Sh. Mubarak Ali, 1949.
3. *Hayat-i Akbar Allahabadi* by Mulla Wahidi, Karachi, Bazm-i Akbar, 1951.
4. *Tarikh-i Sahafat-i Urdu* by Imdad Sabri. Delhi,Churiwalan, 1953.
5. *Sahafat Pakistan wa Hind mein* by Abdul Salam Khurshid, Lahore, Majlis Tarraqi-i Adab, 1963.
6. *Yadon ki Duniya* by Yusuf Husein Khan, Azamgarh, Darul Musaniffin, 1967.
7. *Ilm Tafsir awr Mufassirin* by Rashid Ahmad Jalandhari, Lahore, al-Maktaba al-Ilmia,1971.
8. *Adabi Aiyne* by Sakhi Ahmad Hashmi. Karachi, Maktaba Shahid, 1974.
9. *Mashahir ke Khutut* by Abdul Latif Azmi. Delhi, Maktaba Jamia, 1975.
10. *Hakim al-Ummat Maulana Thanwi Akabir awr Muasirin ki Nazar mein* by Syed Mahmud Hussain, Karachi, Kutubkhana Mazhari, 1976.

11. *Chehra Chehra Dastan* by Suleman Athar Javed. Hyderabad, National Book Depot, 1977.
12. *Akbar Allahabadi* by Khwaja Muhammad Zakariya. Lahore, Majlis Tarraqi-i Adab, 1980.
13. *Tazkiratul Mufassirin* by Qazi Muhammad Zahidul Husaini. Atak, Pakistan, Darul Irshad, c. 1980.
14. *Tazkirah Muasirin* by Malik Ram. New Delhi, Maktaba Jamia, 1982.
15. *Mauj-i Kausar* by Sheikh Muhammad Ikram. Lahore, Idara Thaqafat-i Islamia, 1982.
16. *Mutala-i Akbar* by Zulfiqar Ghulam Hussain. Lahore, Sang-i Mil, 1984.
17. *Urdu Asalib-i Nasr* by Amirullah Khan Shaheen. Meerut, Amir Nishan, 1985.
18. *Allama Syed Suleman Nadwi Shakhsiyat wa Adabi Khidmat* by Muhammad Naim Siddiqui Nadwi. Lucknow, Maktaba Firdaus, 1985.
19. *Deed-o-Shunid* by Rais Ahmad Jafri, Karachi, Rais Ahmad Jafri Academy, 1987.
20. *Urdu Khud Nawisht: Fan-o Tajziya* by Wahajuddin Alvi. New Delhi, Maktaba Jamia, 1989.
21. *Hum Qabila* by Ali Jawwad Zaidi, Lucknow, Uttar Pradesh Urdu Academy, 1990.
22. *Shakhsiyat aur Waqiyat Jinhon Ne Mujhe Mutathir Kiya* by Junaid Ahmad, Patna, Khuda Baksh Oriental Public Library, 1991.
23. *Nuqush-i Raftigan* by Muhammad Taqi Usmani, Deoband, Zam Zam Book Depot, 1994.
24. *Qalmi Chehre* by Agha Shorish Kashmiri, Karachi, Majlis-i-Yadgar-i Shorish, 1999.
25. *Purane Chiragh* by Syed Abul Hasan Ali Hasni Nadwi, Lucknow, Maktaba Firdaus, 2000.
26. *Yad-i Raftigan* by Mahirul Qadri. Delhi, Markazi Maktaba Islami Publishers, 2000.
27. *Khyalat* by Muhammad Yunus Nigrami, Lucknow, Yunus Nigrami Educational and Welfare Society, 2001.
28. *Urdu Tafsir Bisween Sadi mein* by Syed Shahid Ali. New Delhi, Kitabi Dunya, 2001.
29. *Mulaqatein* by Syed Abdul Bari. New Delhi, Institute of Objective Studies, 2003.
30. *Mashahir-i Ahl-i-Ilm ki Muhsin Kitabein* by Maulana Muhammad Imran Khan Nadwi and Faisal Ahmad Bhatkali Nadwi. Lucknow, Idara Ihya-i Ilm wa Dawat, 2004.
31. *Tarikh-i Adab-i Urdu* by Ram Babu Saxena, Lucknow, Nawal Kishore, n.d.
32. *Bazm-i Raftigan* by Syed Sabahuddin Abdur Rahman, Azamgarh, Darul Musaniffin.

33. *Lucknow Ka Dabistan-i Nasr* by Iffat Zarrin. Delhi, Maktaba Jamia, 2011.
34. *Urdu Safarnamon ka Tanqidi Mutala* by Khalid Mahmood. New Delhi, Maktaba Jamia, 2011.
35. *Fahm-i Quran* by Said Ahmad Akbarabadi. Delhi, Nadwatul Musaniffin, 1359H.

Reviews on Daryabadi's *tafsir* in English

1. M.A.M. "Review on Daryabadi's English translation of the Quran", *Islamic Culture* 181:1 (1944), 103-104.
2. M.H. "Review on Daryabadi's English translation of the Quran", *Islamic Culture* 20:3 (1946), 337-338.
3. Jeffrey, Arthur "The Holy Quran by Abdul Majid Daryabadi", *Muslim World,* 35:4 (1945), 160-161.
4. Kidwai, Abdur Raheem. "Review on *Tafsir-ul- Quran* by Daryabadi", *Muslim World Book Review,* 5:2 (Spring 1985) 14-16.
5. Kidwai, Abdur Raheem. "Maulana Daryabadi and the Quranic Exegesis", *Hamdard Islamicus* 7:2 (1985), 63-70.
6. The Daily *Leader,* Allahabad, 1 June 1943.
7. The Daily *Times of India,* New Delhi, 13 August 1943.
8. Kidwai, Abdur Raheem, "Abdul Majid Daryabadi" in *Bibliography of the Translations of the Meanings of the Glorious Quran into English 1649-2002: A Critical Study.* Madina, King Fahd Quran Printing Complex, 2007, pp. 156-161.
9. Kidwai, Abdur Raheem, "Abdul Majid Daryabadi" in *Translating the Untranslatable: A Critical Guide to 60 English Translations of the Quran.* New Delhi, Sarup Book, 2011, pp. 35-39.

Daryabadi's *tafsir* in English – Editions

1. *The Holy Quran:translated from the original Arabic with lexical, grammatical, historical, geographical and eschatologicalcomments and explanation and sidelights on comparative religion,* Lahore, Pakistan, Taj Company, 1957, 2 Vols., Vol. I 456 pp. Vol. II. 513 pp.
2. *The Holy Quran with English translation,* Karachi, Pakistan, Taj Company, 1970, 611 pp.
3. *The Holy Quran,* Karachi, Pakistan, Taj Company, 1971, 2 Vols., Vol. I 456 pp. Vol. II. 513 pp.
4. *Tafsirul Quran:Translation of Commentary of the Holy Quran,* Lucknow, India, Academy of Islamic Research and Publications, Vol. I 1981, 464 pp. Vol.2 1982, 508 pp. Vol.3 1983, 503 pp. and Vol. 4 1985, 560 pp.
5. *The Glorious Quran: Text, Translation and Commentary,* Leicester, UK, Islamic Foundation, 2001, 1149 pp. ISBN: 086037-360-6.
6. *The Glorious Quran: Text, Translation and Commentary,* Lucknow, India, Sidq Foundation, 2006.

Editors and Contributors

ABDUL MAJID DARYABADI (1892–1977), contributed *tafsir* in both English and Urdu. Author of 70 books and numerous articles, and a leading Muslim scholar.

SYED ABUL HASAN ALI NADVI (1914–1999), recipient of the prestigious King Faisal award, a towering Muslim scholar, thinker and writer of our time and Rector, Nadwatul Ulema, Lucknow.

AKHTARUL WASEY (1951), presently National Commissioner for Linguistic Minorities in India, is Professor of Islamic Studies and Hony. Director, Dr. Zakir Husain Institute of Islamic Studies, Jamia Millia Islamia, New Delhi. Various international and national awards and honours, including Padmashri, have been conferred upon him in recognition of his substantial contribution to Islamic Studies and Urdu. He has authored a spate of books and articles.

ABDUR RAHEEM KIDWAI (1956), Professor of English and Director UGC Human Resource Development Centre, Aligarh Muslim University, Aligarh and Visiting Professor, School of English, University of Leicester, UK has written more than 30 books and scores of articles on Islam, the Quran, and English and Urdu literature.